Collaborative Public Management

American Governance and Public Policy series
Series Editor: Barry Rabe, University of Michigan

Collaborative Public Management

New Strategies for Local Governments

Robert Agranoff
and
Michael McGuire

GEORGETOWN UNIVERSITY PRESS / WASHINGTON, D.C.

Georgetown University Press, Washington, D.C.
© 2003 by Georgetown University Press. All rights reserved.
Printed in the United States of America

10 9 8 7 6 5 4 3 2   2003

This volume is printed on acid-free offset book paper.

Portions of this book have been published previously. Unless noted, the authors of each of the following journal articles are Robert Agranoff and Michael McGuire. Parts of chapter 3 appeared as "American Federalism and the Search for Models of Management," *Public Administration Review* 61 (November–December 2001): 671–79 (copyright 2001 by Blackwell Science, Ltd.; reprinted by permission of Blackwell Science, Ltd.). Parts of chapter 4 have been published in "Expanding Intergovernmental Management's Hidden Dimensions," *American Review of Public Administration* 29, no. 4 (winter 1999): 352–69 (copyright 1999 by Sage Publications; reprinted by permission of Sage Publications, Inc.). Some of the data in chapter 5 appeared in "Multinetwork Management: Collaboration and the Hollow State in Local Economic Policy," *Journal of Public Administration Research and Theory* 8 (January 1998): 67–91 (copyright 1998 by Transaction Publishers; reprinted by permission of Transaction Publishers). Chapter 6 is based on Michael McGuire's "Collaborative Policy Making and Administration: The Operational Demands of Local Economic Development," *Economic Development Quarterly* 14, no. 3 (2000): 276–91 (copyright 2000 by Sage Publications; reprinted by permission of Sage Publications, Inc.). Portions of chapter 7 have appeared as "Big Questions in Public Network Management Research," *Journal of Public Administration Research and Theory* 11 (July 2001): 295–326 (copyright 2001 by Transaction Publishers; reprinted by permission of Transaction Publishers).

Library of Congress Cataloging-in-Publication Data

Agranoff, Robert.
    Collaborative public management: new strategies for
local governments / by Robert Agranoff and Michael McGuire.
        p.   cm.
    Includes bibliographical references and index.
    ISBN 0-87840-896-7 (hardcover : alk. paper)
    1. Local government—United States.   2. Intergovernmental
cooperation—United States.   3. Public-private sector cooperation—
United States.   I. McGuire, Michael, 1964–   .   II. Title.
JS356   .A37   2003
352.14'0973—dc21   2002014315

CONTENTS

PREFACE

Our concern in this book is with the formidable task of dissecting the extent and nature of the process whereby public and nonpublic organizations work together. The era of the manager's cross-boundary interdependency challenge has arrived, as has the world of working in the network of organizations. Public functions are no longer the exclusive domain of governments. Many seemingly private domains, such as those of business creation, are at the core of public-sector developmental functions. The term "intergovernmental" has new meaning beyond federal–state, state–local, and interlocal connotations, to include quasi-governmental and myriad contractual, regulatory, subventional, reciprocal, and other interactive relationships with organizations outside the public sector. More needs to be known about the core nature of collaborative management, the kinds of collaborative activities that exist, and what can be discovered about the processes of managing collaboration.

This study attempts to go beyond the arguments about the importance of interorganizational management by breaking it down into its parts and sequences as well as to make suggestions regarding how to manage the process. As such, the book can be used as a research source by scholars, as well as a supplemental text in many different areas, such as courses in intergovernmental relations, managing networks, urban management, economic development, and general public management.

Researching at the boundaries of governments and other organizations, career-long endeavors for the authors, requires a very high level of tolerance for ambiguity. Some say it is a gift and others say it is acquired; we don't know, but we do know it is not for everyone. Being able to think, talk, and write outside the hierarchy, about transactions *between* formal entities, may be equivalent to social psychologists looking at interpersonal interactions. The study of boundaries is sometimes avoided because of a lack of concreteness. Clearly, in politics and administration, boundaries are harder to study than those within an organization. But their accelerating prominence means that they cannot be put aside as foci of study.

The empirical database used here is both quantitative and qualitative, with a survey of cities and their collaborators' interactions in economic development. Though designed for this study by the authors, it follows a 1994 economic development survey conducted by the International City/County Management Association (ICMA), sampling respondents to that survey. For that assistance, we thank Barbara Moore and Woody Talcove of ICMA for allowing us to follow along their survey. The collaboration study itself was initially funded by the Ameritech Foundation Research Program in Management and Organizational Studies, Institute for Developmental Strategies, Indiana University. For this support and for their encouragement, we thank Charles Bonser and Daniel Knudsen of the institute. This large-scale study depended mightily on their backing.

Portions of this book have appeared elsewhere in professional journals, usually with different data displays, somewhat more preliminary data interpretations, and in most cases in attenuated form due to journal space limitations. The full bibliographic information for each of these journal articles is given on the copyright page. Here, we simply give their titles. Parts of chapter 3 appeared as "American Federalism and the Search for Models of Management." Parts of chapter 4 have been published as "Expanding Intergovernmental Management's Hidden Dimensions." Some of the data in chapter 5 appeared in "Multinetwork Management: Collaboration and the Hollow State in Local Economic Policy." Chapter 6 is based on "Collaborative Policy Making and Administration: The Operational Demands of Local Economic Development." Portions of chapter 7 have appeared as "Big Questions in Public Network Management Research."

This work on collaboration could not have been accomplished without extensive collaboration. First and foremost are the problem-oriented joint learning experiences of the two authors over the years. Our exchanges have been on an equal plane, each contributing his strengths and filling in the weaknesses of the others. Indeed, McGuire's propensity to "crunch numbers" and in many ways to represent the "new" and Agranoff's "old" literature perspectives and enjoyment of "stepping in the mud" in the field have enriched our collaboration a great deal. But the real richness has really come in the joint efforts of design, data collection, analysis, interpretation, and writing. Together and regardless of age, we try hard to develop the "dog tricks" necessary to experiment and grow in this murky field of study.

Many people have helped in the preparation of this study and book. Nora Wittstruck, Ann Tillery, and Dawn Lenzie were instrumental at various stages of data collection. We offer thanks to our principal contacts in the field case studies: Paul Rasmussen in Beloit, Susan Paddock in Cincinnati, Noreen Kuban in Garfield Heights, Troy Feltman and Don Schurr in Ithaca, Gary Walton in Salem, and Tim Clifton in Woodstock. Three people, in addition to the anonymous reviewers for the various journal submissions and for this book, read the manuscript in draft form and offered helpful suggestions at an early stage: Dale Krane, Larry O'Toole, and Beryl Radin. To the three go our profound thanks for tolerating a work in progress. The manuscript itself and its many versions were produced by Monica Boyd at Indiana University and Dawn Lenzie at the University of North Texas, both of whom were invaluable to the finished product. We also give our thanks to Georgetown University Press editor Gail Grella and series editor Barry Rabe for their support and encouragement in bringing this book to their list.

We would be remiss without acknowledging family support and tolerance. The first author will never forget that Saturday, on the first trip to Texas to work on the study, when the McGuire boys were deeply disappointed as we left for the office to go to work. Corey, for one, thought that "Bob" had come for the weekend to play. Keenan, being the younger one, quickly followed suit and looked equally peeved. There were many, many other such days when Michael went off alone to crunch numbers and to write, leaving his family to wonder how writing a book could possibly be more important than playing baseball or watching a movie together (which, of course, it is not). Most of all, we acknowledge the patience and perseverance of our spouses, Susan Klein and Sharon McGuire, who were supportive in so many ways.

I

Collaboration at the Core

The government of Beloit, Wisconsin, works actively with Beloit 2000, a nonprofit redevelopment association, to transform a blighted area on the Rock River that runs through the heart of town into a combined venue of civic center, industrial site, and moderate- and low-income housing. Among other activities, Beloit 2000 mobilized neighborhood groups, the business community, local elected officials, and the city administration behind its goals. The city was called upon to tackle infrastructure improvements, handle building and other permits, and devote federal Community Development Block Grant money and U.S. Department of Transportation Urban Rivers Program funds to this effort. The Rock County government was asked to contribute tax funds and to either relocate some office space or build a new facility in the redevelopment area. Both the city and county governments used their state-authorized powers to establish tax increment finance districts, grant tax abatements, and reduce or eliminate regulations that thwarted development. Both of these public entities worked with Beloit 2000 in seeking additional project grants and loans from the state and federal governments to finance portions of the project. Finally, numerous interactions took place between nonprofit associations, industries and housing interests, and all levels of government over financing arrangements, regulatory permits, and taxation questions. The Wisconsin Department of Development assisted local interests in working through these interorganizational and intergovernmental questions, not only with regard to programs in their own department but also with other state departments, particularly those dealing with highways and environmental protection programs.

The principle that managers often must operate across organizations as well as within hierarchies is becoming an accepted component of contemporary management theory.

I

This includes the work of governments connecting with other governments and with the nongovernmental sector. Through partnerships, networks, contractual relationships, alliances, committees, coalitions, consortia, and councils, managers in public and private agencies jointly develop strategies and produce goods and services on behalf of their organizations.

For the greater part of the twentieth century, the processes of hierarchical management occupied practical and academic attention. But such a focus captures too few of the challenges faced by today's managers. In the twenty-first century, interdependence and the salience of information have resulted in an environment where organizational and sectoral boundaries are more conceptual than actual, and collaborative managerial responses are required to complement, and in some cases even displace, bureaucratic processes. This type of cross-boundary collaborative management is the subject of this book, which is based on an empirical study of 237 cities and their officials as they work with other governments and organizations to develop their city economies.

Cities and their public managers operate in a complex intergovernmental and interorganizational environment. The past few decades have brought home the ubiquity of interdependence among jurisdictions, government agencies, nonprofit associations, and for-profit entities at the local level. In many functional areas, cities contract with private-sector agencies to deliver basic services to citizens. Metropolitan areas continue to grow in number, size, and density, making the daily work of each city a direct determinant of work in other nearby cities; managing externalities is synonymous with governing in central cities and their surrounding suburbs. Rural communities as well must seek out governing resources externally due to decades of out-migration and rapid shifts in their economic bases. Functional responsibilities viewed for a half-century as national in scope have become increasingly subnational partnerships (i.e., the Personal Responsibility and Work Opportunity Reconciliation Act of 1996, known as the welfare reform act), whereas responsibilities that have historically been subnational have become more national in scope (i.e., the Individual with Disabilities Education Act of 1997 and the Elementary and Secondary Education Reauthorization of 2002).

In the wake of the terrorist attacks on the United States of September 11, 2001, national defense is being redefined as cities—large and small—prepare to be on the front lines in the war against terrorism. This war has clearly been defined as one of collaboration between law enforcement agencies at all levels of government and private-sector security firms, business and industry, civic associations, and many others. Even within the global economy where nations and regions ostensibly are the focal points, cities occupy a more and more critical strategic position as the venues for bringing together potential partners. As intergovernmental programs evolve, nongovernmental organizations expand their scope of operations, and policymaking resources are held by entities other than the government, collaboration is becoming a tool that cities can use to strategically pursue their political and economic objectives.

The decision by a city (or other entity) to exploit this increasingly complex and interdependent environment through collaborative management, however, is variable. Cities examine the environment and decide whether collaboration is a productive strategic tool, a necessary evil, or simply not important. Some cities view collaboration as an opportunity, but others view it as unnecessary at best and a burden at worst. Some cities choose to collaborate in any way possible, but others avoid it. Some cities collaborate as a means to achieve local aims, others as a mechanism for not opposing the achievement of external aims. Many cities collaborate with other levels of government, thus operating in the administrative web of federalism; some cities work with local bodies, capitalizing on the resources of profit-making and nonprofit organizations; some cities exploit the advantages of both.

Collaboration does not just happen. Like operating within the city hierarchy, collaboration must be managed, albeit in a different way. Such processes of collaboration are examined in this study of cities and their officials. In economic development in general, as in the many specific policy arenas that constitute economic development, critical policymaking resources—finances, information, labor, knowledge, legal authority, and expertise—do not reside exclusively in the public agency but with other levels of government, counties, water districts, utilities, chambers of commerce, and development corporations. The complex interorganizational, intersectoral, and intergovernmental policy context of cities provides an opportunity for a city to strategically and collaboratively pursue its political and economic objectives—an opportunity exploited by some but not all cities.

Our argument is consistent with recent urban studies that demonstrate economic development is a deliberate, predetermined, city-level activity. Cities make conscious decisions about the form and content of economic development policy; such choices are strategic, thus political (Pagano and Bowman 1992). Empirical studies show the strategic nature of development by linking "correct" and "incorrect" strategies with economic performance (McGuire 1999), and argue that some cities are innovative and entrepreneurial (Borins 1998). Clarke and Gaile (1998) argue that cities have gone through several transformative stages that require increasing amounts of intersectoral and intergovernmental cooperation. Our locus, the city, is the same as these development studies, but our focus is different, because we examine the intricacies of policymaking and the administrative activities of those city officials collaborating in complex multiorganizational environments.

Collaborative management is a concept that describes the process of facilitating and operating in multiorganizational arrangements to solve problems that cannot be solved, or solved easily, by single organizations. Collaboration is a purposive relationship designed to solve a problem by creating or discovering a solution within a given set of constraints (e.g., knowledge, time, money, competition, and conventional wisdom; Schrage 1995). The term "collaboration" should not be confused with "cooperation." The latter refers to working jointly with others to some end, as does the former, but the more accepted definition of cooperation means that those working jointly seek to be helpful as opposed to hostile.

Although a great deal of collaboration is cooperative—meaning working jointly with others—collaborative management sometimes entails engaging one or more organizations in a purposive and official partnership or contractual arrangement, and it sometimes amounts merely to assisting others in a particular effort. Collaborative management can be formal or informal, ranging from simple acquisition of information to a negotiated agreement that paves the way for more extensive projects. For example, in Cincinnati, the city government makes dozens of contacts monthly with agencies in state and federal government through its department administrators, its lobbyists on retainer, and the city manager's office. Some of these contacts involve reaching compliance with state or national regulations, but many emphasize meeting city goals. Recently, one such transaction involved city-initiated negotiated agreements with Hamilton County and the U.S. Department of Energy to extend water service into the city's Water West project area. The service was initiated to provide an infrastructure boost that would in turn generate several million dollars in federal funds for an area revitalization strategy.

Collaborative management can involve developing policy, planning and carrying out projects, or managing finances. Salem, Indiana, a city of 6,600 people in the south-central part of the state, follows the practice of many cities today by joining voluntary partnerships and networks to promote its economic development. Anchoring Salem's activity is the Washington County Economic Growth Partnership (WCEGP), a local development corporation whose members include the city and county governments, the Chamber of Commerce, the Salem Redevelopment Commission, and private-sector firms. Salem is also part of a consortium of thirteen small cities that uses the grant procurement and administrative services of Administrative Resource Associates and regularly engages the River Hills Regional Planning Commission in Jeffersonville for planning services. As a small city, it contacts state and federal agencies less frequently than does Cincinnati, but its mayor and the WCEGP executive director have monthly interactions with state and federal agencies, particularly with those dealing with the environment, highways and transportation, commerce, and housing.

Some collaboration is voluntary, and some is mandated by the state or federal government. Cities need to deal with their regulatory burden, particularly with environmental agencies, to make land available or to otherwise move development projects along. For example, Woodstock, Illinois, successfully negotiated a U.S. Environmental Protection Agency (EPA) Cleanup Order regarding a city-owned dump, trading off initial site preparation and clearing plus subsequent pump and treatment of waste for twenty years in exchange for the EPA-proposed method, at about half the estimated cost of the original cleanup order. All city work is being conducted by city public works crews. At some point, the city hopes to use this site for other purposes.

The government of Cincinnati is collaborating when it joins forces with two different multiorganizational institutions—Downtown Cincinnati, Incorporated, which is a public–private organization and policy initiator, and the area Chamber of Commerce—to jointly design policies for the city's economic development and undertake creative financing activities intended to combine and/or leverage funds from multiple sources. Ithaca, Michigan, a town of about 3,000, collaborates often through Greater Gratiot Development Incorporated (GGDI), a venture that involves three cities, one village, a county government, and the city and county chambers of commerce. Ithaca spends city revenues to improve land for development, provides support to contractors renovating older buildings, and participates in job training with the support of grant money from the State of Michigan, along with the policymaking and administrative assistance of GGDI and the Ithaca Industrial Development and Economic Association.

The Framework

The intent of this book is to (1) demonstrate the various ways in which multiorganizational, multiactor collaboration is utilized as a public policymaking and management tool by cities, and (2) consider the underrecognized practical and theoretical issues at the forefront of public management that suggest a more complex and more interesting world of public management in practice. Drawing on the literatures of intergovernmental relations and management, urban affairs, network management, and public management, we argue that collaborative management exists at the intersection of activity and strategy. The dependent variable of concern in this study is collaborative management, which is measured in terms of activity level and the purpose of the collaborative effort. We hypothesize that the city-level "values" of collaborative management vary across cities and that explanations can be found for how it differs, why it differs, and what determines the differences. Our framework is based on four straightforward propositions, which guide our analysis.

The first proposition: *The collaborative mechanisms available to a city for achieving its strategic objectives are multifarious and abundant.* Our argument: Cities operate in a complex web of jurisdictions, agencies, businesses, and nonprofit organizations, each of which has some claim on the governing activities of the city. Empirical support for this proposition will be found in cities that engender useful transactions with these entities.

The second proposition: *The extent and purpose of city government collaborative management varies across cities.* Our argument: Some cities choose to avail themselves of the opportunities present in the intergovernmental and multiorganizational environment, and some do not. It follows that as the level of collaboration varies across cities, so will the purpose of such connections. Empirical support for this proposition will be found in the actual variation in activity and purposes among cities.

The third proposition: *The choices of whether, why, or how to collaborate are based on structural and administrative considerations, along with economic and political imperatives.* Our argument: Many factors are associated with the variation in collaborative activity levels and purpose, only some of which are the traditional explanations of politics and economics. Collaboration is associated with the condition of the local economy and the type of local government, but factors related to organizing and managing the collaborative enterprise may also prove relevant. Empirical support for this proposition will be found in the linkages between such factors and collaborative activity.

The fourth proposition: *Given a distinct number of mechanisms, levels, and purposes of linking activities, numerous types or patterns of collaborative activity exist in practice.* Our argument: Within the variation of collaborative management are combinations of activity and purpose that distinguish a city's approach to the intergovernmental and multiorganizational environment. Empirical support for this proposition will be found in identifiable models of collaborative management in cities.

Given our expectation that we would find empirical support for these propositions, we set out to derive models of collaborative management from these various patterns of activity. More specifically, we sought evidence of management whereby collaboration is viewed as an opportunity to exploit rather than an activity to be avoided. In the midst of the multiple players, activities, and purposes that can be involved in collaboration, we sought out cities that practice a form of strategic management that capitalizes on the complex interorganizational and intergovernmental system for the purpose of advancing the interests of the city.

The critical empirical case to be made is not just the extent of collaboration per se—and we will demonstrate just how extensive it can be—but how such activity is inconsistent with the approach of researchers and practitioners weaned on bureaucracy and direct provision of public goods and services. Focusing empirical research nearly exclusively on the single-organization and bureaucratic dimension of public management will ultimately provide little guidance to practitioners operating in a collaborative managerial environment. We show that the capacities and skills required for contemporary policymaking and administration are different from the capacities and skills associated traditionally with public management. Providing an understanding of these differences both for the practitioner and for the scholar is the mission of this book. If managers adept at navigating through government agencies, private-sector organizations, and nonprofit associations are potentially more consequential to agency success than their bureaucratic counterparts of the past (O'Toole 1997c), the need for catalyzing a renewed research agenda cannot be overstated.

We argue for a new conceptual and empirical approach to the study of public management. Some important theoretical questions are approached, and an empirical foundation upon which theory may be built is provided through the findings. The motivation for our emphasis on managing across rather than within organizations comes not from the position of the advocate who wishes to persuade his or her peers that management approach X or management technique Y is the "most efficient," "most effective," or just plain "best" and therefore should be incorporated into the repertoire of the public manager. Rather, our position is empirical, not prescriptive: Collaborative management is a governing mechanism available to cities on a daily basis, and in many cities it has become a dominant activity of public management. However, our lack of knowledge about such management is constraining the field's ability to accurately portray and effectively convey to managers just what public management and governing entail. We thus do not proclaim that collaborative management is a new approach that managers should adopt, but, instead, that such managing occurs, and we know too little about its use as a policymaking and administrative tool.

Methods

The unit of analysis in this empirical study of collaborative management is city government, and the policy sector we study is economic development. Cities are useful units of analysis for examining the various characteristics of collaborative management, especially the potentially strategic nature of the activity. Cities offer large numbers and types of potential collaborators with governments. It is not certain that a typical city government agency official will pursue collaboration; but when one does, the variation of actors across cities is desirable, from the standpoint of explanation.

Similarly, economic development is also an excellent context because, in practice, economic development involves several policy areas—housing, finance, public works, environment, and transportation, to name just a few. Indeed, "economic development" is really a summary term that comprises multiple policy areas. Given the wide range of experience that is possible in cities' pursuit of economic development, if management patterns can be discovered across a few hundred cities in this context, we believe the findings can be viewed as credible and valid, both internally (causal) and externally.

The findings are drawn from both survey research and qualitative case research. Data were collected from 237 cities in the Midwest by survey, and from within the large sample, six purposively selected cities through site visits and extensive interviews (see appendix A for a complete description of the survey design). The case study cities are all active collaborators in the policy context of economic development, but each operates from the posture of its location, economic condition, and status as a city, and not all approach collaboration strategically. For example: Large central cities would be expected to be different in some notable respects from suburban cities or small towns; large inner-ring suburbs would be expected to be in different situations than small outer-ring suburbs; and cities imbedded in rich collaborative settings would be expected to act differently from those that must work to seek out potential collaborators. The cases were selected to illustrate such differences. The field research was designed to enable cities to clarify or elaborate on certain key responses and findings, which allowed for an in-depth discussion about how cities collaborate.

Case studies used in this research provide an opportunity for elaboration, for adding richness and understanding to the data, and for supplementing the quantitative survey. We used a discussion guide with a common format, and the same questions were asked in all settings and the discussions were guided, but open-ended, resulting more in structured conversations than rigid interviews. In addition, numerous types of materials were collected from the cities, such as descriptions of partnerships, brochures on economic development practices, and government organizational information. Brief sketches of the six case study cities follow.

Cincinnati

Cincinnati is the largest of the case study cities, with approximately 340,000 persons, and is the central city of a metropolitan area of nearly 2 million persons that includes counties in Ohio, Kentucky, and Indiana. Cincinnati has employed the council–manager form of government since 1926 and affirmed its preference for this form in August 1995 by voting nearly two to one in a challenge referendum. A charter reform in 1999 provided for an elected mayor but retained the city manager. At the time of the study, the city Department of Economic Development (DED) was the city's primary economic development unit. It was staffed with more than fifty employees, many of whom were professionals in planning and development.

As is the case in most large central cities, Cincinnati maintains an active intergovernmental presence. It has formally adopted an intergovernmental policy, and it pursues many discretionary grants and negotiates regulatory programs as a routine part of its operations. The city government has a broad and deep experience with federal discretionary and entitlement programs, dating back to the Model Cities and War on Poverty programs. On an annual basis, it has literally hundreds of grants or federal and state programs operating within the jurisdiction. The city retains lobbyists in Columbus (the Ohio capital) and Washington, D.C., and the city manager's office is a focal point of near constant communication with state offices, members of the state legislature, the congressional delegation, and federal offices in many locations. State contacts are regular and face-to-face, either with a governor's representative, who serves the entire region but is located in Cincinnati, or by a one-hour trip to Columbus for visits to state agency headquarters.

Many interlocal partnerships for development are forged in Cincinnati, especially with the area Chamber of Commerce, Downtown Cincinnati, Incorporated, and with local developers and entrepreneurs. As evidence of decentralized collaboration and development, the city has taken its strategy to the neighborhoods through the Cincinnati Neighborhood Action Strategy (CNAS). The DED staff and structure reflect the city's commitment to the CNAS by providing extensive outreach to neighborhoods, neighborhood associations, and local development corporations.

Beloit, Wisconsin

Beloit is a city of 36,000 persons located on the Wisconsin–Illinois state line in a small two-state metropolitan area of more than 150,000 persons. The city has operated under the council–manager form of government since 1929, one of only twenty-one Wisconsin cities to adopt such a charter. At the time of the study, the thirteen-employee Department of Community Development (DCD) was the city's primary development arm and main representative in collaborative ventures. It was staffed by five professionally trained planners.

Although it is relatively small, Beloit's low-income status makes it eligible for a number of federal and state programs, such as federal Community Development Block Grants (CDBG) and programs offered by the Economic Development Administration, as well as State Development (Enterprise) Zone assistance. Professional managers in the executive office and in DCD have been aggressively pursuing federal funding for capital improvements and are seeking discretionary grants. In a given year, the city administers between forty and fifty state and federal grants. The city government maintains an active presence in Madison, the state capital, seeking development assistance, help with potential business start-ups or expansions, and assistance in getting regulatory permits and adjustments.

Interlocal collaboration is also prevalent in Beloit. The local development corporation, the Beloit Economic Development Corporation (BEDCOR), serves the City of Beloit, the Township of Beloit, and South Beloit, Illinois. It is funded by the three government jurisdictions and by private sources, particularly the Beloit Area Chamber of Commerce. BEDCOR has an experienced industrial recruiter on staff, and its executive director makes contacts with business prospects, both in the Beloit area and through state agencies. Recently, BEDCOR shared a role in a development project with DCD. Beloit has entered into a number of multipartner development projects over the years, the most notable being a major riverfront revitalization project, Beloit 2000.

Garfield Heights, Ohio

Garfield Heights is an inner-ring suburb of 30,000 persons in the Cleveland metropolitan area of 2.9 million people. The city has operated with a mayor–council charter since its incorporation in 1932. At the time of the research, the director of economic development, who constituted a one-person department, worked along with the mayor on major development projects. Eight other city departments provided public services.

The city's vertical presence is maintained by the mayor and the director of economic development, who doubles as city grants coordinator. About fifteen discretionary grants are submitted by the city annually to federal, state, and Cuyahoga County governments, and about ten are in force in a normal year. Because the city is a suburban jurisdiction in a metropolitan area, it has the county government as a regular point of contact, not only because Cuyahoga is an entitlement CDBG county, but also because the county serves as a source of expertise and as a regulatory body. The city is very involved with state agencies located in the Cleveland area (the regional offices of two state agencies, transportation and employment security, are within city borders) and with members of the congressional delegation.

Although the Garfield Heights government had no formal partnerships with other local entities at the time of the study, it was actively working with public agencies and private developers in opening up office complexes near its two Interstate highway exchanges. The city also teams with cities and special districts in its part of the county, particularly for sanitation, water resource, land use, and recreation promotion.

Woodstock, Illinois

Woodstock has 17,000 residents and is the seat of McHenry County, a northwestern "collar county" of the Chicago metropolitan region. It is a town that has evolved into a small outer-ring suburb. Woodstock was incorporated in 1852 and is governed by a council–manager charter. At the time of the study, major city functions related to economic development, such as planning and zoning, were housed in the Department of Community Development.

Woodstock selectively engages in federal program participation, writing only a few grants each year. As a relatively prosperous and growing community, it is ineligible for programs such as those offered by the federal Economic Development Administration. It occasionally and cautiously contacts the State of Illinois, interacting more frequently with the Department of Transportation than with other agencies. It does have good working contact with the field representative of the Illinois Department of Commerce and Community Affairs, but it has much less frequent contact with officials in Springfield, in the state capital. Woodstock regularly accesses state-authorized development programs: state-pooled bond and direct loan programs, a state-funded revolving loan fund, tax increment financing, and selective use of tax abatement.

Owing to the leadership efforts of the city manager, Woodstock is very active in developing lateral intergovernmental agreements with adjacent local governments. Economic activities are promoted within the town by the Woodstock Economic Development Corporation, which is a cooperative venture of the Chamber of Commerce and the city but operates within the city government orbit. The city maintains a close working relationship with the McHenry County government. Such contact is expected to increase, because McHenry became an entitlement CDBG county in the mid-1990s.

Salem, Indiana

As the only incorporated area in Washington County, Salem, a city of 6,600 people, is located in the south-central part of Indiana in a rural area outside the Louisville two-state metropolitan area. Salem was permanently incorporated in 1868 and was upgraded from a town to a city in 1936. It has a mayor–council form of government, the only type allowed in Indiana except for those communities chartered as towns. Although the city had seven departments at the time of the study, only the Building Department had any direct involvement in economic development, whereas a Planning Commission and a Board of Zoning Appeals played a more indirect role.

Salem is a small city that "operates big" in terms of external support and contacts. The city taps into county Economic Development Income Tax funds, uses tax abatement extensively, and occasionally uses tax increment financing and state-sponsored loans. It is exploring enterprise zone designation. Local leaders pursue many external funding sources. As a result, the city has been able to receive a fair share of federal discretionary development grants, Indiana CDBG funds for small cities, and state discretionary funds, totaling fifteen grants in a five-year period. External funding has led to major highway improvements, airport renovation, and industrial park expansion in the economic development area. Salem also negotiates jurisdiction interests with the state and federal governments, particularly regarding water and other environmental regulations.

Although Salem does not have a core professional staff, its major collaborative actors are the mayor and the executive director of the Washington County Economic Growth Partnership, organized by the City of Salem, Washington County, the industrial community, and the city–county Chamber of Commerce. Salem is part of Administrative Resource Associates, a nonprofit consortium of thirteen small cities for grant procurement and administration, and it works with its regional planning commission for city planning services.

Ithaca, Michigan

Ithaca, the smallest of our case study cities, has a population of about 3,000. It is the seat of nonmetropolitan Gratiot County, which is located in the center of lower Michigan, about 45 miles north of Lansing and clustered with surrounding jurisdictions. Ithaca became a village in 1869. In 1961 it became a city and the council–manager form of government was adopted. The primary economic development actors are the mayor, the city manager, and the staff of GGDI, a multicommunity development organization. GGDI is the shared enterprise of three of the county's cities and one village, the county government, and the Ithaca and the county chambers of commerce.

GGDI provides Ithaca with considerable development capacity, enabling it to use professionally written grants and research-based regulatory negotiations to support its economic development strategy. During the study year, Ithaca had ten discretionary grants in effect for economic development. GGDI staff members represent the city in Lansing and in Washington, giving it a very active vertical presence for a small town.

Ithaca's government, in turn, provides local support through physical infrastructure improvements, a countywide tax abatement policy, a revolving loan program, and tax increment financing. Ithaca intends to seek state and federal funding to upgrade its water and sewer systems, and to develop another water well to support its nongovernmental partners in industrial expansion. Considerable infrastructure support is also given to private contractors involved in renovating older buildings, often with the help of CDBG funds for small cities pursued in Lansing. Most of Ithaca's lateral connections are through joint planning and policy work with other GGDI member communities and with the county government.

Managing in the Matrix of Levels and Sectors

Collaborative management is a core activity for today's public manager. Interdependencies with the nongovernmental sector, and the complexity of the horizontal and vertical intergovernmental domains, bring on ever new challenges and potential partners. The purposes, players, linkages, and strategic choices differ from one jurisdiction to another, as will be demonstrated, but more and more governments are deeply in the game of managing at their borders.

Our study indicates that collaborative management is considerably more differentiated than the literatures on intergovernmental relations and network management might suggest. Managers are involved in numerous contacts with many different public agencies and private entities, and in a fashion that is compounded by multiple differentiated efforts to promote local interests. Also, managing within the intergovernmental arena is not just a state–federal vertical undertaking; it involves a host of other local governments and nongovernmental actors. Many communities have boundary spanners promoting economic development through horizontal and vertical collaboration. Specialists bring the public and private sectors together to work within city departments, local development corporations, and other nongovernmental organizations such as chambers of commerce. Intergovernmental (vertical) and interlocal (horizontal) activity is linked in practice: Vertical activity is often stimulated by efforts or projects that are being generated through community-level collaboration, whereas a great deal of interlocal action is the result of stimulation from federal and state programming and/or regulations.

The study reveals, describes, and explains collaborative management. Intergovernmental collaboration involves a set of identifiable managerial actions that go beyond simple "meetings," and "proposals for a change," on one hand, and the technical details of preparing an industrial site, transacting a loan, or establishing a workforce training program on the other hand. Numerous collaborative activities were probed, and virtually all of them had some level of real world grounding, according to our respondents. Vertical collaborative actions involve different information-related transactions or adjustments to the normal workings of grant, regulatory, and other programs. Horizontal collaborative actions involve jointly developing interlocal policies or strategies, designing projects, and seeking various types of resources.

The relationship between policy approaches and collaboration is also under investigation. Because the research focuses on economic development, the use of various economic policy tools— promotion, subsidies, regulation and deregulation, and growing from within—and their relation to collaboration become important. We find that some approaches are not associated with collaboration, whereas others, such as growing from within, stimulate high levels of collaboration. In this way, we are able to go beyond the contention that collaboration across organizational boundaries is important, but that it also involves discrete and strategically oriented activities.

With regard to how managers collaborate in the intergovernmental game, we hypothesize that dominant patterns or models of
management can be identified in cities, and the test of this hypothesis is the core of the book. We show that some cities are nonplay-
ers in the game and abstain from significant intergovernmental
contact—they do nothing. More frequently, cities and their officials
become involved in some way. They may comply with legal, fiscal,
and other demands and expectations, vertically or horizontally, or
they may undertake some form of negotiation and adjustment
regarding these requirements. These are the conventional means of
managing collaborative challenges (Agranoff and McGuire 2001).

The study was instigated by our belief that a special kind of
active and strategic management exists in some cities. We refer to
this as *jurisdiction-based management*, and it also is prevalent in cities
of all locations and sizes. Jurisdiction-based activity by managers
in cities occurs in administrative contexts that are the most complex, where policy activity is extensive and pressures to perform
are the strongest. Such contexts are illustrated throughout the
book—for example, Cincinnati's land-swap effort mentioned
above. In ways consistent with vertical perspectives of cooperative
federalism and horizontal perspectives of managing in networks,
local managers take strategic action in collaboration with multiple
players and agencies from various governments and sectors, both
inside and outside the city, as a means to adequately serve the
jurisdiction. Thus, we seek to demonstrate that intergovernmental
compliance and bargaining have become a part of managing in the
public sector, and to be sure these activities continue—but something else is also going on. In some situations, a type of jurisdiction-based, strategic management is carried out in complex
systems for the purposes of advancing the interests of the city.

Plan of the Book

The seven chapters that follow use our survey findings and field-
based information as the primary means for discussing collaborative management. In chapter 2, we provide essential theoretical
context for the study. An overview of the many theoretical frameworks that inform the study of collaboration is introduced by
reviewing the literature in these areas. Chapter 3 considers specific

models of collaborative management and hypothesizes that a jurisdiction-based model of public management is present in cities. Chapter 4 examines the collaborative management activities that constitute a city's economic development approach by showing how such activities vary in practice and why.

Chapter 5 focuses on the linkages between player and activity, which are the building blocks of the structure of managing collaboratively. The chapter examines the different types of collaborative arrangements that managers engage in as they work within their communities. Chapter 6 examines the policy approaches of collaboration in detail, focusing on how the adoption of various policy instruments leads to different kinds of linkages and becomes the essence of a city's strategic orientation. Chapter 7 pulls together the empirical findings into an explication of how local agents manage collaboratively in light of the propositions that define the study. In chapter 8, we illuminate the findings and discuss their practical and theoretical implications. This final chapter also discusses how management research might be reshaped and raises issues that must be addressed so that analysis can catch up to, and ultimately inform, the world of practice.

The book documents the significance of collaborative management activity. It demonstrates that cities deal with myriad intergovernmental and intersectoral players that are not immediately thought to be located within a specific policy domain. Often, the number of collaborators needed to make a project work or to solve a problem is considerable. Managers in cities engage these partners while being involved in complex activities that include and go far beyond such visible and commonly recognized intergovernmental tasks as writing grants, meeting regulations, and contracting with other parties. In fact, the activities are multifaceted and go far beyond contacts with other governments. Most important, some cities initiate adjustments and accommodations needed by the jurisdiction. As these players, activities, and linkages are pursued by cities, an approach to management is practiced that is very different from the standard single-organization focus of public management.

As with any analysis, there are limitations to what we can claim in this book. The goal of the book is to demonstrate the broad variation and orientation of city collaborative management: what collaboration looks like, what it involves, and what activities it entails.

The analysis also attempts to provide an explanation for various aspects of collaboration, such as why some cities collaborate more actively than others and whether there is a connection between a city's choice of policy strategy and the extent of its collaboration. The data displayed and discussed in subsequent chapters offer much attraction on their own, for this is the first time that such an extensive picture of collaboration has appeared in print; this documentation, in and of itself, is valuable. However, the intent of the book is not only to demonstrate collaboration, but to take it one step further: to consider what collaboration means for public management, as a field of study and as a profession. What does the extensive presence of collaboration suggest for our models of management? What key questions are raised by our empirical evidence? What does it all mean for the future of public management—and of cities?

The risk in writing a book such as this about a topic with so many unaddressed issues is that readers may have a tendency to look for answers to all of the questions driving this and other research. Eager for answers, we also hope for a grand, definitive statement about the topic that can be used in a classroom or bring closure to the subject matter. What we offer are many pieces of the puzzle, but a piece or two are missing. Although this study cannot test directly each of these pieces, it does cast substantial light on them. We address these still unresolved issues at the end of the book.

2

Managing in an Age of Collaboration

This study is framed from many theoretical and applied management perspectives. As a result, the propositions that we test empirically reflect this vast and disparate literature stream. Researchers from many different academic disciplines and subfields—public administration and management, urban studies, political science, sociology, and business management, to name a few—have contributed observations of the complex governing environment of cities and the processes that cities and their managers experience while operating in such an environment. This chapter discusses these contributions and provides evidence from the case study cities to demonstrate the utility of investigating the ideas across many cases. Initially, we offer a definition of collaboration and make a case for the relevance of studying city-level collaboration within the context of economic development.

The Dependent Variable

Many different labels have been used to describe the interactive patterns of multiple organizational systems, and we employ "collaboration" as our primary descriptor of managing across governments and organizations. In the public administration literature, the term "governance" is often used to describe a wide range of organization types that are linked together and engaged in public activities, enlarging (and changing) the domain of government. Governance connotes that more than public agencies are involved in the formulation and implementation of policy, which suggests "the declining relationship between jurisdiction and public management" (Frederickson 1999, 702). Although Frederickson identifies governance as an emergent managerial phenomenon, others point to the increasing number of structural relationships between public and nonpublic organizations, and the increasingly complex mixes of public and private activities that must be incorporated into frameworks of understanding, regardless of their impact (Campbell and Peters 1988). It is within this latter framework that we look to current governance as involving multiple organizations and connections that are necessary to carry out public purposes.

Collaboration occurs both in a vertical context, with emphasis on levels of government within the U.S. federal system, and in a horizontal context, where the players are local and represent multiple interests within the community. Although horizontal and vertical collaborative actions overlap in practice, we separate them analytically for purposes of description; all such activity is included when we use the term "collaborative management." Horizontal actions emanate from the array of public and private interests that often must be locally mobilized. The horizontal environment of public policymaking and administration includes the interlocal resources held by nongovernmental organizations, private agencies, and area local governments. On a vertical plane, the city government operates within the policy and regulatory frameworks of state and federal governments, while gaining access to available resources. Much of the management in the vertical environment has been viewed historically as finding and operationalizing the proper balance between the national or regional purposes embodied in an intergovernmental program and the special needs of the city. A public manager may be involved in managing across governmental boundaries (vertical collaboration) within the context of one program or project, while simultaneously managing across organizational and sectoral boundaries (horizontal collaboration) within the context of another program or project. Operating in each environment simultaneously can also occur within the context of the same program or project. It is often impossible in practice to distinguish where the boundaries lie between these phenomena.

We define economic development broadly to encompass opportunities for linkages in many different policy domains, for example, transportation, environment, commerce, and community development. Local economic development is the ideal empirical laboratory for observing policymaking and managerial collaboration because, as any astute mayor or city manager will attest, nearly everything a city does is considered as economic development. Cities certainly have many challenges in intergovernmental, interorganizational, and intersectoral collaboration in other policy areas. In human services, for example, from the 1970s movement to integrate services to welfare reform in the 1990s, interorganizational linkages and intergovernmental connections became a standard governance component for cities (Agranoff and Pattakos 1979). Rural (or nonmetropolitan) development depends heavily on state actions to support and mobilize communities (Agranoff and McGuire 2000), usually within collaborative networks of public and private actors (Radin et al. 1996). Similar linkages have also been found at this level in workforce development (Harrison and Weiss 1998) or job training (Jennings and Krane 1994).

Examining collaboration in city-level economic development thus provides the opportunity to examine collaboration in overlapping policy domains. The more commerce-oriented activities of economic development have always been one area where many governmental and nongovernmental actors have interacted routinely, although with varying levels and types of activity. Indeed, early federal involvement with state and local governments was, to a large extent, based in promoting internal improvements and other means of fostering the development of the young U.S. economy (Elazar 1962). This intergovernmental tradition has been followed substantially by industrial and business development programs, only with greater complexity and involvement by a large number of nonprofit and private-sector agencies.

Relevance of Collaboration

That the study of collaborative management is relevant needs little justification. Local officials have, to varying degrees, experimented, dabbled, and sometimes depended on nonbureaucratic methods of service production and provision for decades. City government officials will readily point out this phenomenon by emphasizing the importance of contracting; how their agencies are moving gradually from provision and production to provision only; how intergovernmental grants to their cities foster administrative activity that is often nongovernmental; how finances are leveraged from multiple sources; and how the incidence of joint production and problem resolution places agencies from their jurisdictions in the position of being just one between many governments and/or organizations involved in programs.

In spite of the apparent salience of collaborative management, however, a knowledge base equivalent to—or even close to—the paradigm of bureaucratic management does not yet exist. Instead, perspectives on collaboration among public agencies come from a variety of disciplines and theoretical traditions: interorganizational relations from sociology; regimes from urban scholars; federalism and intergovernmental relations from political scientists and public administrationists; strategic alliances from business management; multiorganizational networks from scholars in public management; and, it seems, on and on.

Collaborative arrangements are a unique institutional form, consisting of processes different from the spontaneous coordination of markets or the conscious management of hierarchy (Powell 1990). A critical issue to understand is why collaboration emerges at all and, if we are to believe the expanding research on the topic, why collaboration is increasing in incidence and importance. One dominant perspective argues that the pace and quality of social change at this point in history are the primary determinants of collaborative management. This social change thesis is prominent in the writings of futurists (Toffler 1980), business consultants (Lipnack and Stamps 1994; Peters 1992), and organization theorists (Clegg 1990), and in much of the literature on public management networks. Just as the bureaucratic organization was the signature organizational form during the industrial age, the emerging information or knowledge age gives rise to less rigid, more permeable structures, where persons are able to link across internal functions, organization boundaries, and even geographic boundaries. The world is characterized by extreme complexity and diversity (Dunsire 1993; Kooiman 1993), where power is dispersed, not centralized; where tasks are becoming de-differentiated, rather than subdivided and specialized; and where society worldwide demands greater freedom and individuation, rather than integration.

O'Toole (1997c) suggests five important reasons why managing across organizations in structures such as interorganizational networks are common and also likely to increase. First, policies dealing with ambitious or complex issues are likely to require such structures for execution. This is a problem change thesis, which asserts that the types of problems or issues society seeks to address collectively are increasingly wicked, or "problems with no solutions, only temporary and imperfect resolutions" (Harmon and Mayer 1986, 9). Tame problems are readily defined and easily decomposable into neat, technical solutions, but these have given way in large part to wicked problems. For most of the problems that emerged in the first part of the twentieth century, a bureaucratic organization was ideal—the problem was easily defined, goals were clear, and objectives were measurable. The metaphor of the wicked problem stands in contrast to traditional bureaucratic policymaking and implementation. For wicked problems, agreement is forged by jointly steering courses of action and delivering policy outputs that are consistent with the multiplicity of societal interests. Other more nonconventional modes of organizing, like collaboration, have emerged to do just that.

Second, O'Toole (1997c) argues that limitations established on the reach of direct governmental intervention encourage rather than dampen network-based solutions. In a sense, collaborative structures may be required to achieve results in particular problem areas when public preference is simultaneously for more government action and less government involvement. When the public demands action on certain public issues, multiple players are drawn together to fulfill that demand because it can only be done through collaboration. Third, political imperatives elicit networking beyond what might be necessitated by policy objectives; administrators often must balance technical needs for clear and concentrated program authority with political demands for inclusion and broader influence.

Fourth, as information has accumulated regarding second-order program effects, efforts have been made to institutionalize the connections, such as through interorganizational task forces and planning bodies. Fifth, layers of mandates, including crosscutting regulations and crossover sanctions, provide additional pressure for managing networks. For intense policy spheres like economic development or welfare, different programs have different intents, funding sources and priorities, mandated criteria, and targeted stakeholders. As a result, O'Toole (1997c, 46) suggests that "setting ambitious objectives in contexts of dispersed power makes networking imperative for program managers."

Another key reason for an emphasis on collaboration is the growing prominence of knowledge as a factor in social and economic production, while land, labor, and capital are becoming secondary factors. Moreover, knowledge-related work is increasingly specialized, which presents greater challenges for organizations. Contemporary specialized knowledge is what Reich (1991) refers to as symbolic-analytic (as opposed to routine production and personal services) workers, who do the problem solving, problem identifying, and strategic brokering, elevating the role of human capital in the workplace. Their work is tied less to an organization than to an internal team of complementary symbolic-analytic workers, as well as to interorganizational webs that are often global in reach. Thus, the challenge is to make disparate knowledge productive by integrating it into common tasks (Drucker 1995).

Finally, an important perspective based in the robust theory of urban regimes presumes that the effectiveness of governing is actually determined by governmental operations across organizations. According to this perspective, as complexity has increased, nongovernmental actors become necessary components of a local delivery system. Multiple actors collaborate within many fields of government action, building long-lasting alliances and forging regimes to do what the government alone cannot do. Like other forms of collaboration, regimes are informal, nonhierarchical, and without a single authority to guide operations. Such characteristics are not prohibitive of effective governance, but rather contribute to a city's capacity to govern. Governments must blend their capacities with those of various nongovernmental actors to be effective and "government capacity is created and maintained by bringing together coalition partners with appropriate resources, non-governmental as well as governmental" (Stone 1993, 1). Just as interorganizational networks improve the chances for effective service delivery in certain policy areas, regimes increase the capacity of cities to design and implement public goods and services.

Collaborative Mechanisms

Not too many years ago, the activities of local economic development officials were relatively simple and direct in scope. Policymaking resources existed primarily with a single city official and perhaps a few local businessmen, and collaboration, if any existed at all, rarely extended beyond a government official and the local chamber of commerce. Very few observed functional interdependencies existed in this sector; a state agency would perform the recruitment function, and local officials occasionally would lobby the agency for help or market their community for consideration by the state. The design and management of local development policy were certainly politicized, as at present, but economic policy objectives were also centralized, functionally based, and hierarchically organized through a single government agency (Fosler 1992).

Collaborative possibilities now exist in abundance. Beloit's vertical intergovernmental relationships involve the multiple modes and frequent contacts typical of a central city. The city manager's office estimates that about one state contact a day and one federal contact a week are made by the city government. The city's local development corporation, the Beloit Economic Development Corporation (BEDCOR), reports that it makes one or two contacts a week with state and federal agencies. The most frequent state contacts are with the Wisconsin Department of Development (DoD), the Wisconsin Housing and Economic Development Authority (WHEDA), the Department of Natural Resources, and the Department of Transportation.

WHEDA is important because it administers the Revenue Bond Program, a direct loan program for business, and various home loan programs. DoD is important for loan and assistance programs, flood assistance programs, securing leads on prospective businesses, and for its single state permit application and processing center. As an entitlement city, federal contacts are primarily with the Department of Housing and Urban Development regarding funds from the Community Development Block Grant Program. Funding from this program represents a notable portion of the city's budget and finances a great deal of its development efforts. Beloit also contacts the Small Business Administration office in Madison, which directly administers other federal loan programs, and the representative of the federal Economic Development Administration in Madison.

The city's horizontal contacts begin with BEDCOR as the lead initiator. BEDCOR's recruiter works with prospective businesses, making contacts with the city regarding location and site issues, and initiating discussions over infrastructure concerns. The city government works directly with prospects by providing and working on infrastructure questions, particularly with local utility companies; making the "land deal" with the buyer if it involves city-owned land; making the needed regulatory changes that are within their powers; and brokering with the state if such efforts are needed.

Other local partners include the Rock County government, which in economic development works more in the rural areas outside Janesville and Beloit, but it has participated in some workforce development, joint marketing, and grant-seeking efforts. There is also a great deal of city–county contact regarding roads and transportation issues. A formal working group, comprising representatives from the City of Beloit, City of Janesville, Rock County, the local Private Investment Council, and Blackhawk Technical College, also coordinates joint economic development efforts, such as in workforce needs for business prospects.

Managers in all cities have the opportunity to be involved in numerous contacts with many different public agencies and private entities, and in a fashion that is compounded potentially by multiple efforts to promote local interests. As the Beloit example demonstrates, cities that choose to govern collaboratively experience a set of identifiable managerial actions that can be differentiated. Collaborative mechanisms available to cities include not just those that are state–federal (vertical), but also a host of others at the intercommunity level that are related to local governments and nongovernmental actors. Indeed, vertical activity is often stimulated by the many efforts or projects that are being generated within the community, as embodied in our proposed model of jurisdiction-based management. By the same token, a great deal of intersectoral interaction can exist due to federal and state programming and regulation contacts.

The multitude of collaborative mechanisms pursued by Beloit are consistent with what Robert Dahl and Charles Lindblom (1953) observed one-half century ago. The authors demonstrated in amazing detail the multiplicity of interventions available to modern societies, many of which necessarily involve more than a single hierarchical organization. In their estimation, the effectiveness of public policies is determined less by bureaucratic administration than by ownership that may be public or private, influence that may not be compulsory, expenditure control that may not be direct, and bureaucratic responsibility that may be lacking. Multiple governing mechanisms are available to the public sector; it is not mega-bureaucratic, as machine-like depictions of organizations would have us believe. Rather, the basic problem and challenge of governance is for multiple governmental and nongovernmental organizations to jointly steer courses of action and to deliver policy outputs that are consistent with the multiplicity of societal interests (Kaufmann 1991).

Academic knowledge of the multiplicity of collaborative players and activities emerged from research on intergovernmental relations, policy implementation, and interorganizational relations, as well as studies from business and economics. Much of the history of the U.S. government "has been the search for methods to provide for the necessary collaboration of the various parts of the federal system while at the same time preserving and strengthening those parts" (Elazar 1964, 248). Recognizing the predominance of collaboration across governments, Grodzins (1966) characterized administrative practices in federalism as "shared functions": Significant decision-making power is exercised both by those in the federal government and by those in subnational governments during program formulation, officials of all governments exercise significant responsibilities in the administration of a given activity, and representatives of all governments exert significant influence over the operation of a given program (p. 11). Studies of the administration of federal grants-in-aid (Derthick 1970; Pressman 1975; Nathan and Doolittle 1987), policy implementation studies (O'Toole and Montjoy 1984; Goggin et al. 1990), investigations of state-level policy innovation (Osborne 1988), and research into local government fiscal woes (Levine 1980) suggest the hypothesis that multiple collaborative mechanisms are available to cities.

Managing across governments involves cooperating in a complex system of rules, regulations, and standards, and taking advantage of opportunities. City officials describe how managing within the federal system involves mobilizing forces within and outside the community to build support; acquiring the necessary financing, expertise, and other resources, while setting a course of action; learning about the external government opportunities and constraints; reading the ever-changing signals of program managers and funding agents; and successfully operating and cooperating within the system (Agranoff 1986; Agranoff and McGuire 2001; Wright 1983).

Federal and state governments enable important local actions by setting policy contexts, providing important program resources, and regulating frameworks that condition local behavior. Intergovernmental transactions appear to expand as programs and regulations increase. Such transactions give rise to multiple decision structures, implying additional multiorganizational arrangements (Pressman 1975; Pressman and Wildavsky 1973). The interacting component units result in a national system of governance. Central statutory authority and financial responsibility blend with local delivery and involvement of subnational governments in national programs to share decision making and adaptation, so that policy can unite what constitutions divide (Rose 1985).

Variations in Activity and Strategy

The choices that managers make in any context define whether the organization will adapt to its environment, influence the environment, or attempt to buffer itself from the effects of the environment. Some managers are more proactive than others and more willing to take risks to exploit the environment. Bardach (1998) refers to "purposive practitioners" leaders who see possibilities and act on collaborative opportunities. Management is strategic; decisions regarding whether to pursue a course of action precede decisions about how to do so.

Cities are no different. Some cities choose to avail themselves of the opportunities present in the multiorganizational environment, but some do not. Certainly, the variations in collaborative activity are determined at least in part by politics. For example, all cities understand, to some degree, that the intergovernmental system poses several barriers. Previous survey-based studies from the 1970s and 1980s concerning grants management and requirements demonstrate the incidence and significance of operating barriers

(ACIR 1977; Agranoff and Pattakos 1985; Richter 1976; Study Committee on Policy Management Assistance 1975).

We have evidence suggesting that variations in collaborative activity are related to local managers' perceived internal political and operational barriers, as well as the conditions inherent in the external intergovernmental system. Important external barriers include the time involved in processes such as grants or loans, the complex nature of such processes, the requirements of program and fiscal accountability, and the difficulty of getting clear and timely interpretations. Key internal barriers are internal opposition, incompatibility between jurisdictional needs and requirements, and the pressures caused by other city business. The internal factors appear to be as inhibitory to collaborative management as are the hurdles of working with other governments. Over time, many cities learn to live with the volatility of internal politics and develop capacities for overcoming the political claims of the federal and state government. But such barriers remain an important consideration for a city's decisions about whether and how to collaborate.

The economy of a city is also an important variable to consider when describing the type and extent of collaborative activity. Differences across cities in the composition of the economic base, the condition of the local economy, administrative capacity to address economic problems, and the rate of capital flow through and within the community suggest that cities' strategies and patterns of interaction with other entities also will differ. Research has shown that the condition of the local economy is a strong determinant of the form and content of a city's development policy strategy (McGuire 1999; Fleischmann, Green, and Kwong 1992; Sharp 1991), and certainly managers from cities of all sizes understand the effect of economic condition on a city's operations. Economic conditions across central cities, suburban cities, and rural towns vary significantly, with suburban cities typically demonstrating better, in some cases much better, performance on the key economic indicators of unemployment rate, poverty rate, family income, and education level. We show later in the book that a city's economic strength and level of collaborative activity are inversely related.

In addition to political and economic concerns, structural and administrative factors appear to be significant determinants of collaborative management. Economic policy has changed at the local level, as both the vertical and horizontal terrain of economic development policy has shifted dramatically (Fosler 1992). Officials in cities determine the degree to which the public sector intervenes in the local economy, decide which policy approaches are best utilized to achieve the desired results, and estimate the intended effects of these approaches. The way in which these various policy approaches are manipulated, combined, and packaged, as well as the pattern of collaborative activity each approach entails, defines the form and content of a city's development strategy. Past research suggests that the types of policy approaches adopted by a city could be related in some way to its level and type of collaborative management.

Cities are critical players in the ever-changing and expanding informational and global economy (Clarke and Gaile 1998). Though designed to stimulate private investment and to alleviate the effects of poverty and unemployment, federal and state programs have also fundamentally altered the policy and administrative structure of local development. As cities have intensified their involvement in economic policymaking, the number of actors that have a stake in developing city economies and thus must be mobilized to effectively influence economic activity has proliferated. Many programs require strong linkages among the city, nongovernmental organizations, and residents, resulting in a new institutional infrastructure designed to support economic development activities.

Such changes in the policy and institutional context of local economic development have resulted in changes in the role and operation of city officials who deal with development issues. The contextual changes—partnerships between public and private sectors, combining and leveraging financial resources from multiple sources, multicity and regional initiatives, and governments assisting in product and market development—place new demands on public officials to act as catalysts for other local government and nongovernmental actors in their pursuit of effective development policy strategies. These new demands are no doubt strong determinants of collaborative strategy and activity.

It is also important to understand the number and types of administrative arrangements in cities, which, in economic development, appear to be vast. One major component of the local institutional development infrastructure is the lead development agency in the city. Such agencies can be classified into three distinct forms: (1) government agencies, where activities are centralized in the chief administrator's office, carried out by several line departments, or housed in a specialized agency or department; (2) private associations, which are agencies, like the chamber of commerce, a manufacturer's association, or a downtown business association, typically sponsored by area businesses yet functioning with the full support of the local government; and (3) local development corporations, which involve business, community, and the local government in a formalized cooperative venture that can perform all the responsibilities assigned to it by government while maintaining a close linkage to private business (Blakely 1994).

A government agency, for example, may have the advantages of political access and the ability to make decisions relatively quickly with government executives and with elected officials (Levy 1990). Officials in such an agency benefit from expertise readily available from players in several crucial program areas, such as planning, public works, or finance. The types of government policymaking structure in cities can be line agencies like an economic development department, an office included in another department, or an office linked directly to the office of a city manager or mayor (Fleischmann and Green 1991).

Conversely, because of its relative lack of access to government, privately funded groups such as chambers of commerce and industrial associations interact more frequently with other private-sector players. Alternatively, a public–private economic development organization can ally itself with organizations from the public or private sectors, thus presumably having access to an expanded set of players with whom to collaborate. The structure of public–private partnerships varies from development corporations, in which the public is represented only through the corporation's governing structure, to agencies funded by the city budget. Our four largest case study cities provide examples of the various types of government agency structures: Cincinnati has a separate Department of Economic Development, Beloit has a Department of Community Development in the city manager's office, Garfield Heights has a line department of economic development, and Woodstock's functions are spread across two departments and a public–private development corporation.

Reliance on the various lead agencies varies by metropolitan status, whereas the variation in the type of lead official varies by size. Suburbs of all sizes rely more heavily on government agencies and less heavily on local development corporations as the lead promoters of economic development in comparison with nonmetropolitan or central cities. Apparently, with economies that are relatively strong and prosperous, suburbs have little desire to create an extra-governmental institution to promote economic development. Suburban citizens with expectations of low taxes and stable local commerce may have greater control of economic development promotion when it is lodged in a government agency. The majority of small municipalities have their economic development activities directed by someone from the chief administrator's office. In contrast, in fewer than one-half of the large cities in the sample does the chief administrative officer or an assistant lead the economic development administration.

We also see evidence of strategic collaboration in cities that undertake strategic planning. Planning in local economic development "encompasses the broad concept of formulating courses of action for socioeconomic change" (Blakely 1994, xvi). Because such planning is a means to find a favorable competitive position in the continual competition for resources, collective consideration of where needed resources exist and from whom these resources must be accessed will result in more and varied collaboration. Strategic and long-range planning is commonly employed in many cities and is regularly undertaken in Beloit, Woodstock, Ithaca, and Garfield Heights. In all these cities, incidentally, a professional planner with a graduate degree heads the economic development operation, within either the city government or the local development corporation.

Types of Collaborative Management

Managing in collaborative settings should not be confused with managing hierarchies. Public administrationists are slow to break free of the bureaucratic paradigm that still dominates the field, especially if one considers textbooks and the curriculum of public administration degrees as representative of the field's bridge between theory and practice. For many years, the issue of "collaboration" was framed myopically in terms of public versus private: debates over privatization, the "new" public management, contract administration, and so on.

In these debates, "public" means hierarchy and bureaucracy, and "private" means markets. This classical management approach, which has informed both public and business administration for more than a century, is mostly intraorganizational and based primarily in the activities of planning (establishing organizational goals), organizing (structuring and designing the organization), and leading (achieving the goals). The approach is based on coordination through hierarchies, strict chains of command, and management that takes place within the confines of separate organizational entities (Mandell 1988). In contrast, collaborative settings are not based in a central authority and cannot be guided by a single organizational goal. The primary activities of the manager in such settings are selecting the appropriate actors and resources, shaping the operating context of the network, and developing ways to cope with strategic and operational complexity (Kickert, Klijn, and Koppenjan 1997). Through collaboration, each player brings and keeps his or her authority, while managing together with others.

Collaborative management is an elusive target to measure precisely, given the multiple players and possible strategies a city may pursue. The allocation and utilization of management resources expended is fluid—it varies across time and space within a given program or project. Managing in collaborative structures involves a complex sequence of moves and countermoves, adjustments and readjustments, actions and nonactions. Some moves are more consequential than others. Some moves merely establish the context for making other moves. Others serve as a breach point between failed and inconsequential moves and the promise of eventual success.

We hypothesize that there is an identifiable and predictable logic of collaborative management that can assist researchers in explaining how and why managers allocate resources in a given context. The finite—though myriad—number of collaborative mechanisms suggests some common, generic models involving unique managerial tasks. We assert that from these various combinations of activity and purpose we can infer a set of models representing the allocation and reallocation of tasks. Even as our research reveals the vast inventory of activities and strategies, it is also important to understand how a city strategically matches tasks with policy context.

One assumption of this logic is that the fulfillment of purposes by a city is contingent on its ability to function in, and its capacity to adapt to, its environment. According to Simon (1981), goal attainment is a function of adapting the many and varied inner environments in a system (i.e., network) to the outer environment. He argues that "in very many cases whether a particular system will achieve a particular goal or adaptation depends on only a few characteristics of the outer environment and not at all on the detail of that environment" (p. 11). With a multitude of collaborative mechanisms encompassing a city's governing (outer) environment, it is necessary to isolate those models of management that accurately describe a unique allocation of managerial tasks.

The need to collaborate emerges from interdependence among players, caused by each player possessing different types and levels of technologies and resources needed for fulfilling a task. Interdependence induces an increase in the frequency and intensity of communication among these organizations, which in turn forces decisions to be made jointly and actions to be carried out collectively to some degree (Alter and Hage 1993). The greater the interdependencies between players, both vertical and horizontal, the greater the need for coordination and collaboration. One common unit of analysis used to describe and assess horizontal collaborative management is known as the interorganizational network, which is the totality (or some demarcated subset) of organizations that have varying degrees of interaction with each other, are linked together with varying degrees of formality, and pursue a common objective. The rapidly expanding literature on interorganizational networks suggests that the practice of management is beginning to extend far afield from earlier studies when critical interdependencies were considered to be an overlay or "just another task" of administration to be addressed after managers attended to internal matters (Thompson 1967). Today's managing occurs routinely at or outside the boundaries of governmental and nongovernmental organizations (Milward 1996).

Network management offers an important class of collaborative management models. Our understanding of network management is derived mainly from theoretically examining, rather than empirically cataloging, its tasks. During a time when observers first became aware of the emerging intergovernmental and interorganizational forms of governing, Hanf and colleagues identified how managers intervene in existing interrelationships, promote interactions, and mobilize coordination (Hanf, Hjern, and Porter 1978). Since that time, researchers have documented that officials from all levels of government perceive managing across governments and organizations as involving a number of discrete but related tasks: mobilizing forces within and outside of the community to build support; acquiring the necessary financing, expertise, and other resources, while setting a course of action; learning about the external government opportunities and constraints; reading the ever-changing signals of program managers and funding agents; and successfully operating and cooperating within the system (Agranoff 1986; Agranoff and McGuire 1999; Howitt 1984; Stone 1989). Kickert, Klijn, and Koppenjan (1997) distinguish the multitude of managerial tasks in terms of purposes or models: those network management activities or strategies aimed at the ideas and perceptions of network members, and those aimed at the interaction of members. The former includes preventing or introducing new ideas, bargaining, and inducing reflection within the network; the latter involve arranging, structuring, and mediating interaction among network participants.

Another method for modeling network management is to examine the impact of public management in general on governmental performance, and then isolate those factors that are network specific. O'Toole and Meier (1999) have developed a parsimonious yet robust framework for modeling management that discerns not only the impact of these functions, but also the managerial resources used to perform them in particular structural contexts. The O'Toole and Meier model is not network specific, but rather it captures the resources that constitute public management in general, which include stabilizing the internal operations of a system, exploiting shocks in the environment of the system, and buffering the system to minimize the impact of environmental shocks. The model is grounded in structural variations that exist within particular program contexts and the way in which such variations determine the allocation of management resources. Network management is thus a particular allocation of resources where environmental management—leveraging external opportunities and buffering the system from unwanted shocks—supplements or opposes more hierarchical functions.

American federalism is perhaps the most enduring model of collaborative problem resolution. Intergovernmental administration operates within a federal matrix rather than a hierarchy sometimes assumed by the existence of three levels of government. In many volumes, Elazar suggests the important idea that federal systems are noncentralized, with constitutional diffusion and sharing of powers among many centers. Along with Anderson (1960), he understood that jurisdictions (Elazar called them civil societies) in the United States possessed sufficient legal, fiscal, and political independence to operate (or had the potential to operate) independently, on their own behalf. There is a constitutional diffusion and sharing of powers among many centers. In a statement with obvious management implications, Elazar argued that "the model for federalism is the matrix, a network of arenas within arenas" (1984, 3). These arenas are distinguished by being larger or smaller rather than "higher" or "lower." The form and character of intergovernmental interaction, based in sharing through bargaining, and negotiated cooperation, are best described in terms of his matrix arrangement. A matrix is one useful metaphor for the sets of linkages connecting cities with other governments and organizations (Agranoff 2001).

"Cooperative federalism" and its attendant intergovernmental relations and administration that emerged in the 1930s is an enduring collaborative model. An early argument that intergovernmental collaboration assumes identifiable characteristics was offered by Jane Perry Clark (1938), who was one of the first to recognize the verity of administrative types available to governments. She described administrative cooperation between federal and subnational governments as distinctly experimental yet routine:

> Much of the cooperation between the federal and state governments has been found in the sea of governmental activity without any chart, compass, or guiding star, for cooperation has been unplanned and uncorrelated with other activities of government even in the same field. Nevertheless, a *certain number of patterns* may be traced in the confusion. Cooperation has frequently been a means of coordinating the use of federal and state resources, of eliminating duplications in activity, of cutting down expenses, of

accomplishing work which could not otherwise be carried out, and in general of attempting to make the wheels of government in the federal system of the United States move more smoothly than would be otherwise possible. (1938, 7; italics added)

The practice of what has been referred to as intergovernmental management (IGM) is the most prominent descriptive metaphor of vertical collaborative management. Since the expansion of federal programs in the 1960s, IGM has emerged impressively but somewhat ambiguously into the public management lexicon. The growth of federal grants and new regulatory programs, increased federal–state and federal–local programming, federal initiatives to nongovernmental organizations, and expanded roles for state government have put a premium on collaborative actions and transactions across governmental boundaries.

The primary players working across governments are generally managers and program officials, although elected officials also become involved in intergovernmental relationships. Intergovernmental management has been distinguished as having a problem-solving focus, involving contacts and communication networks, and understanding and working within the existing system (Wright 1983) as managers confront the political, legal, and technical questions related to the task at hand (Agranoff 1986). Wright and Krane (1998) define IGM as "the process of solving intergovernmental problems under conditions of high uncertainty and complexity through the creation and use of governmental and non-governmental networks" (p. 1162). This type of management includes familiar actions, such as seeking funds from other governments, coping with an expanding regulatory burden, and developing interlocal cooperative agreements. Whereas more formal arrangements like obtaining grants and forming agreements were prominent in an era of abundant resources and numerous programs, the policy context of subnational governments has changed. Intergovernmental management is now more daunting and typically encompasses many different collaborative activities, including managing horizontally.

Present and Future of Collaborative Management

Collaborative public management is on the front lines of the transformation from the traditional concept of bureaucracy, with its emphasis on a pyramid of control and maximum specialization of work, to a postbureaucratic paradigm, where new forms of transactions based on marketlike discipline substitute for the external surveillance of supervision. Weiner (1990) predicts organizational management and transorganizational (network) management will become two parallel but overlapping streams within administrative theory, relying heavily on both behavioral science and management science research and practice. Whereas traditional organization is rigid, postbureaucratic organization is flexible: Choice replaces determinism, and work is less differentiated, demarcated, and multi-skilled (Clegg 1990). As a result, complex and fragmentary administrative transactions emerge across organizational boundaries. Kettl (1996) argues that the most important change in administrative functioning during the past century is the increasing interdependence between public organizations that "has radically changed the jobs of public administrators, who must now not only manage the functions of their own agencies but must also build critical linkages with others" (p. 9).

Collaborative management in cities mirrors the overall societal move toward collaboration and networks—though, as we have acknowledged, the field's knowledge of the former is limited. Although the need for collaboration is not new and different in the present day, its perceived centrality for accomplishing major initiatives and making institutions work has brought it to the attention of many management scholars. Collaboration in the twenty-first century, within and between organizations, is a popular subject in many management handbooks (e.g., Austin 2000; Campbell and Gould 1999; Lipnack and Stamps 1994). In her well-known book, *World Class*, Rosabeth Moss Kanter (1995) extends the locus of collaboration by pointing to the need for communities to be more than magnets for attracting resources; they must also develop their social stock. She argues that "communities also need social glue—a means for social cohesion, a way to bring people together to define the common good, create joint plans, and identify strategies that benefit a wide range of organizations and people in the community" (p. 32).

Robert Putnam's *Making Democracy Work* demonstrates an empirical connection among civic community (norms of civic associations), policy networks, and economic progress (1993). Such linkage-based norms are identified as essential for the effectiveness of a host of institutions. Similarly, Neal Pierce's *Citystates* identifies regional economic success as partially depending on the ability of citizens and civic leaders to plan and develop civic networks, as well as the collaborative leadership skills necessary to address their problems and concerns (1993). Pierce contends that "where norms and networks are lacking, the outlook for collective action appears bleak" (p. 185).

Fountain (1998, 104) refers to social capital as the "stock" that is created when a group of organizations develops the ability to work together for mutual productive gain. Social capital is essential for groups of disparate representatives like those in cities to work toward sharing resources held by individual organizations. She argues further that the important elements of social capital are trust, norms, and operations of the network, which are closely related to the values and objectives of the actors. She suggests that tools that enhance the creation of social capital must be part of policies promoting innovation and productivity growth:

> Like physical capital and human capital—tools and training that enhance individual productivity—"social capital" refers to features of social organization, such as networks, norms, and trust, that facilitate coordination and cooperation for mutual benefit. The notion of social capital extends our understanding of "cooperation" or "collaboration" in two significant ways. First, linking cooperation to the economic concept "capital" signals the investment or growth potential of a group's ability to work jointly. Second, the concept identifies the structure created from collaborative effort as capital. (1998, 113)

Social capital has been linked empirically with increased innovation and economic growth within the biotechnology and information industry, as well as revitalization in manufacturing.

Cities are beginning to recognize the importance of knowledge integration through technology (Milward and Provan 1998). In an insightful set of case studies about "innovators" who have helped the United States keep pace with rapid social and organizational changes, Smith's *Rethinking America* (1995) concludes that size and scale, advantages long enjoyed by the United States, are now often liabilities, and less desirable than flexibility and agility. Moreover, developing technology (once believed to be the U.S. competitive advantage) does not work without also developing the human capital needed to apply technology. Teamwork, production networks, and collaboration are the names of the new game. Today's American success stories demonstrate the dynamic renaissance generated by sharing power and tapping many minds. The old adversarial game is much less effective and has given way to success based on shared interest, common responsibility, and mutual respect. Smith concludes: "The lesson from the Innovators for rethinking America then, is the need to forge integrated strategies—to make connections between elements of American society (p. xxii)."

Contemporary thinking on innovation and problem solving also points to collaboration as a core process in change management. In *The Centerless Corporation* (1998), Pasternack and Viscio note that most knowledge creation and learning occur when people are reacting to someone else's thinking. This is why the concept of linkages and communities is so important and should be part of a knowledge program architecture. From this perspective, communities should be organized around both learning and change, and should be overlapping to enhance diffusion of learning. Knowledge creation involves overcoming what the authors refer to as the four unnatural acts: sharing one's best thinking, using what other people have developed, building on the expertise of others, and improving by synthesizing new ideas and purging prior conventional wisdom. The more automatic these unnatural (and, by definition, collaborative) acts are overcome and ingrained into production processes, the more connections and best practices can emerge, and thus the easier it will be to engineer creation processes.

These internal change processes also apply externally to connections between interests and organizations in communities. Successes in urban development, education, health, and children's services not only achieve tangible results but build civic community: "When collaboration succeeds, new networks and norms for civic engagement and the primary focus of work shifts from parochial interests to the broader concerns of the community" (Chrislip and Larson 1994, 13). Successful collaboration between public and nonpublic organizations usually succeeds with some basic preconditions and procedural steps, which in turn spawn additional higher, broader forms of collaboration.

Collaborative management appears to be an undeniable phenomenon that exists in many different settings, including government and nonprofit organizations. It is characterized by complex combinations of vertical and horizontal activity, only some of which can be considered cooperative, but all of which are multi-party. Management by cities across governments and organizations has been described as "intergovernmental management" and as "network management," and with other general terms. But the idea that management styles and orientations vary across cities has not been addressed in previous research. We believe that such models of management are identifiable across cities. The literature, however, also gives us reason to propose that a jurisdiction-based approach to public management is emerging and is in need of elaboration. This belief drives our research. The next chapter explicates our theory that different models of collaborative management exist and can be identified in cities.

3

Models of Collaborative Management

I s the city government just another actor in an array of organizations and agencies or does it engage in purposive action? If it takes action, how does a city approach its multiorganizational environment? These questions go to the heart of policymaking and administration within governance arrangements. We argue that city governments and their officials possess some legal and fiscal levers that can keep governmental units at the center of collaborative transactions and can be counterweights to any financial, informational, or operational asymmetries that may be brought to the table by nongovernmental organizations.

Although governance theory recognizes that government is one of many organizations, it cannot accurately relegate it to the status of just another organization. Our analysis of collaborative management in economic development puts the municipal government at the hub of both horizontal and vertical connections. Cities engage in contacts and transactions with multiple federal and state agencies and with interlocal players. This chapter presents a continuum of such activity through the presentation of hypothetical models. The next three chapters measure their extensiveness.

Hypothesized Models of Collaborative Management

We model collaborative management as the intersection of two variables or dimensions: (1) a city's collaborative activity level and

(2) the extent to which such activity is strategic. Many different types or styles of collaborative management can be hypothesized to exist if we cross-tabulate the activity and strategy variables; the result is several distinct models of management.[1] For example, a city can choose to exploit its complex governing environment by seeking out opportunities and actively operating with vertical and horizontal actors. Conversely, a city can choose to be inactive and passive toward collaboration, for whatever reasons. We can also consider the situation where a city is moderately, even highly, active collaboratively with mainly vertical actors, but does so passively, not viewing the environment as an opportunity but as a burden or necessary evil. Similarly, a city could be active and occasionally bargain with vertical actors, while collaborating with horizontal actors semi-regularly.

The dominant style of collaborative management for each city can be measured as the joint level of the activity and strategy dimensions. Figure 3.1 illustrates the depiction of possible combinations, which we hypothesize do exist in the real world of city governing. The city names correspond to six different combinations offered as hypothesized models of management. To demonstrate initially the crux of these models, we describe briefly the response of the six cities to a hypothetical state grant program involving matching funds for the purpose of acquiring venture capital for economic development investment (a venture capital matching funds program to be paid out over three years, whereby the state grants 25 percent of the capital fund, city government another 25 percent, the rest financed by private investors). The model we refer to as *jurisdiction-based management*, one we believe is the dominant orientation in many cities including our hypothetical Cityville, occupies one extreme (high activity and opportunistic). The *abstinence* model occupies the other extreme (low activity and passive) and is represented by Nothing Hill. Two venerable models, referred to here as the *top-down* and *donor-recipient* models (Vertville and Bargain City, respectively, in figure 3.1), occupy varying levels of activity and strategy. *Reactive management*, represented as a value hovering near the midpoint of figure 3.1, is the dominant orientation in Centerville. Finally, Richburb practices *contented management*, represented as an extreme value (low activity and opportunistic) located in the bottom-right quadrant of figure 3.1.

Figure 3.1. Models of Collaborative Management

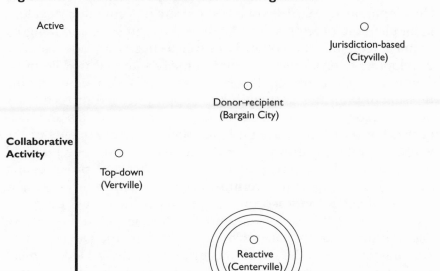

Active

○
Jurisdiction-based
(Cityville)

○
Donor-recipient
(Bargain City)

Collaborative Activity

○
Top-down
(Vertville)

○
Reactive
(Centerville)

○
Contented
(Richburb)

○
Abstinence
(Nothing Hill)

Inactive

Passive   Opportunistic

Collaborative Strategy

Cityville (jurisdiction-based management): Cityville's planning process revealed that government-sponsored venture capital is not presently needed in Cityville, although some city leaders believe such a program may be useful in a few years as the city moves toward developing a high-technology partnership with the local university. The city's main priority is to double the size of its industrial park by developing a parcel of city land adjacent to the city's two interstate highways. The city's collaborative management emanates from two important planning processes that help determine its priorities. First, the city's Department of Community Development regularly conducts a strategic economic development planning process, which involves governmental and nongovernmental organization officials, as well as business leaders and its development corporation. Second, the city's annual update of its Community Development Block Grant (CDBG) plan allows for the revision of priorities in spending to support needed projects. City officials expressed their need for funds to state officials and suggested the possibility of slightly altering the requirements of the venture capital program. After the state declined, they pursued infrastructure development funds from another state program and approached two federal government agencies with other ideas. The city's strategic activity led to adjustments in the CDBG program, a minor redirection of a state infrastructure grant, and extensive negotiations and appeals with the U.S. Economic Development Administration and the state Housing and Economic Development Authority over eligibility for assistance. In the end, the city receives a mixture of state infrastructure funds and federal money, along with enhanced financial support from local investors.

Nothing Hill (abstinence): Nothing Hill refused to apply for the venture capital program because its council opposes any matching fund requirements that bind the city to a program that could be ineffective or outlive its usefulness. The general view of city officials is that economic development will happen with a bit of Chamber of Commerce promotion and old-fashioned charm, not with the state or federal government mandating the direction of development through its ever-present conditions and regulations. Besides, no one in City Hall is willing or able to deal with the application.

Vertville (top-down): Vertville submitted an application for the venture capital program, understanding that such programs have state-imposed requirements and realizing that the program is not perfect, but it is better than nothing. The city would like to expand its industrial park, but it settled for seeking venture capital funds in hopes that such investment might be targeted to the park. City officials do not like grant conditions and complain often about the amount of paperwork and red tape that accompanies each grant, but it dutifully prepared to follow all of the rules related to eligibility requirements, types of enterprises, matching funds, reporting, and auditing. The city discussed each condition and challenge, and it invited a state official to visit to discuss the major operational implications of the mandates. The city manager then worked with an intern from a nearby university to prepare a compliance plan that counts back from the legally designated date for compliance and estimates the costs of each new city effort. Fiscal notes and spending implications were then incorporated into the budget and discussed with the city council. City officials feel that they have little choice but to comply with external programs if they desire the additional funding.

Bargain City (donor-recipient) : Bargain City recognized the value of the venture capital program, but did not view it as a perfect fit for its needs, particularly the funding requirements. City officials applied for the program, but only after a series of negotiations with the state. The city government, including the city manager, is always under heavy fire to broker deals that would keep budget commitments low but not constrain the city's ability to grow. The city wanted to trade off 15 percent of its match for other investment services and a five-year payout, rather than the prescribed three-year funding cycles. Such an arrangement could ease the short-term burden for the city, but also provide a useful and capable recipient for a state agency needing to demonstrate the effectiveness of the program. Although not explicitly designed for industrial park expansion, city staff, through extended negotiations with state government staff, proposed nine industrial projects and generated additional local funding criteria in accord with state criteria. The state and city finally agree to a 20 percent city match and a four-year payout. The city was able to direct a substantial proportion of this state program toward its most pressing priorities.

Centerville (reactive management): Centerville has the staff to deal with the application and they sometimes submit applications for promising programs, but not the venture capital program. The costs are considered to be too high and the city has too little time to plan and carry out such a commitment.

Richburb (contented management): The city's economy is growing rapidly and there is plenty of locally available capital. It is already working with commercial and residential developers who are willing to invest their own money. It has also forged a joint annexation agreement with a nearby suburb to split a large parcel of land that is being sold for development. Why would it want or need the involvement of other governments?

Model Descriptions

Jurisdiction-Based Management Model

Jurisdiction-based management describes the management practiced in our hypothetical city called Cityville. The heart of the model emphasizes local managers taking strategic action with multiple actors and agencies from various governments and sectors. This model portrays the local manager as driven by a strategic rationale that is, as the model name indicates, based in the jurisdiction. For such a manager, the achievement of a local goal and the completion of a particular task are paramount. Strategic behavior in the complex, interdependent world of the jurisdiction-based manager consists of seeking out and contacting the actors who possess the resources (including legal authority, funding, organization, expertise, information) that local managers need to achieve their goals. Goal achievement in complex settings requires interaction and adjustment with critically positioned or endowed actors.

Jurisdiction-based managers in a city may recognize the numerous programs, actors, and agencies—the many possible donors—that constitute the city's policy environment, but contact only those agencies that can provide the targeted, place-oriented resources that directly and strategically affect the manager's jurisdiction. By calculating the costs and benefits of each available program, the manager of the jurisdiction-based model proceeds strategically through the grant-seeking thicket.

The strategic, interactive foundation of the jurisdiction-based model is consistent with a practical and theoretical move away from classical perspectives on management toward an approach based in strategy and managing interdependencies (Bozeman 1993; Bryson and Roering 1996; Kettl 1996). Two essential themes from interorganizational relations and strategic planning provide the theoretical basis for this hypothesized model of collaborative management. Thompson (1967) reminds us that managers' task environments are plural and require management of internal and external interdependencies, which leads to a series of exchange agreements. This contingency approach, which spawned a whole subfield of administrative study, fostered the idea that the public manager operates inside and outside one's organization.

At the same time, strategic planning, which evolved out of several managerial traditions, became widely accepted as a standard approach for designing and launching programs. A series of general accepted steps—such as examining mandates, clarifying mission and values, assessing external and internal environments, identifying strategic issues, formulating action, and assessing actions—is at the core of the process (Bryson 1988). Most important, officials engage in these processes in conjunction with community-level stakeholders that are not formally part of the city government. The process triggers an action agenda that involves the city advancing the interests of those who are actual and potential collaborators. Thus, strategic activities, for example, may involve seeking subsidies or program adjustments as part of an overall jurisdictional strategy. These activities generate and maintain the support of stakeholder collaborators (Krumholz 1995). Strategic moves, therefore, may be made by the city for its own short- or long-term aims.

The types of interactions that characterize vertical jurisdiction-based activity are diverse. Managers actively engaged in jurisdiction-based activity display a complex grid of managerial behaviors that are not merely a special part of the manager's job but constitute the job itself. Such tasks are based not in a constant battle over the distribution of power, but in a daily sorting out of issues within a particular policy area. Bargaining and negotiations are important instruments of jurisdiction-based management, although they are only part of the model. Bargaining by local managers within programs of vertical or horizontal origin provide alternatives to unilateral concession, resulting in a "mutually beneficial solution" (Agranoff and Lindsay 1983).

Adjustments in this model will be initiated by localities requesting treatment that is not technically or apparently within standards or regulations. Adjustment-seeking activity is typically an attempt to redefine program goals from purely federal and state terms to local terms beneficial to all relevant levels of government. The emphasis of jurisdiction-based management is thus on calculation and negotiation rather than accommodation and acclimation.

The horizontal dimension of this model of management describes public policymaking and governance that would take place in networklike arrangements consisting of various players, none of which possesses the power to determine the strategies of other actors (Kickert, Klijn, and Koppenjan 1997, 9), but where the city representative is held accountable for the solutions that emerge from the collaboration. This aspect of jurisdiction-based management is also premised on achieving the goals of the subnational jurisdiction, but it is manifest in interlocal interdependency.

As in the case of vertical collaboration, horizontal jurisdiction-based management extends the analytic focus to intersectoral as well as intergovernmental relationships. Actors in a field of urban communities are dependent on one another because they need each other's resources to achieve their goals: chambers of commerce because they provide policy expertise and support to city government, public–private partnerships because they bring expertise and financial resources, utilities because they are active in projects that affect the city, and so on. Interdependence in the system implies that all actors with a joint interest in a specific activity will benefit in some way. Certainly the local chamber, development corporation, or utilities have a strong interest in fostering and promoting the local economy. In this regard, the interdependence that gives rise to collaborative activity by the city government is, by definition, jurisdiction-based.

Horizontal jurisdiction-based management consists of a variety of public and private actors, each with their own operational goals and policy strategies. Although there are often strong incentives for operating in networked horizontal settings, policy processes in horizontal networks are unpredictable and complex. The preferences of players can often change during the course of the interaction, and players may not know in advance which outcomes are likely to occur and which targets they can meet in the process (Kickert, Klijn, and Koppenjan 1997). However, in spite of the complexities of horizontal, networklike settings, symbiotic relationships occur when interdependent organizations, each possessing different types and levels of technologies and resources needed for fulfilling a collective task, increase the frequency and intensity of communication among these players, which in turn forces decisions to be made jointly and actions to be carried out collectively to some degree (Alter and Hage 1993). The solutions that result from jurisdiction-based management will favor the city itself, but— when involving horizontal players who are also concerned with jurisdictional issues—are adjustments designed to provide a solution that benefits all parties (Kickert and Koppenjan 1997).

Many structural and policy-driven forces in the vertical environment since the 1960s suggest the emergence of jurisdiction-based management. During the Creative Federalism period of President Lyndon Johnson's administration, the massive expansion of domestic programs had profound effects that were to later sow the seeds of city-based steering of programs. As Walker (2000, 124) suggests, "Intergovernmental relations between 1964 and 1968 became bigger (in dollars, programs, and jurisdictions involved), broader (in the range of governmental functions affected), deeper (in terms of intrusive grant conditions and of the expanding number of recipient local governments and nonprofit organizations), and certainly more complicated when compared to the relatively neat, narrowly focused, inexpensive, basically two-tier intergovernmental pattern of 1960." The most important of these trends was a shift in federal aid toward urban and metropolitan areas and the "partnership principle," which took in a growing number of local governments and a range of nonprofit organizations (p. 125). These forces, along with new discretionary opportunities, gave cities some resources and a broader playing field throughout the 1970s.

President Ronald Reagan's agenda in the 1980s of reducing the federal presence included a reduction in federal aid, particularly to urban areas, and an attempt to strengthen the states with block grants and other means of easing national program standards and regulations. Intergovernmental reform, though a small part of a broader agenda to cut taxes and the national domestic presence, was deemed essential; altering the balance of power between the federal government and the states was a core issue (Conlan 1998). State administrative agencies increasingly became the focal point of federal programs in such areas as environmental protection, transportation and highways, human services, workforce development, and CDBG for small cities. Meanwhile, states were in the process of launching their own small programs, particularly to help cities promote their local economies. All these forces left managers in cities with fewer direct aid resources, but with more places to seek them out and a more immediate need to be creative in packaging and proposing. Looking out for the jurisdiction, rather than a specific federal program, became the dominant ethos in many cities.

Changes in economic development policy also suggest the presence of jurisdiction-based management. The Reagan administration's approach to economic development was consistent with its New Federalism approach. Local assistance was reduced because it was believed that national funds for local development encouraged inefficient locational decisions, distorted local agendas, and resulted in a suboptimal national economy. State programs and local efforts were expected to take up the slack, and nonprofit and private-sector organizations were seen as more appropriate development partners than federal agencies (Clarke and Gaile 1998). Cities thus moved from dependence on federal programs to locally initiated action.

Left with fewer resources but a greater demand for economic development, state leaders increased their focus on "homegrown" or indigenous growth programs. States began to realize that helping existing firms and/or attracting new investment required enhancement of their internal "competitive capacities" (Ross and Friedman 1991, 128). As a result, many of the endogenous policy tools that were found to be positively linked to collaboration activity emerged. States enacted programs throughout the 1980s and early 1990s to close capital gaps, modernize manufacturing in small and medium-sized firms, upgrade workers' skills, equip small firms with the latest in information and other technologies, support and encourage exports, and reform basic education. In addition, many states developed various other means of encouraging business expansion, including tax exemptions and incentives, industrial development financing authorities, bonds, loans, and other forms of financial aid. This expansion has not only tied city governments closer to the states, but expanded the collaborative field to include a host of private and nonprofit agencies within communities that are eligible for these programs.

Several forces thus have led to the type of interlocal interdependency that gives rise to the horizontal component of jurisdiction-based management. Even before the proliferation of federal programming in the 1960s, and state programming in the 1980s, the local government scene involved myriad governmental jurisdictions like those studied here, and short of metropolitan reorganization, required cities to work in an interactive problem-solving realm within their local public economies (Parks and Oakerson 1989). The expansion of federal programs brought noncity local governments and nongovernmental organizations into the collaborative field, and later state programs followed suit.

Meanwhile, the Reagan changes encouraged cities to look locally for resources, and all local public and nonpublic organizations found themselves in the same boat on some issues. By the 1990s, collaborative management across jurisdictions moved far beyond mutual servicing among local governments to include a host of public and nonpublic actors. The same trends were occurring in such fields as welfare reform (Jennings and Krane 1994), employment and training (Jennings and Ewalt 1998), environmental protection (Scheberle 1997), and social services (Agranoff 1990).

The forces of change in economic development also reinforce horizontal jurisdiction-based management. Globalization, increasingly sophisticated technology, the realization that existing firm expansions usually produce more jobs than does recruiting new firms, and limits to the scale of state programs all point to changes in economic development approaches. These approaches include further decentralization, less reliance on government as a sole source provider, the use of endogenous economic development instruments, and public leveraging of private resources (Ross and Friedman 1991). Globalization, for example, requires "municipal economic competitiveness" in an interconnected global society (Fry 1995, 33) that involves intergovernmental cooperation, linkages between the public and private sectors, connections with education and workforce training, international connections, and institutionalization of all of the links needed to develop an information-oriented international economy.

Clarke and Gaile (1998) identify the latest era as including new organizational clusters—business incubators, community development corporations, and local development corporations—both in formalized networks as well as in multiple, less formal, structures. These network arrangements, they observe, are increasing at a time when metropolitan government consolidations are at a standstill. They conclude that "the interest in greater metropolitan and regional cooperation on development issues suggests that cities may find economic teamwork more palatable than political consolidation" (p. 83).

Abstinence Model

At the other extreme of the two-dimensional graph (at the lower left in figure 3.1) is our hypothesized model of abstinence, as represented by Nothing Hill. The model suggests that some cities simply abstain from collaboration. Cities can choose not to be involved in virtually all state and federal programs, particularly those of a discretionary nature, as a matter of internal operating policy. Such operational abstinence can be the result of mayor or city council pressure to avoid entanglements or of an administrative decision. Decisions to abstain can be for a host of reasons, including objections to intrusion or a lack of capability to play the game.

From the earliest days of studying city federal grants administration, it was clear that numerous governments chose not to participate in discretionary programs. The only federal contact some jurisdictions had was as a recipient of general revenue sharing when that program existed (Richter 1976). At the state level, there was perhaps more contact, inasmuch as states have more supervisory and regulatory authority over local governments. For some local governments, the major point of contact was minimal, such as the fiscal audit or as recipient of some form of entitlement state assistance like tax sharing (Zimmerman 1995).

Many local governments do not engage in the type of intergovernmental contracts and joint service agreements that have become so familiar in the literature. One benchmark study by the International City/County Management Association (ICMA) revealed that despite an increase in such use, just under half of all cities did not engage in any contracting or services agreements (Henderson 1984). Economic development surveys by the same organization reveal notable levels of intergovernmental nonparticipation in financing.

Although federal and state grants and other state financing mechanisms are among the most important sources of local funding, research in the 1980s and 1990s showed that a large percentage of cities did not use federal funding (Henderson 1984; Farr 1989). In the more recent survey, more than three-fourths of the responding cities were not involved in state grants. Many other state-authorized tools, such as general obligation bonds, revenue bonds, tax increment financing, and special assessment districts, were also available to some cities; but only a small percentage took part. By contrast, local general revenue, which is an indicator of "going it alone," was used by a large majority of cities (Farr 1989).

Many factors suggest the existence of collaborative abstinence. First, some jurisdictions object to the involvement of another level of government, particularly the federal one, in their political and governmental space. They wish to avoid intrusion, excessive paperwork and/or procedures, unwieldy rules and regulations, or attendant crossover sanctions. A related issue is the fear of an external government influencing the spending priorities of the jurisdiction. Required matches are another concern. A perhaps greater concern is a fear that the city will be saddled with another funding burden when the external program ends. Programs often develop local constituencies to whom it is hard to say no when federal funds disappear. As a result, the city council, mayor, or city manager may urge a strategy of avoiding unnecessary federal intrusion. On a horizontal level, one or more of the same challenges may be faced: internal opposition, workload burden, state financing rules, or environmental regulations that would be passed on to a potential cooperating government. The city may not want to assume someone else's burdens.

Second, some cities lack the resources to collaborate. It could be time involved in organizing and preparing an application, or the press of other business. Cities may be too busy delivering basic services and providing infrastructure to get involved with grants or state programs. The city staff could also lack the capability to play the game of preparing applications, negotiating on behalf of the city, carrying out the programs, and reporting. Many administrators are increasingly sophisticated at collaboration, but some are not. Third, some jurisdictions do not collaborate vertically or horizontally because they do not particularly need to be involved. Some relatively wealthy communities do not need to heavily engage in stimulating their economies. The local private sector provides sufficient activity. New businesses locate within their borders and developers open up new areas. As a result, there is less of a pressing need to go after state financial incentives and federal grants, or to engage other entities in the community.

Collaborative abstinence in practice can be a conscious or unconscious practice. For example, stimuli come in the form of a written notice or a state or federal agent's verbal contact. In some cases, a kind of calculation of costs and benefits occurs. It can be a formal calculation, but typically if calculation occurs at all it is more likely a back-of-the-envelope exercise. Conversely, cost is not everything. The press of other business, previous city council resistance, or incompatibility with current strategies may also be factors. At any rate, in abstaining cities opportunities arise and are passed over. In the abstinence model, the jurisdiction is a nonparticipant, leaving the field "smaller" and the governing environment more inviting for others to exploit.

Top-Down Model

The top-down model is part of the federalism heritage that extended from the 1920s through the early 1970s. It was dominant during the period of increasing national programs, slowly through the 1920s, at an accelerated pace in the 1930s, sporadic in the 1940s and 1950s, and culminating in a steady stream of expanded programs, particularly for the cities, during the 1960s and early 1970s. The model is predicated on the growth of national programming and tipping of the federal balance toward central control, mostly executive control, with the federal government managing its programs vertically through state and local government managers.

Cities like the hypothetical Vertville are moderately active in the collaborative environment, but they rarely approach collaboration strategically. The model is based on two normative premises: that the federal system must be considered as a single system and that the de facto interdependence of the federal system mandates the application of executive-centered logic to the system (Sundquist and Davis 1969). The model constitutes the bureaucratic resolution to the basic dilemma of "how to achieve goals and objectives that are established by the national government, through the actions of other governments, state and local, that are legally independent and politically may even be hostile" (Sundquist and Davis 1969, 12). When intergovernmental programs appear to lack an overall strategy, as evidenced by confusing legislative enactments, overlapping program authority, uncertain responsibility, and duplication of effort, state and local officials may complain about these conditions.

The "easiest" solution is for the federal government to use executive instruments through federal agencies to manage by enforcing or requiring coordination. Toward that end, federalism's heritage includes mandated interagency linkages, comprehensive plans, joint boards and councils, special planning areas, and quasi-governmental planning units as common requirements associated with grant legislation. Many of those instruments have emanated from an executive-centered approach in the Executive Office of the President and other presidential instruments (Stever 1993).

A primary aspect of top-down management is local compliance. Coordinating managerial activity, either with higher governments or interlocal partners, is difficult and often not even desirable. Fierce competition for limited resources among localities can result in a kind of impulsive grantsmanship, whereby managers look to the federal government for assistance from numerous programs with little regard for how, or even if, such funds should be spent locally. More demonstrative of top-down managing, however, would be the impact of regulatory programs or government by remote control. Administrative rule making and regulatory and preemptive enactments have been prevalent for the past few decades. This situation has forced some local officials into a compliance management mode, usually in situations where no stream of funding accompanies national mandates. The important internal budgetary and other resource implications for jurisdictions are obvious. In such a bureaucratic environment, the "local manager as agent" perspective emphasizes the risks of discretion and the importance of compliance with external regulations and grant requirements.

For cities, this approach coincided with their becoming conscious of more extended roles in promoting their economies. Early in the twentieth century, factories located in cities where their entrepreneurs lived, where important raw materials were located, in proximity to transportation routes, or some combination. When industrial decline began to show its head in the late 1950s and 1960s, the first response was the attraction of newer, more technologically advanced factories and service businesses to replace lost workers and eroding portions of the local tax base. National programs for local areas included growth programs that would encourage private investment and additional incentives to focus on locational approaches, particularly what Eisinger (1988) calls supply-side programs. These programs were packaged in urban renewal, job training, business infrastructure, and some subsidy programs that were designed to make cities more attractive as business locations. Ross and Friedman (1991) characterize this strategy as low-cost investment locations and public financial incentives. The key players were the private investors, city governments, and federal funders or lenders, with cities being the "agents" for federal "principals."

Management thought is, at least historically, congruent with this hierarchical orientation, particularly the scientific and administrative management approaches. Frederick Taylor (1947) and his followers in the scientific management movement first applied knowledge to the organization of work and production on engineering jobs that led to common methods and procedures, standardized tasks, and specialized roles, which then became a part of the fabric of managing and organizing. Even closer to top-down management was the work of several administrative management theorists. For example, Luther Gulick (1937) identified hierarchical management principles of executives as planning, organizing, directing, and reporting. This in turn led to such practices as requiring single points of contact, delegation of responsibility to agents in subnational governments, and means of enhancing coordination, control, and assessment.

Intellectually, this top-down, compliance-based model originated in Leonard D. White's (1939) classic textbook on public administration (first published in 1926). He refers to the importance of central administration in intergovernmental relations because of the "gradual acceptance of the idea that in certain fields a national minimum standard is in the public interest, and by the intervention and application of nationwide procedures, largely administrative in nature, to secure such standards (p. 144)."

Donor–Recipient Model

The activities in Bargain City are consistent with the donor–recipient model of collaborative management, where collaborative activity may be moderate or even high, and the strategic orientation of the city is neither strong as in a jurisdiction-based city nor absent as in a top-down city. The donor–recipient model is suggested by intergovernmental activity in the mid 1970s, often from programs started in the 1960s, as federal programs become more complicated and scholarly interest turned toward the chain of program implementation. The top-down collaborative management model is based on the idea that some actor possesses the information, expertise, and skill to control policy outputs consistent with multiple social interests. Alternatively, the donor–recipient model involving grantors and grantees is based on actors within a collaborative system who depend on one another instead of operating by control at the top of the system. It recognizes that program collaborators must rely on each other within the parameters of a program that involves varying degrees of mutual, two-party control. Donor–recipient is primarily a vertical model of collaborative management, although a minimal horizontal component may be present in donor–recipient communities.

The empirical basis for this model of management comes largely from policy implementation studies that have looked at the elements of participation. Pressman and Wildavsky (1973) were among the first to understand policy implementation as a process of interaction or shared administration that occurs at the intersection of setting goals and carrying out actions geared to achieve them.

The utility of viewing intergovernmental relations in terms of a donor (the actor providing resources) and a recipient was first identified in Jeffrey Pressman's *Federal Programs and City Politics* (1975). Examining federal aid at the local level, he concludes that any federal partner is dependent upon the actions of others to achieve its own objectives; the recipient may need money but donors need fundable applications and implementation ability at the local level. The donor does not have the time, the resources, the inclination, or, in many cases, the authority to intervene on a regular basis in the recipient's locality. Although donors acknowledge their dependence upon the actions of the recipient, thus leading in part to cooperation, conflict is also a common aspect of managing donor–recipient relations. Pressman argues, "Donor and recipient need each other, but neither has the ability to control fully the actions of the other. Thus, the aid process takes the form of bargaining between partly cooperative, partly antagonistic, and mutually dependent sets of actors" (1975, 106–7).

Other studies demonstrate that grant programs are not necessarily instruments of federal control but opportunities to bargain (Ingram 1977). Though federal agents would like to bind subnational jurisdictions to federal policy, subnational agencies seek the maximum possible leeway to pursue their own separate goals and objectives with federal help. Donor–recipient managing can involve several different approaches: compromise, participation in a problem-solving discussion, or cooperation with a third party who is trying to solve the controversy (Liebschutz 1991).

According to the donor-recipient model, recipient managers often seek some change that is desirable to the jurisdiction. Some action provides adequate resources and discretion for the jurisdiction, some action does not, but (as with the top-down model) all action must ultimately conform to the goals of the donor. Recipient managers might ignore national standards either by inaction or open defiance, placing the jurisdiction at risk of sanctions such as withdrawal of funds, large financial penalties, or even protracted litigation. Other alternative means of navigation include engaging the donor in a forum where adjustments can be made or the recipient's jurisdictional resources can counter the donor's attempt at conformity.

Donor–recipient management became common as intergovernmental programs became numerous, complicated, and then costly. Federal regulations were expanded as funds became more scarce and were targeted to state and local governments, which were, in turn, inextricably tied to the federal government in a wide range of actions. However, the extensiveness of regulatory programming was far beyond the scope of any direct federal control; state and local governments were largely left to themselves to implement these programs, beyond reporting, occasional inspection, and federal post-audits. Moreover, in keeping with Nixon New Federalism, states were made administrators for the federal government. The states, which are closer to communities and other regulated entities, were not only designated as the agents of the federal government, but were expected to make adjustments that accounted for local and state tradition and approaches. Instead of the federal government dealing directly with a grantee, federalism involved a handoff, with more actors at the other end of the intergovernmental chain involved in programming (Elmore 1985). Thus, while the critical component of policy success in the top-down model is that local actors carry out national goals, policies are judged successful in the donor–recipient model when they leave room for local decision making and provide local actors with sufficient policy discretion, resources, and autonomy to carry out national goals while fulfilling local needs.

The shifts in economic development programming during this time resulted in a bottom-up, donor–recipient managerial relationship for many programs. Federal programs to promote economic development in the 1960s included dozens of programs to assist state and local governments in attracting business, provide targeted loans and loan guarantees, give special help to small and minority-owned businesses, and stimulate state and local economies (Eisinger 1988). These programs, such as those administered by the Small Business Administration, Economic Development Administration (EDA), Department of Agriculture, and the Department of Commerce, involved a much wider web of local players in recipient cities.

Federal programs are now dwarfed by state programs and spending, which grew to eventually total three to four times federal efforts. But federal programs began the game of bringing in local organizations, neighborhood associations, and many smaller investors. Cities were encouraged to focus on their economic roles, to assess their economic needs, and to work with private investors on revitalization projects (Clarke and Gaile 1998). Engagement in these processes, as well as involvement of actors outside of city government, brought different ideas about development to the table. City officials thus learned to deal not just with the constraints of a grant, but also with locally generated processes, myriad local concerns, standards, rules, regulations, and other elements of federal programs. Urban Development Action Grants, EDA Titles II and IX, and CDBG all exemplify the programming that encouraged the locally generated involvement of private investors and nonprofit organizations in the participatory mix, in most cases changing the cities' pattern of involvement in national programs.

Reactive Model

We also hypothesize a model of management at the center of the activity–strategy continuum, although we cannot be as specific in its description as in the other models. This model is admittedly a "catchall" category for describing some cities. Our basic premise of the hypothesized models is that a city can be identified by its dominant managerial response as a particular type or model of city collaborative management. A reactive city is one without a dominant orientation—moderate to little activity, and moderate to little strategy. In our formulation, a reactive model of collaborative management is consistent with the "maybe, maybe not" approach of Centerville. Sometimes a city may choose to participate, sometimes not. The decision to participate may be strategically based, or it may not be.

When such a city decides not to participate collaboratively in a program or project, it resembles a kind of capacitated abstinence, which occurs when a jurisdiction chooses to demur on a particular occasion or situation. Though these jurisdictions accept the game and its attendant costs, their capability as intergovernmental actors leads them to somehow decide not to play the game in a particular situation or set of situations. For example, a city may choose not to underwrite matching portions of state-offered venture capital loans to local entrepreneurs because it has decided that the risk factor is too high.

Reactive cities will look at potential involvement and decide that "this program is not for us." There appears to be no single managerial legacy that leads to such noninvolvement, but several might contribute. One would be the autonomy and integrity principle of the jurisdiction as an entity with boundaries. For many officials, each unit of government should be autonomous and left free to make decisions on the basis of citizen preferences, not federal dictates or mandates. As such, external stimuli present potential threats to citizen demand as well as to the organization's integrity. A second justification might be the old politics–administration dichotomy. That is, the council and/or mayor decide that intergovernmental activity is undesirable, and so instruct administrators not to become involved.

A third justification might be that the activity is not mission driven. Some officials view the city's mission in terms of basic specialized services and infrastructure: Economic activity is the role of the private sector, human services that of the county, cultural events that of the nonprofit sector, and so on. As a result, activities other than basic services are considered to be out of bounds. A final managerial justification may be that some other agency or organization is already providing the service. Avoidance of duplication and overlap means that another organization, the city in this case, should not become involved because this smacks of poor management.

Contented Model

A contented city like Richburb is one that is opportunistic and chooses to exploit the economic development environment—it is strategic by our definition. However, it needs less and it seeks very little if any collaboration with other actors. Collaboration that is pursued by contented cities is typically with other cities and development organizations whose policy choices affect the city itself. In other words, spillovers are managed through horizontal collaborative mechanisms, but vertical activity is minimal.

A relatively well-off city in affluent suburban areas worries less about the industrialization or "globalization" of its economy. It relies on more expensive real estate development, both residential and commercial. It does help investors in paving the way for new developments, and it works with adjoining cities on issues like annexation of land, mutual servicing, and perhaps special districting. But it does not feel highly pressed to seek the external vertical grants, loans, or myriad tax adjustments that poor communities need to attract economic investment. Private investments are more likely to come to the city with little promotion. They do not encourage the type of industry deemed strategically undesirable. These cities normally have staff capacities to pursue the intergovernmental game, and occasionally opt for a program like tax adjustments. They do not focus their energies on investment of public dollars, but rather on interlocal facilitation of investment by the private sector.

Contented cities are relatively wealthy and are experiencing a strong growth curve, both in population and in the economy. Any governing activity is designed to sustain the city's favorable pace of economic development. Activity is low, and a local strategy is composed primarily of policy decisions that minimize both the cost of development and the involvement of the public sector, especially federal and state governments.

Collaboration and Models of Managing

Public managers are increasingly concerned with how to collaborate within changing contexts of policy, management, and the federal system. They must confront multiple governments, organizations, programs, and instruments within their field of operations. A greater proportion of a public manager's time is caught up in handling numerous interdependencies between his or her organizations and other organizations (Kettl 1996), including the horizontal and vertical actions discussed throughout this book.

The collaborative models of managing hypothesized here involve a different kind of public management than does "classical" hierarchical work within a single organization. Managing linkages with other organizations is qualitatively different from managing employees in a single structure (O'Toole 1997a). Each of the models implies a different type of management at work. The activity that we believe to be the most collaborative—jurisdiction-based management—induces leadership by forging strategic design and packaging of programs wrapped around dozens of horizontal and vertical consultations, and directed toward programmatic adjustments that meet local rather than external intent. It invokes a form of collective decision making and programming where no one is in charge (Bryson and Crosby 1992), but at least one institution—city government—is held accountable. Jurisdiction-based management geared to the strategic priorities of the city involves a set of cross-agency managerial skills and processes that are substantially different from the core approaches in standard public administration texts.

For the local manager trying to pursue and achieve jurisdictional goals, the contemporary system is a field of intergovernmental and interorganizational complexity. The days when a city could simply fill out a federal grant application and operate a small program attached to a city department are less and less frequent. As the jurisdiction-based model suggests, most vertical transactions are linked to a corresponding set of horizontal connections to the same project effort. Some cities are more likely to propose something that must be worked out with its county government, a development association, a public–private economic development corporation, and state and federal players. Managing the interdependencies may also lead to a variety of somewhat unpredictable connections. This type of complex interorganizational managerialism is rarely limited to a single plane. The hypothesized presence of jurisdiction-based management further underscores the importance of governance. As complexity increases, governmental actors link with nongovernmental actors, who become necessary components of the local delivery system (Stoker and Mossberger 1994).

Other models exist in practice. The top-down approach suggests compliance transmitted through "buzzwords," rules, standards, and expectations. Donors and recipients engage in forms of two-party bargaining across jurisdictions and try to reach mutually agreeable accommodative decisions as a result of give-and-take behavior. The abstainers stay away from collaboration at any cost, whereas reactive cities may approach a program in a top-down fashion, bargain over another program, or simply abstain from the activity, depending on the situation. Contented cities see no compelling reason to collaborate beyond the standard public–private interaction that takes place in a naturally growing economy.

An important implication of our models is that the managers of many organizations who are involved in economic development are becoming "policymakers" as they propose strategies and work through adjustments at the boundaries of their organizations. Decisions are increasingly made by administrative officials acting as organizational representatives. Capital attraction activities have not given way, but growth from within and other endogenous activities have become more prevalent and, according to many studies, more effective. A city thus may deal with potential investors while it also deals with local organizations that can enhance capacities and supply necessary linkages. Organizational representation and decisions are made by administrative officials. City managers, economic development directors, chamber of commerce executive directors, county planners, officers of economic development corporations, utility managers, and foundation executives are the players who make the core decisions. It is their decisions, collective or accommodated, that form jurisdictional positions. And it is from their ranks that collaborative contacts and negotiations emerge across governments and organizations. Representatives of legislative bodies or governing boards are less often in the central loop of this type of economic development decision making. As Wright (1983) has maintained, intergovernmental policy issues place the greatest emphasis upon appointed administrators. This is particularly true with regard to jurisdiction-based management.

We hypothesize a new, compelling approach to public management. The three chapters that follow pick up the broader challenge to show empirically that the jurisdiction-based model, and the other management models, exist in practice. Managing across the boundaries of governments and organizations is not an add-on, but a core activity of public managers that deserves its own conceptual and practical underpinnings. Still, more must be known about such management; a clearer view of the empirical landscape is needed. Thus, we now turn our attention toward developing such an empirical foundation for collaborative management in the public sector.

Note

1. The term "model" employed in this book follows Kaplan's (1964, 266–67) usage as a "scientific metaphor" that directs attention to certain resemblances between the theoretical entities and the real subject matter; where one type of system can be found to be consistent with interpretations of another. As such, our search here is not for characteristic metaphors for federalism or for collaboration, but for how policymaking and management can vary as the governing environment of cities varies both across time and in various policy realms.

4

Collaborative Activity and Strategy

Garfield Heights, like so many cities, engages in a whole complex of collaborative activities. Vertically, its director of economic development, who doubles as city grants coordinator, is involved in the preparation of ten to twenty grants a year. The city regularly contacts the state of Ohio and federal agencies regarding transportation, commerce and environmental issues, sometimes seeking regulatory interpretations, sometimes negotiating the financial impact, and sometimes helping local businesses with problems. It has one partnership for traffic monitoring and control with the state of Ohio Department of Transportation. Horizontally, it has the usual mutual services agreements and contracts for service. The city seeks out technical assistance and financial resources from county government, engages in a number of regional service networks and special districts, works with one enterprise zone, has a joint development project with the neighboring city of Cleveland, and works with its recently revived Chamber of Commerce to forge local development policies and strategies. Garfield Heights therefore engages in many different types of collaborative activities.

The models of collaborative public management discussed in the previous chapter are distinguished in terms of the level and type of collaborative activity as well as the extent to which cities approach such activity strategically. In this chapter, we provide an in-depth analysis of those activities that constitute collaborative management and offer a way to meaningfully categorize such activities. We examine empirically the quantity and quality of activity in cities, and show how and why variation in collaborative management occurs. The evidence supports the idea that strategic orientation and activity level are related systematically as proposed in the jurisdiction-based management model, but it also shows that activity varies in ways consistent with the top-down and donor–recipient models. We also explore the abstaining cities and find that the least active cities are those with strategic orientations and administrative structures quite the opposite from jurisdiction-based cities.

Description of Collaborative Activities

Our description of collaborative activities is parsimonious, yet analytical as well, providing something more than "talk on the phone" or "meet with people" by offering a thorough accounting of activity that parallels our knowledge of bureaucratic management, while clearly distinguishing between the two different contexts. We examine twenty specific collaborative policymaking and managerial activities (see table 4.1). Respondents to our mail survey were asked to identify, from a list of twenty, the activities that had been performed by city officials during a two-year period. The respondents were also asked to identify which players in the horizontal (governments, semipublic organizations, private agencies, and nongovernmental organizations) and vertical (federal and state government agencies) environments were involved in each activity. Totals of eleven activities occur in the vertical environment and nine activities occur in the horizontal environment.[1] Five of the vertical activities (see table 4.2 for examples of vertical activities) are referred to as *information seeking*, activities that constitute a large proportion of collaborative management; the other six vertical activities are *adjustment seeking*, activities that seek program adjustments from the state and federal government, particularly within the context of intergovernmental grants or regulatory programs. Information-seeking activities are pursued by many cities, but those cities that rely heavily on such activities relative to adjustment-seeking activities can be viewed as employing a primarily top-down approach to managing. Adjustment-seeking activities are the prime examples of donor–recipient and jurisdiction-based activities.

The nine remaining activities, all of which are horizontal (see table 4.3 for examples of horizontal activities), include *policymaking and strategy-making* activities, whereby managers include other

Table 4.1. Collaborative Management Activities

Vertical Activities	Type[a]	Horizontal Activities	Type[a]
Seek general program information	IS	Gain policymaking assistance	PM
Seek new funding of programs and		Engage in formal partnerships	PM
projects	IS	Engage in joint policymaking and	
Seek interpretation of standards		strategy-making	PM
and rules	IS	Consolidate policy effort	PM
Seek general program guidance	IS	Seek financial resources	RE
Seek technical assistance	IS	Employ joint financial incentives	RE
Regulatory relief, flexibility, or		Contract for planning and	
waiver	AS	implementation	RE
Statutory relief or flexibility	AS	Establish partnership for a project	PB
Request change in official policy	AS	Seek technical assistance	PB
Seek funding innovation of existing			
program	AS		
Request model program			
involvement	AS		
Request performance-based			
discretion	AS		

[a] IS = information seeking; AS = adjustment seeking; PM = policymaking and strategy-making; RE = resource exchange; PB = project based.

horizontal players, either formally or informally, in the planning, goal development, and decision-making tasks of collaborative policymaking; *resource-exchange* activities, which involve seeking and acquiring resources from multiple players, as well as combining and leveraging resources with many different horizontally positioned actors; and *project-based* activities, which involve a multitude of community and extra-community actors within the context of a particular project, either short term or long term. The variation in horizontal activities is best described in terms of the actors involved in such activities (as will be demonstrated in the next chapter), but jurisdiction-based cities are more likely to pursue all types of horizontal activities than are top-down or donor–recipient cities.

Vertical Collaborative Activities

Information Seeking

The most central vertical collaborative activities involve contacts with state and federal governments for the purpose of seeking out

Table 4.2. Vertical Collaborative Activities

Type of Activity	Example
Information seeking	
General program information	Salem, Indiana, inquires at the Department of Commerce regarding the scope of activities allowed under the CDBG-funded Community Focus Fund Program.
New funding of programs and projects	Garfield Heights submits a grant application to the Ohio Department of Transportation to access ISTEA funds to construct noise walls alongside its freeways.
Interpretation of standards and rules	Beloit checks with the Wisconsin Housing and Economic Development Authority regarding the eligibility of a potential participant in its Revenue Bond Program.
General program guidance	Woodstock discusses with the Illinois Department of Transportation how it might deal with problems of traffic control access to its business districts through possible rerouting or four-laning of a state highway.
Technical assistance	Ithaca asks representatives of the Michigan Small Business Development Center to visit and explain to prospective entrepreneurs what it takes to successfully start a business, deal with the extensive paperwork and compliance requirements, and become eligible for SBA assistance.
Adjustment seeking	
Regulatory relief, flexibility, or waiver	Cincinnati asks the U.S. EPA for a waiver to cease testing for certain contaminates that are highly unlikely to be in its drinking water system.
Statutory relief or flexibility	Garfield Heights, through its Department of Development, asks the Ohio attorney general's office for a zoning law exception to accommodate a new low-density development that overlaps with the city of Cleveland.
Change in policy	Cincinnati requests a review by the Ohio EPA of several of its operating practices said to be prohibited by regulation in its water treatment program.
Funding innovation for program	The Ithaca LDC, Greater Gratiot Development Incorporated, seeks discretionary CDBG funding from the Michigan Jobs Commission and HUD to promote small business networks in its multicity cluster of organizations.
Model program involvement	Beloit seeks special designation in the U.S. Department of Transportation's Urban Rivers Program to develop a new type of recreation–civic–commercial center as a part of Beloit 2000.
Performance-based discretion	Woodstock proposes to EPA a measured results-based cleanup of a contaminated landfill as a substitute for the agency-prescribed method, which would involve extensive monitoring and reporting.

Note: "CDBG" is Community Development Block Grants; "ISTEA" is the Intermodal Surface Transportation Efficiency Act; "SBA" is U.S. Small Business Administration; "EPA" is Environmental Protection Agency; "LDC" is local development corporation; "HUD" is U.S. Department of Housing and Urban Development.

Table 4.3. Horizontal Collaborative Activities

Type of Activity	Example
Policymaking and strategy-making	
Gain policymaking assistance	Garfield Heights regularly uses the planning and zoning expertise of the Cuyahoga County Planning Commission to update its master plan, revise its zoning codes, and for major site preparation issues.
Engage in formal partnership	LDCs are one of the most common forms of partnerships; an example is the Washington County Economic Growth Partnership, a nonprofit arrangement among the city of Salem, Washington County, the Chamber of Commerce, and the industrial community.
Engage in joint policymaking	Beloit city officials regularly meet with the Chamber of Commerce, local manufacturers, local developers, Beloit 2000 leaders, and BEDCOR officials in "strategic retreats" to formulate strategic economic development plans.
Consolidate policy effort	Ithaca regularly works with the Gratiot County government and neighboring cities through its LDC, GGDI, to formulate countywide economic development strategies. The combined group has written policies in business retention, business expansion, new business recruitment, and counseling and case supports for small business start-ups.
Resource exchange	
Seek financial resources	Salem has financed several redevelopment projects by successfully tapping into Washington County's Economic Development Income Tax (EDIT). The city has been able to use EDIT to provide matching funds for numerous federal grants, for a downtown redevelopment project, and for a number of airport improvements.
Employ joint financial incentives	In a creative example of joint financing, Cincinnati initiated a three-way property exchange among the city, school district, and Hamilton County, enabling the school district to work out a stormwater utility debt of $1.7 million to the city. As a result, land in the Downtown—Over the Rhine historic district was made available for a regional shopping complex anchored by a large supermarket.
Contracted planning and implementation	Woodstock contracts with the McHenry County Planning Department for planning and zoning assistance, data gathering, and geographic information systems. It relies on the county health department to implement health inspection permits for septic tanks and wells.
Project-based work	
Partnership for a particular project	Beloit 2000 is a major public–private partnership that plans and raises funds and also acquires property necessary to conduct this riverfront revitalization project. The city of Beloit allocates staff time to a Beloit 2000 technical steering committee for project operations.
Seek technical resources	Salem relies on a variety of sources for technical support beyond that which is provided locally by its LDC staff member: Staff of its regional planning agency, its multicity grants and representation development corporation, and staff and advisers from various Indiana agencies.

Note: "LDC" is local development corporation; "BEDCOR" is Beloit Economic Development Corporation; "GGDI" is Greater Gratiot Development Incorporated.

information. Information is an important policymaking resource in settings where other resources—finances, expertise, legal authority, personnel—are held by multiple players. Information-seeking activities are most closely associated with obtaining and managing grants, but they also include transactions regarding the basic organization and operation of all intergovernmental programs. Because the execution of intergovernmental policy strategies is dependent upon the perceptions of risks, opportunities, levels of trust, and timing on the part of the multiple actors (Pressman and Wildavsky 1973), local officials "build support for the common effort by using information carefully and sensitively, often in an informal fashion" (O'Toole 1988, 433). Managers in cities thus induce collaboration through multiple means: technical assistance, exploring funding options, clarifying program requirements, and jointly agreeing on methods of operation that satisfy donor or regulator specifications while fulfilling local needs. A common approach to information seeking is to convene, identify, and reach agreement on the nature of problems and to search for joint solutions (Agranoff 1986; Radin et al. 1996).

One of the most ubiquitous activities in vertical collaborative management is making contact with state and federal governments for available program and funding information. Because there are many different approaches to development, the act of leafing through a catalog, and thereby resisting collaborative interaction, can add to the confusion. During the era of federal government expansion, grants and other financial resource acquisition stories were legendary. One small-town mayor, for example, attracted more than $16 million in project grants, loans, and credit buy-downs during a ten-year period. His success was said to be related to his regular reading of the *Catalog of Federal Domestic Assistance*, to his working with a series of advisory committees, and to his personally filling out applications and working with many federal officials (Hale and Palley 1981, 80). Many hard-pressed governments have looked for money from various available sources by similarly focusing their efforts on any opportunities. In the present-day funding environment, many cities know all too well that participation in the game has become extremely difficult. Managers interested in acquiring funds from vertical players are adept at seeking and utilizing information by increasing their contacts, improving their knowledge of the targeting of funds, garnering greater support from external groups, and paying more attention to program detail and quality. The activity of seeking program and funding information is thus a critical aspect of collaborative public management.

Cincinnati "aggressively" pursues federal grants and tries whenever possible to "use everybody else's dollars first." At the time of the research, it was awarded a $3 million grant from the State of Ohio to study the feasibility of expanding its convention center, which was its largest ever Capital Improvements Projects allocation (nearly $13.9 million), granted $1.5 million in special Intermodal Surface Transportation Efficiency Act enhancement funds, and leveraged more than $2 million over their normal allocation in Job Training Partnership Act (since replaced by the Workforce Investment Act) incentive dollars. Garfield Heights applies for about twelve grants a year. Some discretionary grants included a $7 million project to widen and improve the main commercial thoroughfare. A federally funded project of several million dollars will raise forty-eight noise walls near the Interstate highway. The city also received a $1 million grant from the county to upgrade its traffic light system in order to improve traffic patterns. Many other projects like these have been funded over the years.

A common but less well-known purpose of using informational resources is to seek administrative interpretations and reach mutual understandings. These information-seeking activities involve the pursuit of guidance and interpretations. Higher-level governments have aims and needs, often to maintain legal program aims and fiscal integrity. Part of public management is its indirect nature, where parties representing different organizations are likely to differ somewhat over aims. Implementing governments may share the same *general* aims, but *specific* adaptations to the situation may engender differences between the parties, or at least potential differences. Such transactions are common in collaborative management, because often the respective interests in making programs work deal in common program aims, not specifications, and because contacts are ongoing. Misinterpretation of program guidelines is often the result of local managers being inexperienced and unaware that the easy aspects of collaborative contact and consultation can turn a costly contract provision or seemingly immutable regulation or standard into an opportunity.

Agranoff (1986) concludes that intergovernmental managers are able to solve many multijurisdictional issues by convening, identifying, and reaching agreement on the nature of problems, searching for and forging joint solutions, and implementing decisions through joint action. Our empirical research more than a decade later confirms this. Most solutions discussed by city officials are basic program accommodations, reciprocal tasks, or adjustments made to intergovernmental programs within requirements and standards. These activities typically involve very routine matters on specific problems that rarely cause conflict once jurisdictional representatives and the other players have discussed them.

Seeking technical assistance is also a common information activity occurring regularly in cities. Program transactions often place knowledge or operational demands that cannot be met with the jurisdiction's existing capabilities. Technical assistance is often more informally arranged than by contract. Many examples of seeking informal technical assistance can be found in the cities. For example, a city government required to test its drinking water supply for a new chemical may not be familiar with the procedure, so it contacts the state environmental agency and asks for a field technician to visit the city and work with the water treatment plant staff.

Similarly, a newly authorized state financial-reporting law requires an accounting technique no one in the city finance department has used, so a deputy finance director of a city calls on the state finance department and, when the city official is in the capital, she receives a one-hour demonstration of the technique. State departments of economic development also hold workshops for small cities interested in becoming a "certified," higher-capacity community. Through the process of requiring communities to plan and develop a community profile, state economic development agencies offer a great deal of technical assistance to communities. Local managers in turn seek help with a variety of tasks, such as brochure production, translations, technical specifications, and advertising layouts. In this and other contexts, state officials in the field work very closely with cities, especially small nonmetropolitan cities, imparting useful assistance and know-how for carrying out a task important to all levels of government.

In some cases, information seeking is an institutionalized aspect of local governance. Because of the sheer volume of information-seeking activity in the city, the assistant city manager's office in Cincinnati serves as a clearinghouse for nonroutine (special) intergovernmental contacts. In this office, department administrators seek information on response mode, fulfillment of conditions, use of funds, intent of new funding opportunities, and, most important, fitting current issues with local priorities. Officials in Cincinnati reported that around seven or eight nonroutine information transactions a week are conducted vertically, usually by program heads, after clearance with the assistant city manager. Information transactions of all types are the routine but nevertheless collaborative lifelines between governments as parties attempt to make programs work.

Adjustment Seeking

A second type of vertical managerial activity apparent in the cities involves seeking latitude in implementation by requesting some form of local asymmetrical treatment or program adjustment that is not technically or apparently within standards, rules, or guidelines, but nonetheless forwards the purpose for which both higher-level and local managers are working. Adjustment-seeking activities typically involve requesting a suspension or alteration of program requirements or regulations, redefining one's program as a model or experiment, or trading off strict compliance for increased flexibility and enhanced performance. Such efforts are often essential to move a program along when the rules themselves constitute an impediment to the general purposes and development aims of that program. Collaboration occurs in this context because city officials must jointly establish a course of action for the city with state and/or federal government officials. Although conflict often develops, a workable and effective solution can be found in these situations only through the process of collaboration.

Seeking regulatory or statutory flexibility and relief are important components of a public manager's vertical collaborative repertoire. Such adjustment-seeking activities involve the common practice of a government seeking to change the application of a regulation or standard to a particular situation if it is excessively costly or impedes a specific development project or effort. Regulatory relief or adjustment can be a very difficult area to pursue because most of the aims of such regulations promote important national purposes (e.g., clean drinking water, access to public facilities for disabled persons, affirmative action hiring practices). However, universal and standard application principles of regulations can be burdensome on jurisdictions, as we heard again and again from the case study cities. Collaborative regulatory management has become most critical in the environmental area, as federal and state standards promulgated by the U.S. Environmental Protection Agency (EPA) and other regulatory agencies affect jurisdictions. National regulations often preempt state and local authority, set tight timetables, detail procedural requirements, and force technological standards in such areas as wastewater treatment, drinking water, air quality, landfills, and groundwater and underground storage tanks. As a result, many managers actively seek collaborative regulatory adjustment.

Regulations place local agencies in positions where they may have to calculate the political and economic costs and benefits of moving a project forward, which is a common practice in large cities like Cincinnati and is prevalent in small cities such as Salem and Ithaca as well. Managers may conclude that it is worthwhile to seek relief from any standards that adversely affect local interests. In this regard, collaboration with, rather than acceding to, national or state officials can result in a successful regulation application for both parties. In many cases, the request for regulatory flexibility is initially denied by the regulating government, but in all cases a settlement is established collaboratively rather than coercively.

For example, Salem has on occasion felt it necessary to maintain its position in a negotiation of regulation. The city's most frequent negotiations are with the State Board of Tax Commissioners over rate adjustment approvals, usually over water rates. Currently, the city has suffered the fate of many small cities: Its sewer system has inadequate capacity and is leaking into a local river. The Indiana Department of Environmental Management issued an order for a system upgrade that would cost the city about $5 million. The city countered with a sludge treatment proposal costing about $500,000. It is expected that some form of negotiated solution will result. The proposed bypass will also involve extensive negotiations over the proposed siting because it involves wetlands.

Ithaca "manages" its regulatory framework when it can. The city regularly negotiates with federal and state officials. Although it is concerned and often frustrated regarding unfunded mandates, it takes a "proactive stance" on most of these issues. For example, when officials from the Public Works Department became concerned about health and safety regulations, the city asked the Michigan Occupational Safety and Health Administration to do an inspection audit, which was discussed and negotiated, and then followed. Recently, the Michigan Department of Natural Resources informed the city that several city streets, some of which blocked industrial and retail access, would have to be closed while the state did repair work. Ithaca called in the department supervisor for a meeting and was able to negotiate a solution that no more than two of the proposed streets would be closed at one time. City officials also proposed to the Department of Natural Resources (DNR) an alternative storage pond for the water reservoir so they could expand their industrial park without having to build a water tower. This action ultimately required an EPA waiver of rule, which was successfully obtained. Another example of adjustment-seeking activity occurred in the early 1990s when U.S. EPA Superfund project officials arrived in town to do testing work for lead on city property. The initial cost to the city would have been $2 million for mitigation, but the city negotiated with the state attorney general and DNR to reduce its liability to in-kind costs only.

Managers who are inexperienced in local government and who may perceive the collaborative environment as top-down might think that there can be no circumstances under which a government—state or federal—would willingly provide a local jurisdiction relief from a statute. Experienced persons know that some situations make such relief a normal way of doing business. Statutory adjustments are attempts to amend a law or to obtain legal sanction for an activity that is currently prohibited (Zimmerman 1995). If this entails enacting a special bill, it may require lobbying or direct representation on behalf of the jurisdiction.

For an example of how statutes can be made flexible, consider the strict setback laws regarding buildings on lakefronts (typically 75 feet) that are on the books in many states, including the states in our research population. Within the boundaries of a rural conservancy (lake management) district, if development around part of the lake is impossible because a preexisting road has resulted in standardized acre lots not fitting into the space, there are few alternatives. Rerouting the road would cause expense and right-of-way problems. Instead, the manager of the district could seek "relief" from the setback statute and pursue a strategy of 50 feet for five of the thirty-five lots to be opened up for development. Such a strategy set in motion a series of inspections and measurements from the state conservation department and state health department, and even a review by the attorney general's office. Legal relief could be granted in this case, but only within certain new conditions imposed on the district, such as requiring the five lots to have septic systems built in a nonstandard way and to have special liners in the holding tanks. Such give-and-take is a typical example of the protracted but mutually beneficial process of statutory relief.

Model programs are often used in some packaged form. State enterprise zone legislation is a model effort that emphasizes coordinated tax incentives and deregulation for local governments and businesses. The most common features of enterprise zones include special job credits, dedicated grants, local property tax abatements, and exemption from state sales taxes on numerous business improvement activities. Cincinnati and Garfield Heights use enterprise zones as part of their overall development strategy, and another fifty-five cities in the sample report the use of such zones.

In addition, we found that local managers often seek a policy change to promote a city's own development efforts. For example, one small community in Ohio sought the same type of property tax abatement for business attraction contained in the state's enterprise zone law, even though the community was not located in a zone. The state granted the small community similar permission as a "demonstration effort," but limited it to all new manufacturing locations, starts, or expansions, and with a five-year time limitation. Other communities also applied for such policy changes.

Similarly, by working with state officials, one Illinois community received a small venture capital loan from a dedicated enterprise zone pool as a "one-time experiment" to allow a locally based firm to introduce the transfer of an engine technology. Ithaca and its public–private local development corporation regularly seek program funding and eligibility changes in the business development and loan programs of the Michigan Economic Development Corporation (called the Michigan Jobs Commission at the time of the study) to accommodate particular businesses they are seeking to attract.

A great deal of vertical collaboration is transacted over whether recipient and regulated governments are legally in compliance, have followed guidelines, and are in conformance with audit principles. Though there is no question that such interaction is appropriate, at some levels of activity it too often becomes the essence of the process. Many localities agree that this is another variation of the state and national government emphasizing form over purpose. To minimize the paralysis that accompanies this compliance mentality, performance management has frequently been introduced as a means of ensuring that the program is being adhered to.

The central issue in this type of management is whether it is auditing or evaluation that is at stake. Auditors, who see control by management as a means of ensuring legal and procedural compliance, have different rules than those of program managers, who need to look at performance and effectiveness. Both may be necessary in intergovernmental programs, but auditing has often been the sole emphasis when evaluation may be what is at stake to account for the worth of a program.

In economic development, there has been movement on several fronts to encourage performance management, thereby allowing local managers to focus on outcomes instead of process. Two programs of the U.S. Economic Development Administration—Special Adjustment Assistance and Public Works Loans and Grants—have been very flexible in conditions and prospective uses. As such, the two programs have moved toward awarding and monitoring localities in terms of the number of jobs created and the potential for replacing declining employment. The shift to evaluation requires some trade-off in administrative time and energy, but one that many local managers are apparently prepared to accept. Indeed, the impetus for a shift from audit to evaluation often comes at the urging of local managers.

In summary, local managers undertake different types of adjustment-seeking activities by attempting to change the application of a statute, regulation, or standard when it impedes a program effort. In many cities, pursuing collaboration over coercion results in the achievement of both local and national goals. Such adjustment-seeking activity is the heart of the jurisdiction-based management we discovered in the case study cities.

Horizontal Collaborative Activities

Policymaking and Strategy-Making

Managing horizontally means working the highly interdependent local policy process, attempting to pool and use differential resource contributions, building bases of support, and determining feasible courses of action. One type of horizontal collaborative activity involves policymaking and strategy-making. Collaborative policymaking and strategy-making in the horizontal realm can be formal, such as when two cities enter into an agreement to plan or share in the delivery of a service, or it can be more informal, involving a relatively stable group with access to institutional resources that enable it to have a sustained role in decision making. Such arrangements are not simply mechanisms for coordination, but also means of addressing problems that cannot be solved by single organizations.

An important and highly prevalent interlocal activity involves cities engaging in shared decision making to enhance the overall purpose. Even when programs are federally or state sponsored, local government managers need to work with other local interests in developing economic development policy strategies. Joint policymaking requires high levels of interaction between local managers and the various horizontal players. As Hanf (1978, 3) has clearly stated: "The ability of individual decision units is so dependent on other units, as well as their own choices, that the major task is serving coordinated policy actions." As a result, collaborative policy development engages interlocal players in a process with city officials. Key actors in economic policy operate through mechanisms of joint production and service delivery within contexts where the resources and outputs of the cooperating organizations are "complementary in much the same way as the pieces of a jigsaw puzzle" (Pennings 1981, 434).

In this regard, nongovernmental actors become necessary partners not only in implementing policies but producing policies as well. Joint policymaking of this sort, which requires high levels of interaction based in a singular purpose and intent, is often held together by a mutually agreed-on program rationale (Hjern and Porter 1981) and by trust (Sabel 1992; Fountain 1994). Many programs are carried out through horizontal structures or relevant parts of organizations, which, while having a variety of individual goals and motives, operate nonhierarchically.

As a small suburban community, Garfield Heights looks extensively to a primary partner, Cuyahoga County, for assistance, particularly to the Cuyahoga County Planning Commission (CPC). Its domain is broad, encompassing economic and social conditions, land use, transportation and utility systems, natural resource development and conservation, and long-range programming and financing of capital projects and facilities. Planning and rezoning has been a consistent source of collaboration between Garfield Heights and CPC. Salem and its home county engage regularly in joint strategic planning. Beloit's economic development pursuits take place through an institution based in the principle of joint policymaking, the Beloit Economic Development Corporation (BEDCOR), which involves the city of Beloit, the township of Beloit, and South Beloit, Illinois. The Woodstock Economic Development Corporation (WEDC) is a cooperative venture of the Woodstock Chamber of Commerce and the city, through which strategies are developed and administration is determined. Program specialists from Cincinnati's Department of Economic Development are cross-trained as area-based generalists, acting as the city's point persons on economic development for a group of neighborhoods and promoting joint problem solving.

Horizontal activity also unfolds through city governments and other entities engaging in formal partnerships. Many variations of collaborative partnerships exist in the United States, given the multiple jurisdictions and layers of types of governmental organizations (Henderson 1984; Shanahan 1991; Zimmerman 1973). A number of collaborative approaches are intended to overcome the disadvantages of fragmentation by handling certain functions on a multijurisdictional basis, achieving economies of scale in providing various services by broadening the basis of fiscal support, addressing spillover problems in servicing, and building cooperation between various actors and groups. For example, informal cooperation can involve collaborative and reciprocal actions between two local jurisdictions that do not require state or other legal authorization. Formal horizontal collaboration that occurs in the cities includes: (1) interlocal service agreements between two or more units of government or firms, in which one pays the other for the delivery of the service to the inhabitants in the jurisdiction of the paying government; and (2) joint service agreements between two or more governments for the joint planning, financing, and delivery of a service to the inhabitants of all participating jurisdictions.

Other horizontal collaborative approaches to service delivery are county-based solutions, which involve either transferring some city government programs to the county government or both jurisdictions sharing in service production and delivery. In addition to the usual mutual service agreements like those for fire, police, and natural disasters and emergencies, there are several interlocal agreements between Woodstock and surrounding municipalities regarding annexation limits for unincorporated areas. Other agreements deal with police liaison, jointly using facilities, and development impact fees. The city and county have developed agreements regarding central purchasing, data gathering, geographic information systems, and the mutual concerns of planning and zoning.

Resource Exchange

Resource exchange is always an important component of a city's managerial activity. After the city government has established its goals, either individually or collaboratively, it must acquire the resources necessary to fulfill them from local actors. City governments in the horizontal development environment are dependent on others because they need their resources to achieve their goals. With the days of federal government abundance long past, policymaking resources are increasingly held by many players, most of which are located horizontally within or apart from the city.

Such resource dependency actually enhances the interdependencies across governments and organizations, because those players that need the resources must work with those players that are willing to contribute resources. Economic development is a citywide policy pursuit, rather than a highly specialized (geographically or otherwise) focus, so possessors of resources have an interest in the success of local economic policies and strategies.

City governments thus will work with development corporations, county or school district governments, and other important actors to acquire additional resources from higher-level government, carry a project forward, or establish policies dealing with business incentives. The interdependence that is characterized by resource exchange implies that all actors involved will benefit in some way.

Local economic leaders often seek resources from horizontal partners to accomplish local objectives and pool these finances among various organizations and governments for the purpose of attracting or retaining businesses (Agranoff 1998). Jointly developing financial or other resource incentives across more than one organization or agency are collaborative activities requiring particular skill in building trustworthy working relationships. The most prominent example we have found in the case study cities of utilizing joint financial incentives is the $12 million riverfront development project involving Beloit, its county, and private-sector firms. Managers are normally seeking assistance to accomplish local plans and projects.

In addition, direct grants, loans, revenue bonds, tax exemptions, and other financing mechanisms arranged by national and state governments have increased dramatically (while funding levels have fallen), and are increasingly conditional (Eisinger 1988). They almost always require that the local development unit arrange for some form of financial participation in the project. Horizontal collaborative management also includes leverage and engagement techniques to attract private nonprofit and for-profit resources to blend with public resources. Through their various financial programs, state and national government agencies encourage other nongovernmental and governmental organizations to commit their resources to supply the good or service in demand.

Contracts are often forged with governments or organizations to carry out specific services for the city on a paid basis. Intergovernmental and interorganizational partnership action has operated since the mid–nineteenth century, but its visibility began in the 1950s. Today, our sample cities contract for a variety of services, including economic development planning or some aspects of that function. Joint purchases, pooled liability, and group employee benefit packages are other examples. Jurisdictions have also voluntarily engaged in tax-sharing agreements. Contracting is exemplified by an annual $100,000 contract between Cincinnati and a public–private entity, Downtown Cincinnati, Incorporated, to provide planning, development, and environmental enhancement. The regional Chamber of Commerce in Cincinnati (for three states and thirteen counties) has a small contract with the city to perform some local business retention services, promote international trade, and collaborate on promoting air service.

Project-Based Work

Some horizontal efforts are designed to execute a specific project or purpose. While engaged in project-based work, managers become partners in projects that are either short-term, such as a county-wide tourism promotion to which all municipalities in the county belong, or much longer lasting projects, such as a major transportation construction that transcends many jurisdictions. As localities seek out funding arrangements to leverage and combine financial resources for a particular project, they may also become a formal partner in a project. Cincinnati regularly works as partners with the area Chamber of Commerce and the downtown development corporation on various projects, and it has cooperated with groups of manufacturers to engage in workforce development projects, many with federal financial assistance. Just as long-term policy strategies demand energetic and dependable managerial structures within which development is formulated and implemented, specific projects also require considerable effort.

Unlike the vertical activity of seeking assistance in areas where a jurisdiction has no expertise, some local jurisdictions access existing local technical information or help to move a project along. Usually, the expertise is in the community but not necessarily in the jurisdiction. Small cities, for example, often rely on substate or regional planning agencies to do their planning, zoning, and codification work. We have found that cities look to their home counties and/or lead development organizations for technical assistance in many different areas. Sometimes this is provided as a free service (although dues may be paid), and sometimes it is by contract, as in Cincinnati. Other bodies not investigated in this research, such as community services councils, the United Way, and Agricultural Extension Service Offices, have community development specialists who can help cities do a host of strategic planning activities. Local economic development corporations possess varied expertise in making local business contacts (e.g., business services), finding site locations, contacting workforce development agencies, and dealing with state permitting and licensing. Utilities provide assistance with development planning, especially to small and medium-sized cities. Finally, chambers of commerce study local economies and have data available that other entities may access to plan grant or loan applications. Most communities have a variety of such resources from which technical assistance can be drawn.

Use of Collaborative Management Activities

The primary collaborative activity variable is the total number of collaborative linkages, measured as the sum of all vertical and horizontal linkages made in the two previous years as reported by the survey respondents. Respondents to the collaboration survey were asked to indicate which actors had been contacted in the two previous years and for what activity. Two separate questions addressed the vertical and horizontal environments. The question pertaining to the first environment, which was referred to as "intergovernmental" on the survey, asked the respondent to select whether the federal government, state government, or both had been contacted; which (any or all) of 11 vertical activities was pursued with each contact (e.g., seeking general program information, seeking regulatory relief); and which of 6 methods of contact was used for each individual contact (face-to-face, written, bargaining, lobbying, through a task force, or a professional association). Cities could have made up to 132 contacts for the vertical activities (11 activities, 2 actors, 6 contact methods). The question pertaining to the second environment, which was referred to as "interlocal" on the survey, asked the respondent to select which (any or all) of 10 local governmental and nongovernmental actors had been contacted, and which (any or all) of 9 activities (e.g., creating joint financial incentives, developing a formal partnership in a project) was pursued for each interlocal contact. Cities could have performed up to 90 horizontal activities (9 activities, 10 actors).

The primary activity variable is thus an additive measure of all vertical and horizontal activities and contacts for each city. Values for this measure variable can range from zero, indicating no vertical or horizontal activities, to 222, indicating that every activity was performed with every actor through every possible contact method. The measure of total activities in the sample cities is not normally distributed (see table 4.4); thus, the incidence of such activity varies significantly. The amount of activity in the sample cities is extraordinary: The vast majority of the sample—195 cities—report both vertical and horizontal activity.

How common are these activities among the sample cities? Cities perform approximately 6 vertical and 5 horizontal activities out of a possible 20 (see table 4.5). Cities average one more information-seeking activity than adjustment-seeking activity (3.4 compared with 2.4). Cities also pursue about twice as many policymaking and strategy-making activities than resource-exchange or project-based activities. The relative frequency of vertical activity among the sample cities is much greater than we anticipated at the outset. Eighty percent of the cities sought general program information and approximately two-thirds of the cities sought new funding, program interpretations, program guidance, and technical assistance.

Managers in the field told us that although there are not many funds available from either the federal or state government, they must constantly pursue those opportunities that are available, and they must be more selective in pursuing opportunities. They also must maintain regular contact with state (and sometimes federal) officials regarding a host of nonfinancial assistance programs. Jurisdictions are not merely acquiring funds and following program rules, but also are actively discussing and managing programs for their jurisdiction. It is also notable that some managers are actively trying to change the system and are not just agents of

Table 4.4. Descriptive Statistics for Collaborative Management Activities

Measure	Total Activity	Vertical Activity	Horizontal Activity
Mean	28.1	18.0	10.1
Median	22.0	14.0	8.0
Standard deviation	23.9	17.5	9.4
High	142.0	96.0	49.0
Low	0.0	0.0	0.0
Total for all cities	6,549	4,263	2,286

the state and federal governments. More than one-half of the cities reported seeking some form of statutory or regulatory relief or waiver, nearly one-half sought a change in policy, one-third sought a funding innovation for a previously awarded program or involvement in a model program, and nearly one-fourth pursued discretion in exchange for performance.

Several conditions trigger these vertical actions: the potential cost or burden of regulations, incompatibility of state and federal expectations with local needs or interests, restrictive eligibility rules or funding regulations, laws or regulations that impeded local development projects, and standards that local partners in a development effort could not meet. These negotiations and bargaining activities that "recipients" or the "regulated" can use are important in dealing with higher-level governments. Given the difficulty of making the appropriate contacts and developing some understanding of the conditions under which the state or federal government is more apt to grant discretion, the substantial amounts of managerial energy that must be expended, and the considerable risks that must be taken, the evidence of cities pursu-

Table 4.5. Percentage of Cities Using Collaborative Management Activities and Mean Usage of Activities

Vertical Activity	Percent	Use	Use	Percent	Horizontal Activity
Information seeking	86	3.4	2.6	85	Policymaking and strategy-making
General program information	80			76	Gain policymaking assistance
New funding of programs and projects	67			70	Engage in formal partnership
				63	Engage in joint policymaking
Interpretation of standards and rules	66			51	Consolidate policy effort
General program guidance	64				
Technical assistance	64				
Adjustment seeking	71	2.4	1.4	65	Resource exchange
Regulatory relief, flexibility, or waiver	52			54	Seek financial resources
				47	Employ joint financial incentives
Statutory relief-flexibility	52			40	Contracted planning and implementation
Change in policy	45				
Funding innovation for program	33				
Model program involvement	30				
Performance-based discretion	24				
			1.4	75	Project-based work
				66	Partnership for a particular project
				58	Seek technical resources
Total	87	5.8	5.2	90	

ing discretion appears remarkable. These activities indicate the existence of managing consistent with donor–recipient and juris-diction-based models.

Seven of the nine horizontal activities were pursued by more than one-half of the cities. The most prevalent policymaking and managerial activities in the horizontal environment include seeking out policymaking assistance from various organizations and engaging in formal policymaking partnerships. This underscores the importance of the city government working with other local entities to develop local economic development approaches and to create development institutions locally. The difficult process of gathering resources for development purposes is demonstrated by the relatively low incidence of city activity in resource-exchange activities, which are the least pursued of all collaborative activities. As will be shown in the next chapter, even when employed, the acquisition and exchange of resources apparently involve a relatively small number of partners. In the case study cities, this was partially explained as organizations more willing to meet and discuss ideas and approaches, but reluctant to part with finances or staff to work together on something that involved resource commitments. Nevertheless, the fact that cities are working at such activity demonstrates that they are active within local, horizontal networks.

Nearly twice as much activity is devoted to the vertical environment as to the horizontal environment (64 percent compared with 36 percent), suggesting the continuing importance of the working relationships between local government officials and state and federal governments (see table 4.6). Information seeking is the most commonly pursued vertical activity. Fifty-eight percent of all vertical activity and 37 percent of total collaborative activity is information-seeking. Cities clearly rely on the guidance and knowledge found in other levels of government, in addition to pro-gramming. Policymaking and strategy-making is the most commonly pursued horizontal activity (55 percent of all horizontal activity), underscoring the importance of involving the expertise and point of view of the community in economic development decision making. More than one-fourth of all collaborative activity involves seeking adjustments in programming or implementation from the state and federal government, whereas less than 10 percent each of collaborative activity is devoted to resource-exchange and project-based activity.

Variation in Collaborative Activity

Examining the determinants of activity variation in cities provides the best evidence of a specialized approach to management that we have referred to as jurisdiction-based. In the previous chapter, we proposed that jurisdiction-based management exists in cities that exploit their complex governing environment strategically. To test this proposition, we defined strategy as any explicit step taken by a city to assume control over the direction and success of its economic development. One important type of strategic activity includes the package of economic *policies* selected by the city; we examine this in chapter 6. Other strategies involve administrative or *procedural* steps (see table 4.7 for the strategic, structural, and economic characteristics of all the sample cities). We looked at three strategies that can be considered proxies for all strategic activity: designing an areawide comprehensive plan that considers the collaborative environment, implementing a formal economic development plan, and establishing performance measures and evaluation processes to assess the effectiveness of development policies.[2]

As is shown in table 4.8, the link between strategic activity and collaborative activity is undeniable.[3] Two findings are notable. First, a locally based strategic orientation is positively and significantly associated with collaborative activity. As cities attempt to

Table 4.6. Level of Collaborative Activity

Collaborative Activity	Percentage of all activity	Percentage of vertical or horizontal activity
Vertical	64	
Information seeking	37	58
Adjustment seeking	27	42
Horizontal	36	
Policymaking and strategy-making	21	55
Resource exchange	7	20
Project-based work	9	24

Note: Some totals do not add up to 100 percent due to rounding.

Table 4.7. Strategic, Structural, and Economic Characteristics of Sample Cities

Characteristic	Total
Strategic (percentage of sample)	
Written development plan	36
Strategic plan	43
Evaluation and performance measures	24
Structural (percentage of sample)	
Development corporation lead agency	24
Government lead agency	52
Full-time director is lead manager	33
Chief administrative officer is lead manager	52
Council-manager	50
Central cities	9
Small suburbs	32
Large suburbs	29
Independent cities	30
Economic (entire sample)	
Unemployment rate (percent)	5.9
Poverty rate (percent)	9.9
Median family income (dollars)	39,429

gain control of the local economy through administrative means, high levels of collaboration occur. The causal relationship is unclear from the data, but we contend that strategizing breeds collaboration, which cultivates continued or enhanced use of strategic approaches, and so on. A city that undergoes a planning process must necessarily consult key local actors such as developers, the chamber of commerce, or the county government—or perhaps all of these and more. As the interaction between the city and local actors commences, the city recognizes the policy resources available to them and seeks out joint processes, financial resources, and the capacity to implement projects.

Collaboration locally also reveals the level of local implementation capacity and thus can allow a city to confidently pursue vertical collaboration, such as grants and regulatory adjustment. The level of collaborative activity also appears to be cumulative, in that the greater the strategic orientation—as measured by the presence of multiple strategic procedures—the greater the activity level. Cities encountering just one strategic procedure are less active than cities with two or more procedures.

Procedural strategies are also associated with qualitative differences in a city's collaborative activity. Strategic cities emphasize

Table 4.8. Difference of Means Tests, Active Cities with Procedural Strategies Compared with Active Cities without Strategies (n = 195)

Procedural Strategy	Time Spent[a]	Total Activity[b]	Vertical Activity[b]	Horizontal Activity[d]	Information Ratio[e]	Adjustment Ratio[f]	Policymaking Ratio[g]	Resource Ratio[h]	Project Ratio[i]
Areawide plan (n = 63)	26.6*	39.9*	25.3*	14.6*	62.1*	37.9*	54.9	20.9**	24.2
No plan	19.2	29.2	19.0	10.2	68.9	31.1	58.1	17.0	24.9
Development plan (n = 72)	26.0*	37.3*	23.5	13.9*	65.7	34.3	54.9	21.3*	23.7
No plan	19.1	29.9	19.6	10.3	67.3	32.7	58.3	16.4	25.3
Performance and evaluation (n = 57)	22.3	43.3*	28.3*	15.0*	60.7*	39.3*	61.5**	18.1	20.4*
No evaluation	21.3	28.3	18.0	10.3	69.2	30.8	55.2	18.3	26.5
Two or three strategies (n = 57)	24.9	44.0*	28.4	15.6*	61.1	38.9	57.6	19.5	22.9
Any strategy (n = 63)	26.0	37.6*	23.8	13.7*	64.5	35.5	56.1	20.6	23.3
No strategy (n = 75)	14.5*	24.8*	16.5*	8.3*	70.3*	29.7*	58.6	14.5*	26.9

* = statistical significance at p = .05.

** = statistical significance at p = .10.

[a] Time spent = percentage of time spent on collaborative activity.
[b] Total activity = total number of activities.
[c] Vertical activity = total number of vertical activities.
[d] Horizontal activity = total number of horizontal activities.
[e] Information ratio = percentage of vertical activity that is information seeking.
[f] Adjustment ratio = percentage of vertical activity that is adjustment seeking.
[g] Policymaking ratio = percentage of horizontal activity that is policymaking and strategy-making.
[h] Resource ratio = percentage of horizontal activity that is resource exchange.
[i] Project ratio = percentage of horizontal activity that is project based.

adjustment-seeking vertical activity to a much greater extent than other cities. For example, a city with both types of plans in force devotes 39 percent of its vertical activity adjustments, which is far greater than the mean of 33 percent (for the 195 active cities). Although all cities devote the majority of their vertical activity to seeking information, the extra activity in strategic cities is adjustment seeking, suggesting a jurisdiction-based approach. A top-down city is characterized by a willingness and capacity to accede to the requirements of state and federal governments; seeking information is one component of that approach. All things being equal, a city that relies more heavily on information rather than adjustment activity practices a top-down management approach.

The relationship between horizontal activity and strategy is not as clearly defined as vertical activity, but some differences do exist. Strategic cities rely more heavily on resource-exchange activities than other cities. For those 195 active cities as a whole, approximately 18 percent of all horizontal activity is dedicated to resource exchange, whereas cities with at least one strategic plan in place devote 21 percent of such activity to resource exchange.

Structure clearly explains the quantitative variation in collaborative activity (see table 4.9). Cities where the public–private development corporation is charged specifically with leading the economic development effort have significantly greater levels of activity. Similarly, cities where the person most responsible for development policymaking and administration is a full-time agency director—regardless of the locus of the agency—are significantly more active. Conversely, when the lead policy agency is located in the government structure or when the lead official is the city's top administrator (e.g., city manager, mayor), collaborative activity is significantly lower than average. One structure that does not explain city variation is the form of government. Council–manager governments (as defined by the International City/County Management Association) spent significantly more time on collaborative activity than mayor–council cities, but the amount of activity and the mix of activity types do not vary across government forms.

The economic condition of a city is also a statistically significant determinant of collaborative activity, although substantively it does not explain much of the variation across cities. Unemployment and poverty rates are both positive predictors of the level of

Table 4.9. Difference of Means Tests, Active Cities with a Certain Structure Compared with Active Cities without Structures (n = 195)

Procedural Strategy	Time Spent[a]	Total Activity[b]	Vertical Activity[c]	Horizontal Activity[d]	Information Ratio[e]	Adjustment Ratio[f]	Policymaking Ratio[g]	Resource Ratio[h]	Project Ratio[i]
LDC lead agency (n = 48)	23.4	42.8*	26.9*	15.9*	64.7	35.3	57.5	19.4	23.1
Other	20.1	29.3	19.1	10.2	67.4	32.6	56.9	17.9	25.2
Government lead agency (n = 102)	21.8	29.6*	19.2	10.3*	66.8	33.2	54.1*	19.3	26.6
Other	21.4	36.0	23.0	13.0	66.6	33.4	60.3	17.0	22.6
Director is lead official (n = 70)	29.4*	40.0*	25.7*	14.3*	64.7	35.3	52.7*	20.1	27.2
Other	16.8	28.5	18.4	10.1	67.9	32.1	59.5	17.2	23.3
City CAO is lead official (n = 105)	15.0*	28.9*	18.9*	10.0*	67.8	32.2	58.5	16.3*	25.1
Other	29.0	37.0	23.5	13.5	65.5	34.5	55.4	20.4	24.1
Mayor–council (n = 89)	18.0	33.2	21.8	11.4	66.0	34.0	57.9	17.3	24.8
Council–manager (n = 106)	26.2*	31.9	20.1	11.8	67.6	32.4	56.1	19.3	24.6
Central city (n = 20)	24.2	64.2*	44.7*	19.5*	50.6*	49.4*	59.8	19.5	20.7
Suburban city (n = 116)	17.3	27.0*	17.7	9.3*	69.9	30.1	58.0	16.3*	25.7
Independent city (n = 59)	29.4*	33.1*	19.5	13.6*	66.0	34.0	54.4	21.4	24.1

* = statistical significance at p = .05.

Note: "LDC" is local development corporation; "CAO" is chief administrative officer.

[a] Time spent = percentage of time spent on collaborative activity.
[b] Total activity = total number of activities.
[c] Vertical activity = total number of vertical activities.
[d] Horizontal activity = total number of horizontal activities.
[e] Information ratio = percentage of vertical activity that is information seeking.
[f] Adjustment ratio = percentage of vertical activity that is adjustment seeking.
[g] Policymaking ratio = percentage of horizontal activity that is policymaking and strategy-making.
[h] Resource ratio = percentage of horizontal activity that is resource exchange.
[i] Project ratio = percentage of horizontal activity that is project based.

Table 4.10. Correlation Coefficients for Measures of Economic Condition and Collaborative Activity ($n = 195$)

Economic Condition	Time Spent[a]	Total Activity[b]	Vertical Activity[c]	Horizontal Activity[d]	Information Ratio[e]	Adjustment Ratio[f]	Policymaking Ratio[g]	Resource Ratio[h]	Project Ratio[i]
Unemployment rate	.201*	.168*	.143*	.157*	−.149*	.149*	−.068	.144*	.028
Poverty rate	.182*	.245*	.207*	.230*	−.147*	.147*	.001	.090	−.071
Median family income	−.295*	−.229*	−.188*	−.226*	.091*	−.091	.059	−.232*	.108

* = statistical significance at $p = .05$.

[a] Time spent = percentage of time spent on collaborative activity.
[b] Total activity = total number of activities.
[c] Vertical activity = total number of vertical activities.
[d] Horizontal activity = total number of horizontal activities.
[e] Information ratio = percentage of vertical activity that is information seeking.
[f] Adjustment ratio = percentage of vertical activity that is adjustment seeking.
[g] Policymaking ratio = percentage of horizontal activity that is policymaking and strategy-making.
[h] Resource ratio = percentage of horizontal activity that is resource exchange.
[i] Project ratio = percentage of horizontal activity that is project based.

activity, as expected, and median family income is a negative predictor of activity (see table 4.10). Cities with a high unemployment
rate rely more heavily on resource-exchange activities, and cities
with a high median income rely less so on such activities. But no
more than 5.5 percent of the variation in activity usage is explained
by these particular measures of economic condition. The small correlation coefficients lend support for our proposition that strategic
and administrative factors—not purely economic conditions—are
the most important predictors of activity level and mix.

Finally, we offer a word about the abstainers. These cities,
which choose not to be involved in virtually any state or federal
program, have few interlocal collaborators. Our examination of the
variation in collaborative activity actually included those 195 cities
that reported both horizontal and vertical activity. A total of 42
sample cities proved to be abstainers by our definition. Only 5 of
those 42 cities (fewer than 12 percent) were without both types of
activities, and for those, they report the use of two or three strategic
procedures. As one might expect, more than one-half (22 of the 42)
employ no strategic procedures. There are other indicators of lack
of strategic effort. Only 8 of the abstainers have a local development corporation that is a lead development agency, and only 8
report that the lead official is a full-time director. A total of 22 cities
report that government is the lead agency, and nearly one-half (19
of the 42) use the chief administrative officer of the city as the lead
official. This type of in-house operation further indicates the lack of
collaborative action. Thus, nonengaged cities employ few strategic
procedures and tend not to engage other entities or staff in their
development activities. These findings present additional evidence
that strategy and activity are significantly and positively related.

Conclusion

Local managers seek grants and comply with regulations, but they
also intergovernmentally manage programs through negotiations
and pursuit of program adjustments with state and federal officials. As managers work within the vertical and horizontal systems, they pursue more than eleven discrete collaborative
activities, encompassing nearly two-thirds of all the collaborative
activity explored. Working within the vertical system is important,

as the literature suggests, but it is a more complex interactive process than that of typical portrayals. Managers also operate horizontally by engaging other local governments and nongovernmental organizations in program developments and exchanges of specific development efforts. These joint-engagement activities broaden the concept of interlocal cooperation and adjustment beyond interlocal agreements.

Managing interdependencies has indeed become more pervasive, routine, and complex (Kettl 1996). Notably, the policymaking resources demanded by the greatest number of cities, in both the vertical and horizontal environments, are information and expertise. Just as a public manager in a particular government agency learns the value of reducing uncertainty and amassing information to improve decision making, so also does a collaborative manager seek to improve policymaking and strategy-making. Apparently, however, the collaborative manager seeks to achieve the goals of the jurisdiction by accessing the needed information and expertise from sources outside the government agency, thus managing at or beyond the boundaries of the jurisdiction, on behalf of the jurisdiction.

Managing at the boundaries of government is considerably more complicated than has been depicted in earlier eras. Managing involves seeking relevant operating information, asking about interpretations related to running a program, seeking guidance regarding a proposed course of action on a program, and asking for and applying technical assistance. Dealing with intergovernmental regulation does indeed include those activities related to compliance, but not every regulated government complies in every case. Some manage by seeking discretion. They do this by one of several means of "tweaking the system," learning how to ask for, negotiate, and perhaps bargain for greater measures of discretion. Though not every local government in our sample reported doing this, a notable percentage (up to one-half) had done so in the two years before the survey. These managers attempted some basic regulatory or statutory adjustment, sought a policy change, or some other form of "loosening" up the compliance game. The frequency data on vertical collaboration suggests that many managers are actually working the system to adapt federal and/or state programs to jurisdictional needs.

The horizontal activities also expand earlier notions of interlocal adjustments and cooperative agreements. Governments at the local level not only work with one another in the form of city–county, city–township, or city–special district relations; they also engage a variety of nongovernmental partners. Contacts and collaborations are between cities and chambers of commerce, public–private partnerships, and local utilities—and, to a lesser extent, with job-training programs, neighborhood associations, and a few other organizations.

The findings suggest that the work of the manager entails non-traditional activities, such as seeking out policymaking information, negotiating partner arrangements, practicing interorganizational policymaking, leveraging and arranging multiple-source financing, creating financial incentives, contract management, finding and operating formal partnerships, and using and giving technical assistance of various kinds. Although these managerial actions are less often employed than those of a vertical nature, they are called upon nonetheless. These emergent collaborative management skills do not supplant the traditional list of interlocal managerial actions, structural adaptations and joint purchasing or servicing, but they add to the expanding nature of what needs to be known about managers' collaborative activity within communities.

Managing collaboratively is ingrained in the core of the public manager's repertoire. Managing has become far more involved than "coordinating" programs from the top or "complying" with them from the bottom. For some cities, collaborative public management means adjusting, coping, partnering, brokering, contracting, exchanging, informing, and performing many other managerial actions across the boundaries of organizations. Along with the city officials studied here, other managers promote and maintain lines of contact and communication, propose actions, make accommodations and adjustments, exchange resources, and execute programs between multiple governments and organizations. As cities strategically pursue opportunities within their complex governing environment, their level of collaborative activity is quite strong. This is jurisdiction-based management in action.

Notes

1. A varimax rotated-factor analysis of all twenty activities (measured as the usage of each in each city) initially revealed three total factors: the

two vertical activity types and a third factor that included the nine remaining activities, all of which are horizontal. We categorized the nine horizontal activities according to their use in practice into three different activity types. Purely as a means to further test the reliability of these groupings, Cronbach's alpha coefficients were computed, which are based on the average covariance of items with each other. The higher the coefficient on a scale from 0 to 1, the greater the correlation between each item (in this case, collaborative activities) and all other items in a category. Large values for the alpha coefficients for both the horizontal and vertical categories of activities indicate a high degree of internal consistency and strong measurement reliability in the scales. The alpha coefficient for the eleven vertical activities is .93; for the five information-seeking activities, .88; and for the six adjustment-seeking activities, .90; whereas the coefficients for the three horizontal categories of activities are .87, .75, and .71, respectively. The strength of these coefficients provides a high level of confidence that these factors do, indeed, exist in the real world of collaborative management, and that the categorization is both an intuitive and empirically grounded way to differentiate collaborative activities.

2. We also tested other strategic procedures, including city use of databases for seeking and accessing resources, as well as leveraging resources from various actors. The relationships between these procedures and collaborative activity are much the same as those shown in table 4.8. We believe the planning and evaluation strategies are the most compelling and highly demonstrative of a local strategic orientation, and thus we chose to display them in tabular form.

3. We examine both the absolute number of activities and the qualitative mix of activities. Although the summary tables earlier in the chapter described activity for the entire sample, our examination of activity variation focuses on the 195 cities that reported both horizontal and vertical activity. We look at the "abstainers" later in the chapter.

5

Linkages in Collaborative Management

Beloit had just over two days to put together a competing bid for the location of a large electronics factory. City officials secured the cooperation of the Chamber of Commerce and the Beloit Economic Development Corporation (BEDCOR) in formulating a plan and facilitating permits and licenses, and they gained financial commitments from the Rock County government and job-training supports from the state of Wisconsin to accompany its own Community Development Block Grant (CDBG) expenditures and tax increment financing. Meanwhile, BEDCOR worked with the substate vocational-technical program to prepare a workforce development plan, and with the Small Business Development Center and the U.S. Department of Commerce's Economic Development Administration (EDA) to help support the creation of area-based supplier businesses of small components. Although unsuccessful in their bid, local officials became more adept at developing links and forging agreements across jurisdiction and organization boundaries.

The variation in collaborative activity across cities is explained in part by the strategic orientation of each city. We have shown that when a city adopts strategic and policy planning processes, measures and evaluates its development programs, and employs basic administrative structures focused on achieving its development goals, high levels of collaborative activity ensue. A city's management approach can also be defined in terms of the actors with which the city collaborates. As the Beloit example suggests, managing across governments and organizations is evident not simply in the extent to which collaboration has become the primary organizational setting for designing and executing policy, but also in the number and type of collaborative linkages that exist within the policymaking realm of a single city. Like the hub of a multi-spoked wheel, many managers in cities are linked to all of the spokes, each representing a different strategic activity; each consisting of collaborative linkages of different composition, scope, and size; and each with its own set of management challenges and responsibilities. The game of engaging multiple partners is increasingly played.

The focus of this chapter is on the dimensionality or variation of strategic collaborative activity, as well as the depth or extent of collaborative partners. The basic unit of analysis involves the collaborative *linkages* through which local economic development policy is designed and executed. Provan and Milward state that "the basic building block of any network study is the linkages among the organizations that make up the network" (1995, 10). Although the research reported in this book does not address networks per se, the principle is still applicable. Contacts and interactions by the sample cities at the local level provide the foundation for the findings reported here.

Because our data were collected from survey responses and interviews with local development officials, we have mapped out the collaborative linkages as they exist according to those actually involved, rather than through objective observation. When survey respondents were asked to select which of ten actors in or around the locality (governments, organizations, and agencies from all sectors) they collaborated with, as well as whether they collaborated with the state or federal government, they were also asked how frequently the actors were engaged and for which specific strategic activity they were contacted. This chapter thus involves empirically linking activities with actors and identifying whether certain linkages occur more frequently than others or whether such linkages occur in patterns.

The Beloit electronics factory attraction example given at the beginning of the chapter clearly is not a singular event. Most economic development efforts, whether led by city government or some other entity, require extensive horizontal and vertical collaborative linkages to make them go forward as successful projects. The first page of the Cincinnati Department of Economic Development's brochure identifies the importance of federal and state financial assistance to business, of public–private partnerships, and of local interagency cooperation.

What is striking is the sheer extent and complexity of interorganizational linkages in cities. Although our research has been able to track more than 200 different collaborative linkages, the true complexity of a city's governing environment may, in fact, be understated by our analysis. It is important to note that we are only examining linkages for the purposes of economic development; additional collaborative linkages are created for programs addressing social issues, crime and delinquency, parks and recreation, housing, and many other matters.

Furthermore, we examined linkages from the perspective of the city official most responsible for economic development only over the previous two years and only in terms of ten core potential horizontal collaborators as well as several agencies in the state and federal governments. We did not explore other potential collaborators, such as housing and building developers, financial institutions, and redevelopment corporations and school districts, all of which no doubt complicate the work of collaborative managers.

Who is contacted by city officials and for what purposes are perhaps the most fundamental questions to be answered in our analysis of jurisdiction-based and other forms of collaborative management. To answer these questions, we take an extensive look at the linkages within cities. Also, we show how and why such linkages occur—the "who" and "what" of collaborative management.

Vertical Linkages

The collaborative linkages made by cities with vertical actors are extensive, but the level of involvement varies across cities. In Beloit, vertical intergovernmental relationships involve the multiple modes and frequent contacts typical of a central city. The city manager's office estimates that about one state contact a day and one federal contact a week are made from the city government. BEDCOR reports that it makes one or two contacts a week with state and federal agencies. The most frequent state contacts are with the Wisconsin Department of Development (DoD), the Wisconsin Housing and Economic Development Authority (WHEDA), the Department of Natural Resources (DNR), and the Department of Transportation. DoD is important for loan and assistance programs, flood assistance programs, securing leads on prospective businesses, and applying for state permits. As an entitlement city, the city's federal contacts are primarily with the Department of Housing and Urban Development (HUD) concerning CDBG funds, which represent a notable portion of the city's budget and finance a great deal of its development efforts. Beloit also contacts the Small Business Administration (SBA) office in Madison, which directly administers the 504 Certified Development Company Program and other loan programs, and the state representative of EDA in Madison.

Similarly, both Ithaca's city manager and the local development corporation (LDC) director are constantly making state and federal contacts, particularly with officials based in Lansing, about 40 miles to the south. Their interactions are about the feasibility of funding and opportunities, program rule changes, and potential midcourse changes in previously funded programs. They submit ten to fifteen grant proposals each year, but they report that many more of their contacts are over such issues as acquiring permits and licenses, arranging loans or other forms of credit, and making general inquiries regarding state programs on behalf of existing and prospective businesses in the community.

The experiences of Beloit, Ithaca, and the other case study cities suggest that a variety of vertical contacts are maintained in the same policy arena. We examined ten federal and eight state departments and agencies that have arguably become the most active in and most responsible for the various intergovernmental programs that affect economic development. Survey respondents were asked to rate the extent of vertical collaboration by indicating how many times each year the city government engages in contacts with these agencies. Respondents could select ten or more (frequent), five to nine (moderate), one to four (occasional), or zero (no contact). Table 5.1 displays the proportion of cities that report development-oriented contact with federal agencies.

The pattern of federal interaction illustrates the diversity of policy activities that constitute the development efforts of local

Table 5.1. Percentage of Cities Contacting Federal and State Government Agencies

Agency	Any[a]	Ten or more[b]	Five or more[c]
Federal			
Environmental Protection Agency	63	10	22
Department of Commerce (any)	56	8	19
Department of Transportation	55	8	21
Department of Housing and Urban Development	53	11	19
Small Business Administration	46	5	13
Department of Labor	42	1	9
Economic Development Administration	41	6	15
Department of Agriculture (FmHA)	28	1	5
Department of Agriculture (RDA)	14	0	2
Department of Health and Human Services	21	2	4
State			
Department of transportation or highways	92	35	66
Department of development or commerce	91	33	62
Legislature	90	30	61
Environment agency	83	20	49
Governor's office	75	8	17
Department of education or training	54	6	18
Small business development center	48	9	20
Science- or technology agency	24	2	5

Note: "FmHA" is Farmers Home Administration; "RDA" is Rural Development Administration.
[a] Any = percentage with at least one contact with the agency.
[b] Ten or more = percentage with ten or more contacts with the agency.
[c] Five or more = percentage with five or more contacts with the agency.

governments. At the federal level, the Environmental Protection Agency (EPA), the Department of Commerce, HUD, and the Department of Transportation (DOT) are the most frequently contacted. Very few cities report frequent yearly contacts with any of the federal agencies, but more than half report some degree of contact with these four agencies. It is interesting that, though the Department of Commerce offers the most specific economic development programs through EDA and the Small Business Administration (SBA), the agencies providing a seemingly more ancillary role in development, such as EPA and DOT, receive comparable levels of contact. Indeed, EPA was the federal agency contacted by the greatest number of cities, demonstrating how broadly defined is the policy context of economic development. Even HUD, with a clear mission of housing and community development, is contacted by no more cities than EPA and Commerce.

The number of cities that make any contact with the Department of Labor is comparable to the number that make contacts with EDA and SBA. A small percentage of cities make contact with the Department of Health and Human Services, or such key Department of Agriculture agencies as the Farmers Home Administration (FmHA) and Rural Development Administration (RDA) (agencies that have reorganized since our survey). However, thirty-three sample cities still included RDA in their extensive vertical operations. It is notable that forty-one cities (17 percent of the sample) report absolutely no contact with any of the listed federal agencies for economic development purposes; thirty-two of these cities could be classified as contented cities, or simply as abstainers.

City government interaction is not federally dominated and is considerably more frequent with state-level agencies. As federal funding has tightened or has devolved to the states, managers set their sights toward state capitals. Six of the eight state entities investigated are contacted by more than half of the cities in the sample, whereas only 5 of the 237 cities reported no contact with the listed state agencies. The state department addressing transportation and highways, which provides planning expertise and funding for infrastructure, was contacted most frequently, followed closely by the state department of commerce or development and the state legislature. Although state departments of commerce or development provide direct financial and technical assistance to cities for explicit economic development purposes, city contact with these agencies is not much greater than with environment departments and the legislature, which provide support for economic development only indirectly.

Environmentally oriented departments provide permits and other programs for water, sewer, and other critical areas of local improvements that can influence the implementation of economic development policy. The extremely high proportion of cities making contact with state legislators indicates that these elected officials are an important source of information for local officials. It also suggests the importance of the elected official serving as an "inside-lobbyist" for local projects or intergovernmental adjustments. It also should be noted that many of these more frequent state contacts actually concern federal programs administered by the state, for example, transportation and commerce.

Vertical intergovernmental contacts with the state by Ithaca are illustrative. The city makes about ten contacts a month, and Greater Gratiot Development Incorporated (GGDI) makes about three a week. The GGDI executive often makes two trips to Lansing a week for a statewide committee meeting or to deal with issues involving access to programs. The single most frequent contacts are with the Michigan Economic Development Corporation, a mega-department that claims to offer one-stop shopping for grants, loans, interest-buy-downs, workforce development, and permitting programs. It uses a team approach with an area-based accounts manager to handle each case. The team is joined by a regulatory ombudsman, a business research associate, a workforce development specialist, and an infrastructure development specialist. Very close links are maintained with the accounts manager who covers the region that includes Gratiot County but is located in Lansing (twelve others are based in other locations). Some contact is made with Michigan First, Incorporated, a public–private statewide marketing corporation.

In addition, contact with the Michigan Department of Transportation is regular; an annual grant request is submitted for off-road or street improvements. Regular contact—sometimes three times a month—occurs with DNR on environmental regulatory issues, the city's superfund site and underground gasoline storage tanks. DNR has been sometimes difficult for businesses to work with, so the practice has been to work through the jobs commission accounts manager. Frequent contact is also made with area legislators, and occasionally for special legislation. Legislators are also contacted to help break the bureaucratic logjam or to solve "bureaucratic snafus." Normally, the intergovernmental working style is to "get close to the people who do the work."

Not untypical of large central cities, Cincinnati has extensive federal and state interactions. It is the only city among the case study cities to have state and federal government work plans and retain lobbyists in Columbus and Washington. Both work plans include monitoring information regarding pending legislation, informing the city of any efforts to reduce funding streams or increase tax burdens, monitoring the availability of bond funds, seeking revisions to some laws affecting the city, facilitating the introduction of special legislation related to the recovery of city funds, pursuing special project funding, and representing local governments. Special state initiatives during the study period included promotion of multimodal transportation, a utility franchise fee, telecommunications legislation, funding for a new athletic stadium, and several special bills. Federal highlights include an Army Corps of Engineers flood protection project, restitution legislation for the University of Cincinnati College of Medicine, and a proposed amendment to the Community Development Banking Act.

The variety of vertical collaborative contacts begs an important question: How do city officials interact with these players? Can it be said that city and vertical players (state and federal officials) actually collaborate to the extent that formal or even political processes are pursued toward a particular goal, resulting in a change in the system? Or is the relationship more routine, built on periodic contacts through informal means? Woodstock's intergovernmental contact style is triggered by the actions of the city manager, who regularly initiates discussions, which lead to the exploration of mutual concerns, which then lead to agreed-upon courses of action and ultimately to intergovernmental agreements. His approach, according to an official from another jurisdiction, is to open the door and say, "Can we talk?" State and federal contacts are described as informal in the same way. Initial personal visits are followed by telephone calls. Bargaining and negotiation are also important: The city and county worked out an agreement regarding central purchasing, data gathering, geographic information systems, and mutual concerns regarding planning and zoning.

Woodstock and other cities employ several different methods for establishing contact with the vertical players just examined, and six methods were investigated: *telephone and face-to-face* communication; *written* communication; *lobbying*, through the use of a city-retained representative to advocate with agencies and legislative bodies; engaging in a *formal bargaining* session to resolve an intergovernmental impasse or other such obstacle, sometimes using a formal arbitrator; use of an *association*, such as a state municipal league or a national group like the U.S. Conference of Mayors; and forming a *joint task force* consisting of representative local government and higher-level officials. The first two methods are informal (or at least minimally formal) and routine. The more formal approaches of lobbying and bargaining and negotiation are political methods of contact, whereas involvement in an association or a task force entails a group or joint process of collaboration.

The variation in the composition of linkages between vertical players and the five information-seeking and six adjustment-seeking activities demonstrates the complexity of the vertical environment and the preeminence of multiple modes of collaboration. Whereas a larger percentage of cities seek information from the state government than from the federal government (85 percent, compared with 57 percent), an equivalent number of cities pursue adjustment-seeking activities with the state and federal government (see table 5.2). Twice as many cities work with their states regarding funding, interpretations, guidance, and technical assistance as they do with federal officials. More than one-half of all the sample cities report establishing linkages with the state for seven of the eleven activities, whereas more than one-half report establishing linkages with the federal government for only one activity—seeking program information—which is perhaps the least difficult or involved of the vertical activities.

For all vertical activities, a majority of collaboration is through written, telephone, or face-to-face communication, as the routine columns in table 5.2 indicate. A somewhat higher proportion of the average city's overall contacting with the state government is with the telephone or face-to-face (38 percent) as compared with the federal government (30 percent), whereas a higher percentage of federal contacting is through the written word (45 percent). Cities are twice as likely to use political methods of contact (lobbying and bargaining) when seeking program guidance and technical assistance from the state government than when seeking the same from the federal government.

Overall, it is clear that for most of the collaborative purposes pursued in the vertical realm, the state government is the targeted venue of contact. Respondents in the case study cities suggest that state agency representatives are more approachable and less formal than many federal officials. As a result, managers in cities report a greater "comfort level" with city–state linkages because contacts are more professional yet more relaxed in both presentation and acceptance of locally generated ideas, and the real decision makers are easier to access.

This situation may explain why states are more apt to pursue information through political means. In comparison with the federal government level, lobbying in a state is perhaps less contentious when conducted with the city's state representative, and bargaining can be conducted in a less threatening environment.

Table 5.2. Percentage of Cities Using Various Vertical-Activity Methods to Contact Federal and State Governments

Method	Any Contact		Routine[a]		Political[b]		Formal[c]	
	Federal	State	Federal	State	Federal	State	Federal	State
Information seeking	57	85	76	71	12	15	12	15
Seek general program information	52	81	73	65	13	18	14	17
Seek new funding of programs and projects	36	68	69	70	15	16	15	14
Seek interpretation of standards and rules	33	68	74	72	16	16	11	13
Seek general program guidance	33	65	86	74	5	12	9	13
Acquire technical assistance	28	66	84	76	5	9	11	15
Adjustment seeking	73	72	63	63	23	22	14	15
Regulatory relief, flexibility, or waiver	32	52	60	61	28	25	13	14
Statutory relief or flexibility	26	52	57	58	28	26	15	16
Change in official policy	24	46	62	59	24	22	14	19
Funding innovation of existing program	21	31	78	73	16	17	7	11
Model program involvement	14	31	61	69	16	16	23	14
Performance-oriented discretion	15	24	71	66	17	19	12	15
Total contact	75	76	75	76	20	17	5	7

[a] Routine = total written and telephone contact.
[b] Political = total lobbying and formal bargaining or negotiation contact.
[c] Formal = total formal association and task force contact.

State officials are more accessible, less rule-bound, and more oriented to local problems.

Adjustment-seeking collaboration is conducted differently than is information-seeking activity. It is not surprising that such activity is, overall, less routine and more political. Whereas just 5 percent of city activity that sought federal program guidance or technical assistance was political, 28 percent of all federal regulatory and statutory adjustments were sought through political means. Thus table 5.2 indicates that there is a notable "political cluster" for seeking these program adjustments. Indeed, nearly 20 percent of federal regulatory and statutory activity was worked out through formal bargaining and negotiation. It is also notable that federal model program involvement is clearly most often pursued through an association or task force. The difference in contact methods between information-seeking and adjustment-seeking activities with federal agencies is substantial relative to contacts with state agencies. Finally, city–state collaboration for adjustments was more political than for information, but to a lesser extent than city–federal activity.

Our data suggest that states are not intermediaries in the intergovernmental system as much as they are focal points for intergovernmental programs, particularly in economic development (Walker 2000; Clarke and Gaile 1998); they may be the first actors to which cities turn when in need of resources. Information is gained by cities through communications with state-level elected representatives, and deals are struck more easily for information. Sometimes local jurisdictions pursue both federal and state governments for resources, but the process of seeking either information or adjustments from the state appears to be steadier and less subject to drastic changes in how the city approaches the vertical actor.

Our empirical evidence of the ratio of contact methods in the vertical system confirms that the management of vertical affairs is mainly about the resolution of issues on a routine, day-to-day basis, rather than tackling problems requiring "fundamental changes in the [social] structure" or "substantial realignment in the federal system" (Agranoff 1986, 1–2). The vertical context of local development policy is, for the most part, not based in one-time or occasional occurrences, formal agreements, or inflexible legislative action and judicial decisions. Instead, contacts with vertical partners are "patterned, purposive, and persistent" (Wright 1988, 23). However, the prevalence of telephone calls, face-to-face meetings, and letters to a state or federal official does not mean that the overall vertical context is tidy or a particularly unsophisticated system within which to operate. Nor does it necessarily mean that the most nettlesome of issues or largest of projects do not require more political or joint methods. In Ithaca, for example, governor's office contact does happen for special help, but "you only pull that string when you need it and they appreciate it."

In most cases, and for a large percentage of city development managers, managing the system requires bargaining, working through powerful interests and associations, or participating in joint task forces. Major redevelopment projects and contentious regulatory adjustments almost always include the application of political leverage and protracted negotiations. Whichever type of collaborative means is emphasized, vertical activity does not merely entail completing federal grant applications and complying with external rules. A great deal more is going on in the system.

Horizontal Linkages

As was shown in the previous chapter, the strategic orientation and the administrative infrastructure of a city are significant determinants of the level of collaborative activity. These variables were not as strong, however, at predicting the variation in horizontal activity usage patterns. The best explanation for differences in activity usage is found in the linkages between horizontal players and activities. Cincinnati's attempt to redevelop its central commercial and entertainment core almost always involves strategic and project partnerships with the Chamber of Commerce and an LDC, Downtown Cincinnati, Incorporated. We demonstrate in this section how reliance on particular types of horizontal activity is a function of the types of players, and the salience of the players, available to the city.

We examine horizontal collaborative management by using an empirically derived measure. The unit of analysis is what we refer to as a cluster, which is defined here as city government contact with two different players. Although our research reveals considerable dyadic interaction between a city and one player, for the purposes of demonstrating actual real world complexity, we measure collaboration as the relationship of three players (always including the city as one of the three) interacting within the context of a specific activity. Relationships of three or more players exist in a context of multiple goals, often conflicting agendas, and potentially high interaction costs, all of which cannot be assumed to exist to the same degree as in one-to-one relationships.

Another reason for examining clusters of three players is to emphasize how the addition of one player to an existing network or group increases the level of complexity exponentially. For example, assume a city (A) has established a collaborative policymaking and strategy-making relationship with a chamber of commerce (B) and the county government (C). This relationship is what we refer to as a cluster and would count as one cluster (ABC) for this analysis. Suppose that the city included a development corporation (D) in its policymaking and strategy-making activities. The addition of the development corporation increases the complexity threefold; the city would thus operate in policymaking and strategy-making clusters involving the chamber and the county (ABC), the chamber and the development corporation (ABD), and the county and the development corporation (ACD). For this example, three total clusters are involved in that city's policymaking and strategy-making activities. If another player (E) collaborated with the city for that specific type of activity, the number of clusters attributed to the city for that activity would increase to six (ABC, ABD, ACD, ABE, CDE, and BDE).

Our use of triads as the unit of analysis does not suggest, as in this example, that each of these six clusters is separately conceived by the city. On the contrary, all evidence points to the fact that B, C, D, and E in the above example are uniquely linked to A, as a part of the city's economic policymaking. Delimiting our analysis to three-player linkages simply allows us to discuss the composition and complexity of collaboration in cities more systematically and quantitatively.

Our analysis of collaborative linkages is multidimensional. First, a *simple count of clusters* was performed for all players reported by the survey respondents to be involved in horizontal activities. Second, the *total number of linkages in the clusters* in which each collaborative player was involved was computed for the sample cities. For example, we looked at how many linkages involved counties, how many involved chambers, and so on. Third, subtotals of the number of such *linkages were computed for the clusters performing each of the nine horizontal collaborative activities* discussed in the previous chapter, which were then aggregated into the three broad categories of activity. This third measure indicates how frequently cities and their collaborators engaged in joint policymaking, sharing in funding a project, or any of the nine horizontal activities.

Fourth, three *measures of player involvement and integration* were developed from the three previous types of calculations: a measure of density and two different measures of centralization, or centrality. Density is simply a measure of the extent to which all organizations are interconnected or linked to one another, whereas centralization measures whether collaborative links and activities are organized around any particular player or small group of players (Provan and Milward 1995). The following analysis cross-tabulates collaborative linkages across activities and players.

Overview of Linkages

The extent of collaborative linkages within cities is greater than expected at the outset of this research. A total of 2,240 clusters (consisting of 4,480 linkages between a city and horizontal players) is reported by the survey respondents. The most frequent collaborative linkages within the sample cities involve the LDC, the county government, and the chamber of commerce (see table 5.3). The table shows that the city–LDC–chamber cluster occurs 182 times, the city–county–LDC cluster 156 times, and the city—county–chamber cluster 151 times. These three distinct types of linkages account for nearly 22 percent of all collaborative linkages involving the sample cities.

We have also converted the frequencies from table 5.3 into percentages in table 5.4, which displays the distribution of clusters among the ten horizontal players. The cluster distribution can be discerned by reading the table in a columnar direction, with each number representing the percentage of all linkages involving the player listed at the column heading that also involve each player listed in the left-hand column. For example, 19.8 percent of LDC clusters (a city plus an LDC) also involve a county government. The number in each column with an asterisk indicates the most frequent collaborator.

Table 5.3. Frequency Distribution of Clusters among Players

Player	LDC	County	COC	Util	Other	SD	Hood	Town	PIC
County	156								
COC	182	151							
Util	135	118	116						
Other	72	81	77	40					
SD	72	76	68	34	35				
Hood	43	40	54	32	23	27			
Town	41	62	42	13	29	32	14		
PIC	52	33	32	37	17	11	16	5	
Fnd	34	34	26	23	15	5	11	10	14

Note: county = county government; COC = chamber of commerce; LDC = local development corporation; util = local utility; other = other city government; SD = special district government; hood = neighborhood association; town = township government; PIC = private industry council; fnd = local foundation.

The LDC, county government, and chamber of commerce are clearly involved in the largest percentage of clusters. It is notable that six of the remaining seven horizontal players have a higher percentage of linkages with these three players than with any other player. The most frequent contact for each of the three major players is also one of the other three players: county governments are linked with LDCs the most, followed closely by chambers of commerce; LDCs are involved in clusters with the chamber of commerce most frequently; chambers of commerce are clustered with

Table 5.4. Percentage Distribution of Clusters among Players

Player	LDC	County	COC	Util	Other	SD	Hood	Town	PIC	Fnd
LDC		20.8*	19.8	24.6*	18.5	20.0	16.5	16.5	24.0*	19.8*
County	19.8		23.1*	21.5	20.8*	21.1*	15.4	25.0*	15.2	19.8*
COC	23.1*	20.1		21.1	19.8	18.9	20.8*	16.9	14.7	15.1
Util	17.2	15.7	15.5		10.3	9.4	12.3	5.2	17.1	13.4
Other	9.1	10.8	10.3	7.3		9.7	8.8	11.7	7.8	8.7
SD	9.1	10.1	9.1	6.2	9.0		10.4	12.9	5.1	2.9
Hood	5.5	5.3	7.2	5.8	5.9	7.5		5.6	7.4	6.4
Town	5.2	8.3	5.6	2.4	7.5	8.9	5.4		2.3	5.8
PIC	6.6	4.4	4.3	6.8	4.4	3.1	6.2	2.0		8.1
Fnd	4.3	4.5	3.5	4.2	3.9	1.4	4.2	4.1	6.5	

*Most frequent collaborator.

Note: county = county government; COC = chamber of commerce; LDC = local development corporation; util = local utility; other = other city government; SD = special district government; hood = neighborhood association; town = township government; PIC = private industry council; fnd = local foundation.

an LDC most frequently. For a city, clusters involving the county, LDC, and chamber of commerce make up the most frequent linkages in economic development.

The triad of partners was borne out in our field study of the six active communities. Five of the six have developed extensive working relationships with their county governments—in particular the two suburban cities, Garfield Heights and Woodstock, where CDBG funds and other discretionary grants were available; and Salem and Ithaca, where other funding streams and political support were essential. Four of the six (all but Garfield Heights and Cincinnati) operated with an LDC that combined the sectors, and Cincinnati actually operated with several development corporations (one for downtown, one for the new stadiums, one for the performing arts complex, etc.).

Chambers of commerce existed in all six communities, as LDC partners, as partners in planning, and in general development activities. In three of the cities, Beloit, Woodstock, and Salem, the LDCs were positioned very close to the city government in operation, and in Beloit and Salem they were co-located with the chamber of commerce. In all six cases, city officials gave the impression that any researcher would not be able to get a feel for the economic development workings without understanding how these three entities become involved in local economic development.

The occurrence and importance of county–LDC–chamber of commerce linkages are most consistent with horizontal activity in cities like Woodstock, where a not atypical division of labor occurs. The city works most closely with the McHenry County government, the Woodstock Economic Development Corporation (its LDC), and the Woodstock Chamber of Commerce on virtually every core economic development project. Indeed, linkages involving the city, chamber, and county resulted in the establishment of the LDC, which is housed in city hall. The LDC plays a greater role in new business development; the city focuses more on land use and annexation, community development and infrastructure, and business retention; and the chamber is instrumental in planning and public relations.

Most of the other players exhibit surprising patterns in the way in which they are linked together in clusters. For utilities, other cities, special districts, neighborhood associations, township governments, and private industry councils, the most frequent linkage involves another player from the same sector. A utility—which, however structured, is a mixed-sector organization—links most frequently with another mixed-sector player, an LDC.

Similarly, private industry councils, which are explicitly public–private ventures, link most frequently with LDCs. Special district governments, other cities, and township governments are most frequently linked with county governments. Neighborhood associations are linked most frequently with chambers of commerce, both of which are private-sector organizations. Only private foundations do not follow this trend, because they link equally with LDCs and county governments. Although the local development manager must work with multiple collaborative arrangements, often consisting of different actors, there are some combinations of actors with which a manager rarely works.

Density and Centrality

Network or collaborative density is both a player-specific and activity-distinct measure. For this city-based analysis, density measures the degree to which the city (city government officials and managers) links with each of the players. We thus conceptualize density in the simplest terms: How many linkages does the city have with player A (or player B, and so on)? To make the measures comparable across particular activity types, we consider only those cities that reported having collaborative contact with each player.

The overall density of collaboration in the sample cities is thus computed by adding the number of clusters involving each of the ten horizontal players and dividing by the number of cities actually reporting clusters with that player. Higher values of the measure indicate greater numbers of linkages with the player in question. The density measure employed in this analysis is thus a type of multiplexity measure for each player, representing the mean number of linkages per player for each city reporting collaboration with that player.

The actual number of linkages reported by the cities is astonishing, especially considering that cities report multiple collaborative linkages with all ten partners. The mean number of linkages between collaborating cities and the ten players within the context of a city's economic policy is 61.3 (see table 5.5). This means that

Table 5.5. Density and Centrality of Collaborative Linkages

Player	No. of Links	Density (percent)	Centrality (percent)
Local development corporation	787	11.10	17.6
County government	751	10.60	16.8
Chamber of commerce	748	9.62	16.7
Utility	548	7.49	12.2
Other city	389	5.03	8.7
Special district	360	5.22	8.0
Neighborhood association	260	3.30	5.8
Township government	248	3.24	5.5
Private industry council	217	3.10	4.8
Foundation	172	2.63	3.8
Total	4,480	61.32	

the average collaborating city operated through more than sixty horizontal linkages during a two-year period, as part of many larger multiorganizational clusters, which is a remarkable finding. Just more than sixty different types of interactive relationships were built and maintained to some degree, for some purpose.

There is also considerable variation in the number of linkages across the horizontal players investigated. Cities are involved in 11.1 total linkages with an LDC, 10.6 linkages with county government, and 9.6 with a chamber of commerce. On the other end of the density scale, collaborating cities make approximately 3 linkages with a neighborhood association, township government, private industry council, and private foundation. High density results not only from the many linkages with LDCs, counties, and chambers of commerce, but from the sheer number of players as well. Even the least linked player is involved in nearly 3 triad clusters, suggesting that relationship building and collaboration is a nearly ubiquitous part of economic development policymaking and administration.

As was shown above, the local development corporation, county government, and the chamber of commerce are the most central players in a city's total collaborative economic development activity. The centrality measures displayed in table 5.5 mirror the density measures: Approximately 17.6 percent of all city-based collaborative linkages include an LDC, 16.8 percent involve county government, and 16.7 percent involve chambers of commerce, so fully one-half (51.1 percent) of all horizontal collaborative management involves these three players. According to the measures of mean involvement, private industry councils and foundations, comparatively speaking, are not as central to the average city's economic development effort.

The findings demonstrate a very dense, complex collaborative context for cities in their pursuit of economic development; the number of collaborative linkages appears formidable for even the most experienced manager. All ten horizontal entities studied for this research are contacted heavily. The measures clearly indicate that cities serving higher-level economic functions like central cities and nonmetropolitan cities operate in more dense collaborative settings than do suburban cities with stronger economies; but even the latter operate extensively outside the boundaries of the municipal jurisdiction. Measures of centrality, discussed in the next section, help to demonstrate which players are most central to a city's effort and which activity is most central to a particular player.

Player and Activity Centrality

The centrality measures used in this analysis indicate how collaborative linkages and activities are organized around the ten horizontal players within the context of city-level economic development. In other words, to what degree is a city like Salem involved with the county or LDC for policymaking and strategy-making purposes? For resource exchange? For project-based activity?

Centrality measures were computed for each player and for activity. To determine *player centrality*, the total number of linkages for each player was converted into a percentage measuring the aggregate relative involvement of each player within a specific policy activity. The question is as follows: To what extent does the average city collaborate with player A while pursuing activity A (or activity B, and so on)?

Player centrality thus represents the percentage of activity that involves each horizontal player. The higher the percentage, the greater the number of linkages involving the player in a specific collaborative activity relative to all other players. The players with the highest percentage of the ten players can be viewed as the most central to a particular activity. For example, if a city reported a grand total of forty collaborative linkages, and eight of those linkages were with the county government, player centrality for all collaborative activities for the county would be 20 percent (8 divided by 40). If the percentage of involvement for all other horizontal players were less than 20 percent, county government would be considered the most central player in that city's collaborative activity.

For *activity centrality*, the total number of linkages for each of the nine activities was converted into a percentage measuring the aggregate relative involvement of each activity for a specific player. The question is as follows: To what extent is the involvement of player A devoted to activity A (or activity B, so on)? For example, if a city reports that county government is involved in a total of eight clusters and six of these clusters involved policymaking and strategy-making, then centralization for the county government within that activity type would be 75 percent (6 divided by 8). In this example, 75 percent of all county collaboration would be devoted to policymaking and strategy-making activities. Such activity would thus be viewed as the most central to the county government's involvement with the city's economic development effort.

The findings demonstrate that each horizontal activity possesses its own unique operating dynamic, which can only be executed with a particular player or combination of players; all players do not become involved with all activities equally. Referring to the player centrality data in table 5.6, variation in collaborative linkages is observed by comparing centrality measures in the columns across the three activity types. Looking at the first numerical cell of table 5.6 as an example, the number 17.0 indicates that 17 percent of all policymaking and strategy-making activity in the sample cities involves linkages with LDCs. The next number in the same cell indicates that 20.8 percent of all resource-exchange linkages involve LDCs, and the final number in the cell shows that 17.4 percent of all project-based linkages are with LDCs. If LDCs play a consistent and regular role in the economic development activities of cities, those three numbers would be equivalent. However, the data in that cell suggest that LDCs play a slightly more central role in resource exchange than in the other two activity types. The different compositions of player-activity linkages are further illustrated in the third cell in the first column. Although the chamber

Table 5.6. Centrality of Players and Activities in Collaborative Linkages by Activity Type

Player	Activity Type	Player Centrality (percent)	Rank	Activity Centrality (percent)	Rank
LDC	Policymaking and strategy-making	17.0	2	61.5	6
	Resource exchange	20.8	2	14.2	5
	Project-based work	17.4	1	24.3	5
County	Policymaking and strategy-making	15.8	3	59.8	7
	Resource exchange	22.3	1	16.0	3
	Project-based work	16.5	3	24.2	6
COC	Policymaking and strategy-making	18.3	1	69.4	3
	Resource exchange	8.4	5	6.0	9
	Project-based work	16.7	2	24.6	4
Util	Policymaking and strategy-making	11.0	4	57.1	8
	Resource exchange	12.6	3	12.4	6
	Project-based work	15.2	4	30.5	2
Other	Policymaking and strategy-making	9.3	5	67.6	4
	Resource exchange	4.8	8	6.7	8
	Project-based work	9.1	5	25.7	3
SD	Policymaking and strategy-making	8.0	6	63.3	5
	Resource exchange	11.0	4	16.4	2
	Project-based work	6.6	6	20.3	8
Hood	Policymaking and strategy-making	7.0	7	76.2	1
	Resource exchange	2.6	10	5.4	10
	Project-based work	4.4	8	18.5	9
Town	Policymaking and strategy-making	6.4	8	73.4	2
	Resource exchange	3.9	9	8.5	7
	Project-based work	4.1	9	18.1	10
PIC	Policymaking and strategy-making	3.9	9	51.2	10
	Resource exchange	6.1	7	15.2	4
	Project-based work	6.6	6	33.6	1
Fnd	Policymaking and strategy-making	3.3	10	55.2	9
	Resource exchange	7.4	6	23.3	1
	Project-based work	3.4	10	21.5	7

Note: county = county government; town = township government; COC = chamber of commerce; PIC = private industry council; LDC = local development corporation; fnd = local foundation; util = local utility; other = other city government; SD = special district government; hood = neighborhood association.

of commerce plays a fairly similar role in both policymaking and strategy-making (18.3 percent) and project-based (16.7 percent) activities, it is much less central to the economic development efforts of cities when such efforts involve resource exchange (8.4 percent).

It is useful to identify the actual players and the specific role each plays. For example, the most central player for cities is different for each of the three activity types: The chamber of commerce is the most central player in policymaking and strategy-making, the county government is the most central for resource exchange, and the LDC is the most central for project-based activities. LDCs play the most consistent role in collaboration with cities across all activity types, as is evidenced by the rankings. Even foundations, which are the least central for policymaking and strategy-making and project-based activities, are reasonably important for resource-exchange purposes, particularly for the smallest and largest cities.

This same pattern exists with other players: Foundations are more than twice as central in resource-exchange activity as in policymaking and strategy-making or project-based activities, other cities are nearly one-half as central to cities seeking finances as when cities pursue policymaking and strategy-making or project-based activities, and utilities are slightly more central to cities pursuing projects than they are to policymaking and strategy-making or resource-exchange activities.

The data suggest a very important aspect of collaboration that speaks to the often strategic nature of jurisdiction-based management: Cities seek out a collaborative player for a specific purpose and for a certain type or types of resources; each player may play a strategic role for the city. The set of collaborative players that are linked to cities varies by activity and need. It is not as important to know the players with which cities actually link as it is to understand that these linkages can be jurisdiction-based. That is, a city seeks to achieve specific goals, and thus it makes linkages that place it in the best position to achieve its goals.

Analyzing the centrality of players in a collaborative effort is a common way to identify which players constitute the totality of a city's linkages, but it does not indicate the activity or activities in which a collaborative player is primarily involved. Horizontal players simply do not play the same linkage activity roles. For example, Cincinnati and Woodstock strategically plan with their chambers of commerce, targeting such issues as the central business district, historic and core neighborhoods, and other geographic areas as the basis for planning.

In addition, county governments are important sources of funding and policy support for many suburbs. Garfield Heights relies heavily on CDBG entitlement funds from Cuyahoga County for many of its own development projects, as well as a small business loan program. This large suburb also has secured planning and zoning technical assistance from the county Board of Planning. Woodstock receives planning assistance from McHenry County and a number of state–county funding projects. By contrast, none of the six chambers of commerce contributed funds to projects or exchanged resources with the city. Beloit funds and locates a downtown developer and small business ombudsman in its Chamber of Commerce, whereas Cincinnati has a $100,000 contract with its chamber for certain types of industrial recruitment. LDCs, conversely, do raise private money for projects, particularly in our two smallest communities, Ithaca and Salem.

Activity centrality measures indicate how central a particular activity is to the collaborative players. In the first numerical cell of the "activity centrality" column of table 5.6, the number 61.5 indicates that 61.5 percent of all collaborative linkages with LDCs are for policymaking and strategy-making activities. The cell also shows that 14.2 percent of all linkages with LDCs are for resource exchange, and 24.3 percent are project based. Each cell thus provides a breakdown of how linkages with each player are divided among the three activity types. For all players, the majority of linkages with the city are for policymaking and strategy-making activities, but the extent to which each player is involved in other activities varies from one player to another. For example, fewer than 10 percent of the linkages involving chambers of commerce, other cities, neighborhood associations, and township governments are devoted to resource exchange; relatively, resource-exchange activity is not central for these players.

Linkages with a private industry council (PIC) are much less centralized in policymaking and strategy-making activities (51.2 percent) than are the linkages with other players, and much more centralized in project-based activities. Approximately one-third of all collaboration by cities with PICs is project-based. The ranking corresponding to that measure indicates that the proportion of total collaborative linkages with PICs devoted to project-based activities is greater than for all other players. The same pattern of activity centrality is present with utilities. Also, the players with the highest percentage of activity centralized in resource exchange are foundations (23.3 percent), special district governments (16.4), and county governments (16.0).

Linkages between Player and Activity

Many cities link with players strategically. Linkages with state and federal agencies, and horizontal clusters, do not form by accident; managers build them for strategic jurisdictional purposes. City officials pursue different collaborative linkages, depending on the activity, making collaborative management a complex undertaking, owing not only to the number of players who are involved but also to the many different combinations of players that must be addressed in different situations.

There are several notable differences in the composition of collaborative linkages. First, cities operate routinely and informally in coordination with state and federal officials. Written and telephone communications appear to be the preferred mode of interaction in the pursuit of any vertical activity, but such contacts can also have a political component. States are more likely than the federal government to be contacted through lobbying or formal bargaining, although federal agencies may be contacted through such means when a city seeks adjustments to applicable regulations or statutes.

Second, a horizontal collaborative arrangement charged with producing policies and strategies with the city government will most likely consist of the chamber of commerce, an LDC, the county government, and either the local utility or another city. The chamber or the LDC, working with the city government, will play the most central role, and only a minimal role will be played by a local foundation or PIC, if either exists in the community.

Third, resource-exchange networks are the most distinctive in structure and composition. Special district governments and local utilities are more likely to link with cities, compared with chambers of commerce, and counties and LDCs are the most central partners in this type of collaboration. Other cities are rarely involved in resource exchange and almost never collaborate for the purposes of developing joint financial incentives or contracting out some aspect of economic policy.

Fourth, project-based collaborative linkages are not as dense as other types of linkages. An LDC is most likely to play the central role in project-based collaboration, and the local utility is much more likely to be involved in these activities than in policymaking or resource-exchange activities.

These results indicate the richness of collaboration to promote economic development. From the perspective of the city government, there is not one cluster of linkages to manage but several clusters—some horizontal, some vertical, and some that include both within the context of a single project or program. Although a city may have numerous linkages, rarely does a city engage a large number of entities in such working relationships. It is common for four or five players to join with the city; the norm is two to three organizations working with the city on a particular effort. This array of connections gives cities great flexibility and power in the marketplace to add and subtract players, but it also adds to the work of the administrator who must develop and maintain these collaborative arrangements (Milward 1996). The tasks of the most active and strategic player—the city's jurisdiction-based manager—clearly are numerous.

Horizontal players can usefully be distinguished by sector. Clusters are formed by cities that, intended or not, are often primarily, sometimes exclusively, one sector or another. Public-sector players are more likely to work together on resource exchange and projects. Private-sector players work the most together on policy-making and strategy-making and the least on resource exchange. Public–private entities appear to work nearly equally on all three activity fronts. The city remains central across the sectors, with the city and two members of the same sector involved.

Place also seems to matter across several of the analytic categories. Central cities appear to engage the most partners in several respects, but they are less likely to collaborate with their county governments. This no doubt demonstrates the go-it-alone ability of larger cities, and the fact that in many metropolitan areas the county government often serves the urbanized areas outside the central city. Nonmetropolitan cities collaborate with fewer partners, perhaps because organizations like neighborhood associations and foundations do not exist. These cities do, however, more frequently collaborate with county governments.

This view of vertical and horizontal linkages demonstrates that the variation of collaborative management is a function of the players and activities that are pursued by the city. The local manager faces an extensive field of potential linkages. The clusters that make up the city's governing environment are complex in that they differ from one strategic purpose to another. The large number of clusters reveals that in economic development there are multiple forms of collaborative interactions, transactions, and contacts through formal and informal networking. The city government does not go it alone in economic development, but rather partners, operates, and reciprocates with key local actors. It is an exemplar of the governance function within modern public management.

At the intersection of strategy and activity, we find a city's governing style or dominant approach to collaborative management. In the next chapter, we will look at another important aspect of strategy: a city's approach to economic development policy. We will show that a city's overall policy mix is a significant determinant of collaborative activity, and thus of jurisdiction-based management.

6

Policy Design and Collaborative Management

Cincinnati sought to use virtually every type of development policy instrument in its arsenal as a means to grow the local economy, especially those that targeted small business development and expansion in service, medical and health care, chemicals and printing, tourism, and international industries. To accomplish this new approach, city economic development managers and leaders of development-based organizations recognized that they needed to do more than employ city staff to provide business assistance programs. More work needed to be done in packaging tools used to promote the city overall, to attract advanced technology, to market and promote new products, to enhance the city as a tourist magnet, and to maximize the advantages of having an airport that is a "hub" for a major U.S. carrier. Links with workforce training and technical institutes, university and industrial research laboratories, purveyors of entertainment and prospective conventions and conferences, and global enterprises were accelerated. Development officials understood that the city could not exclusively rely on traditional grants, loans, or interest-rate subsidies, but also must use many players and many different strategic tools to help the metropolitan economy.

This chapter shows that the instruments of development are a significant component of a city's collaborative management approach. We demonstrate that a city's economic development policy strategy involves both policy instruments and an associated assortment of collaboration activities engendered by the instruments. The findings provide an important piece of the collaboration puzzle by showing a strong empirical association between collaborative management and the policy approach adopted by the jurisdiction.[1] It appears that cities depending heavily on regulations, boosterism, and directly provided instruments for their economic development effort operate in a policymaking and administrative environment that reaches beyond city hall or the chamber of commerce only to limited degrees. Similarly, the findings suggest that cities depending heavily on instruments that capitalize on local strengths, using approaches such as workforce development and business incubation, operate in a manner consistent with jurisdiction-based management.

Policy Instruments and Policy Strategy

One of the most extraordinary changes in local government during the past twenty years has been the proliferation of economic policy instruments. A policy instrument (or tool) is a mechanism or technique at the disposal of governments to implement their public policy objectives (Howlett 1991) that is intended to affect a fundamental aspect of the economy or society (Linder and Peters 1990; Elmore 1987). The critical building blocks of a city's development policy strategy are such instruments as financial assistance, deregulation, tax increment financing, and enterprise zones.

Through the creation and use of new policy instruments, the economic development policy area has become a hotbed of policy innovation and adaptation (see appendix B for a profile of the five state economies over time). This design revolution, mostly generated by state government authorization, has resulted in countless new mechanisms for affecting local economies. Researchers have diligently cataloged and classified these instruments (Clarke and Gaile 1989, 1998; Eisinger 1988; Fleischmann, Green, and Kwong 1992; Hanson and Berkman 1991; McGuire 1999; Pelissero and Fasenfest 1989; Reese 1993; Sternberg 1987) and evaluated their effectiveness (Bartik 1989, 1991; Bowman 1988; Clarke and Gaile 1992; Gross and Phillips 1997; Marlin 1990). In addition to identifying new instruments, some scholars have argued that the emergence of certain types of instruments and strategies constitutes the foundation for entirely new approaches to local economic development policy (Clarke and Gaile 1989, 1992; Eisinger 1988, 1995; Ross and Friedman 1991).

The collaborative linkages that connect player and activity to a city take place within a specific public policy context. Jurisdiction-based management activity is not only strategic, in the sense that a city seeks out a player or players to carry out an activity. It is also embedded, in the sense that a city's particular approach to some real or perceived policy problem drives the form and content of collaboration. A city that perceives few problems with its local economy, or that perceives little can be done to assist its economy, will conceivably have little need or desire for collaboration. Conversely, a city that puts forth a strong effort to affect the local economy may find that collaboration is a necessity, desired or otherwise. Furthermore, a city can attempt to affect its economy through the use of policy instruments that entail collaboration, such as by promoting business incubators or involvement in workforce development, or with policy instruments that are typically noncollaborative, such as adjusting building regulations or traffic improvement.

Woodstock, for example, has adopted eight different types of public services, facilities, and infrastructure improvements; pursues eight different promotional activities; uses tax abatements and loans and loan subsidies; and has not adopted job-training, building rehabilitation, technical assistance, or shared equity efforts. Ithaca, conversely, engages in as many public improvements as Woodstock, but the smaller town also relies on eight different types of financial assistance to promote business, and becomes involved in building rehabilitation, technical assistance to management, shared equity, sale–leasebacks, and business incubation. In each case, the pattern of instrument adoption or strategy undertaken is connected to the amount of collaboration a jurisdiction will have to undertake. For example, engaging in strategies that promote the city through brochures, videotapes, websites, and industry fairs are stay-at-home activities, whereas strategies based on business expansion, developing local capacities through venture financing, employee retraining, and business incubators imply a great deal of reaching out beyond city hall.

One of the primary analytical questions guiding policy research in this area addresses the effect of adopting a certain type of development instrument, endogenous development policy instruments (Teitz 1994), or what has been referred to elsewhere as demand-side instruments (Eisinger 1988; McGuire 1999; Reese

1993, 1997). Endogenous instruments focus on promoting the development and expansion of indigenous firms, capitalizing on the strengths and assets of the city, and growing economic activity from within the city rather than by luring mobile capital. They are designed to facilitate business expansion through the process of growth and development by launching a new enterprise, creating new technology and products, and identifying new markets for new and existing products (Leicht and Jenkins 1994).

Endogenous instruments are designed to facilitate private (ostensibly local) capital's ability to exploit new demands—an objective quite different from traditional instruments that are used to attract resources to a specific location by reducing producer costs (Clarke and Gaile 1989). Just as traditional policy approaches are associated with more traditional (bureaucratic) administrative approaches, the innovative use of endogenous instruments is shown here to be a primary predictor of collaborative activity in city economic development.

The city of Cincinnati, as depicted at the beginning of this chapter, employs a variety of tools to promote its economy. In addition to the standard promotional, regulatory, and tax reduction programs, it offers several programs designed to grow its economy from within: three neighborhood enterprise zone programs, three different venture capital or financial assistance programs for launching small businesses, a neighborhood outreach program geared toward business retention and expansion, targeted job training and workforce development assistance, and new product development assistance. The last is done in cooperation with the University of Cincinnati. Each of the other approaches also entails a partner or set of partners. For example, most workforce development efforts are partially funded by the city out of federal Job Training Partnership Act funds (since changed to Workforce Investment Act funds), but assessment and referral are undertaken by the Private Industry Council staff. Actual job training and development are delivered by one of Cincinnati's area vocational-technical colleges, with University of Cincinnati School of Engineering technical assistance. In a similar fashion, other business enterprises in need of development enter into partnerships as they determine the educational and technical resources required to meet particular development challenges.

The presupposition that the adoption of endogenous (or other) instruments by cities like Cincinnati activates (or constrains) collaborative activity is not novel. Recent research in many policy areas suggests that the choice of a particular type of policy instrument is linked strongly to the extent of collaborative policymaking and administration. In a groundbreaking study of the problems of job creation, Hjern and Hull conclude that external intermediaries "help firms define problems, identify resources which are available for tackling those problems, as well as mobilize resources" (1985, 141). The authors show that collaboration with external, intermediary actors explains as much as 30 percent of new small-firm job creation in German regions, even after accounting for regional sector mix and investment strategies (Hull 1987). Harrison and Weiss (1998) use numerous cases to demonstrate how effective workforce development is based in networks of interorganizational relationships that connect the residents of low-income neighborhoods to employers with training positions through mediating institutions such as community colleges, government agencies, and various community-based organizations.

In another case, when federal grant support for municipal wastewater treatment was replaced with state revolving loan funds, essentially a swap of one type of policy instrument for another, the result was more complex governing configurations involving new actors with needed resources and technologies. O'Toole concludes that "decisions to shift programs to the states, deregulate, privatize, and employ market-based mechanisms have consequences for interorganizational arrangements and programs in practice" (1996, 239).

Similarly, as the acceptable technology for treating people with severe mental illness shifted in the 1960s from directly provided institutionalization to a reliance on services provided by community health and social service organizations, collaborative production networks of these provider agencies emerged (Provan and Milward 1991, 1995; Weiss 1990). Even in small nonmetropolitan cities, the level of interaction and cooperation between local leaders and external actors increased substantially after strategic planning and information-based instruments were incorporated into their community development processes (McGuire et al. 1994).

Analysis of Development Policy Instruments

We gauge policy and collaboration the same way we have approached most issues in this study—empirically and grounded in practice. Each survey respondent selected from a list of forty-four development policy instruments on the collaboration survey those instruments the city "used in the last two years, or is currently using." Respondents were also asked on the International City/County Management Association (ICMA) survey if they engaged in several different development policy activities, nineteen of which are included in this study. The broad array of development instruments studied in this research can be organized conceptually into one of many different classification schemes, and the literature is replete with descriptions of the function and utility of policy instruments as indicators of development policy activity. However, few of these studies employ a common definition of a development instrument.

Development Instrument Classification

Eisinger (1988) engendered an economic policy perspective based on a supply versus demand dichotomy, employing the terms "demand-side" and "entrepreneurial" as its main description (Clarke and Gaile 1989, 1992). Sternberg (1987) cross-classified nine types of development instruments against a typology of nine business functions for an informed but far from parsimonious typology. In past surveys, ICMA divided a large list of economic development instruments into four functional categories: marketing activities, governance tools and public infrastructure investments, land and property management activities, and financial tools. Fleischmann, Green, and Kwong (1992) and Reese (1993) derived, respectively, nine and thirteen instrument types from the ICMA categories using factor analysis. Development instrument typologies in the literature are based on such diverse qualities as development function (Eisinger 1988; Green and Fleischmann 1991; Hanson and Berkman 1991), pursuit of goals (Pelissero and Fasenfest 1989), and governmental roles (Clingermayer and Feiock 1990; Rubin 1986). Some policy research also examines the cost and the level of visibility inherent in a policy instrument (Cable, Feiock, and Kim 1993; Feiock and Clingermayer 1992; Furdell 1994; Pagano and Bowman 1992).

We describe development policy instruments in terms of their operational features. Improving physical infrastructure such as roads and parking lots requires the costly and active participation of local government, whereas modifying the zoning process or improving a building inspection system requires action by a zoning commission and a less visible but nonetheless highly skilled local bureaucracy. It must be remembered that all instruments are designed for one objective: to improve the city economy, either directly or indirectly. How a jurisdiction goes about affecting an economy and what policymaking and administrative processes are employed, however, differs substantially across instruments. Policy instruments such as the rehabilitation of buildings, donation of land, acquisition of land, and condemnation of land are alike in one regard: Each addresses land and/or buildings.

Rehabilitating a building, however, involves a more extensive operational and administrative process than does donating land. The former involves improving an indigenous asset, presumably to be used for a local business or product. The latter is a gift to a developer or other entity for the purpose of moving to the city or expanding production in the city—a classic subsidy. The rehabilitation of a building by a city does not presume some reciprocal task on the part of a business. Condemning land is regulatory and authoritative, in that orders and not money are used to affect behavior. Different officials and agencies, using different techniques, seek to affect the local economy through land and buildings, but all can do so in entirely different ways. The instrument classification scheme employed in this book to examine collaboration is intended to capture these differences (see table 6.1).

The classification employed in this research is based on the differences in institutional structures across each instrument type and thus emphasizes operational concerns. Four general categories of instruments are derived from Linder and Peters (1990) and applied to the sixty-three development instruments examined in this research: direct provision, exhortation, orders, and subsidy. A fifth category—endogenous instruments—is derived from Reese (1993) and Eisinger (1988).[2] Examples of endogenous policy instruments include venture capital financing, developing export markets, business incubators, targeted employee training, and research and

Table 6.1. Examples of Economic Development Policy Instruments

Classification	Policy Arena	Policy Instrument
Direct provision	General policymaking	Public investment
	Economic development	Physical infrastructure improvements
Exhortation	General policymaking	Public promotion
	Economic development	Solicitation of foreign business
Orders	General policymaking	Quality standard
	Economic development	Pollution controls
	General policymaking	Procedural guidelines
	Economic development	Consolidated permit issuance
Subsidy	General policymaking	Loan
	Economic development	Direct loan to businesses
	General policymaking	Tax exemption
	Economic development	Property tax abatement
Endogenous	General policymaking	Job training
	Economic development	Business incubator

Source: Adapted from Linder and Peters (1990).

development. The twelve endogenous instruments studied here are intended to create capital from within the community and are thus based heavily in the process of goal clarification, market studies, and strategic planning. In contrast, the twelve direct provision instruments examined for this research are instruments where government is the sole sponsor or provider of public goods. Infrastructure provision, government utilities or publicly operated liquor stores, and direct investments in enterprise are examples of this type of instrument. Exhortation instruments, of which there are thirteen in this study, include promotions and promotional materials prepared by government, advertising campaigns and slogans, and general marketing practices. Examples of exhortation instruments include a groundbreaking ceremony for the construction of a new highway in a city or brochures, short films, and web sites touting the economic and cultural benefits of a community.

Orders like the nine studied here involve the use of government as an instrument. They are made up of both regulatory and authority-based instruments. The former restricts or prohibits a particular behavior or activity, whereas the latter confers on persons the right to perform a task or activity, in a manner specified by the government. Orders can thus be environmental quality standards assigned to water, soil, or the reuse of old industrial sites; road and land use restrictions; zoning practices; and franchise or building permits. The seventeen subsidy instruments induce persons or agencies to perform a task in exchange for resources. Tax instruments, such as tax breaks, abatements, or increment financing, are forms of subsidies that work through changes in a person's or organization's tax liability. Loans and loan guarantees are also examples of subsidies.

Development Instrument Use

Cities are often described in the most general sense in terms of size and geography. For example, economic development research is typically focused on cities with populations of at least 50,000 that are located in metropolitan areas (McGuire 1999). Similarly, many case studies of intergovernmental programs have been conducted in metropolitan areas, especially focusing on central cities that are believed to have more extensive dealings with the federal government than other types of cities. This bias toward large cities, however, results in a lack of understanding about smaller suburban and rural communities, and in potentially inaccurate policy prescriptions for the vast majority of American cities. Differences across cities in the composition of the economic base, the condition of the local economy, the level of administrative capacity to address economic problems, and the rate of capital flow through and within the community would suggest that their strategies and patterns of interaction with other entities would be different.

To accurately describe policy differences, we profile cities through four categories of cities: *nonmetropolitan cities*, which are located outside the metropolitan areas defined by the U.S. Census Bureau; *small suburbs*, which are cities with a population of less than 25,000 that are classified by the Census Bureau as suburban; *large suburbs*, which are cities with a population of 25,000 or more that are classified by the Census Bureau as suburban; and *central cities*, which are large cities that perform many higher-level functions in a region's economy and thus act as the economic center of a metropolitan area. Thirty percent of the sample ($n = 71$) consists of nonmetropolitan cities, 29.1 percent ($n = 69$) of small suburbs, 31.6 percent ($n = 75$) of large suburbs, and 9.3 percent ($n = 22$) of central cities. These four categories are commonly used in economic development research.

The directly provided instruments used by the greatest percentage of cities are those that are considered core services of city government: water systems, traffic and streets, sewage systems, and recreation provision (see table 6.2). More than one-half of the cities report that these instruments are part of a comprehensive economic development effort. Approximately one-half of all cities report using each of the twelve direct provision instruments, with the exception of those instruments dealing with property: acquiring land, clearing land, and consolidating lots. Garfield Heights, for example, makes extensive use of many direct provision instruments, including construction of noise-walls between its freeways and residential and commercial areas, improving sites for the development of office parks, converting old landfills into usable property, and making numerous arterial street improvements linking freeway exits to major commercial and industrial sites.

It is not surprising that most cities use directly provided instruments extensively. These instruments not only are completely within the power of the city, but they also can be used with city resources, particularly city equipment and personnel. Moreover, direct provision instruments are designed to improve the city's overall physical infrastructure. Seven of the twelve instruments are used no more frequently in one city type than in another. Only the

Table 6.2. Direct Provision Development Instruments (percent)

Instrument	All	NM	SS	LS	CC
Improve water systems	59.9	63.4	68.1	53.3	45.5
Improve traffic circulation, streets	58.7	53.5	56.5	61.3	72.7
Improve sewage systems	54.9	64.8	58.0	41.3	59.1
Improve and expand recreation facilities	53.6	62.0	46.4	48.0	68.2
Aesthetic improvements	51.9	50.7	44.9	53.3	72.7
Improve street cleaning-garbage	45.2	43.7	46.4	44.0	50.0
Improve and expand parking	44.7	46.5	34.8	42.7	77.3
Improve public safety services	43.0	35.2	47.8	42.7	54.6
Improve pedestrian amenities	40.5	36.6	36.2	42.7	59.1
Acquire land	30.0	32.4	21.7	22.7	72.7
Clear land of unusable structures	29.5	38.0	15.9	17.3	86.4
Consolidate lot to create large sites	16.5	12.7	13.0	20.0	27.3

Note: NM = nonmetropolitan cities; SS = small suburban cities; LS = large suburban cities; CC = central cities.

instruments used to acquire land, clear land, improve parking, and make aesthetic improvements—all of which concern property—are used more frequently in central cities than in the other cities.

These central cities need to be aggressive in promoting their economies, particularly landlocked central cities that are in competition with their suburbs. Cincinnati regularly engages in site assemblage and arranges for the transfer of city-owned property. The city also occasionally offers land equalization grants and write-downs in transferring property for redevelopment purposes. This finding is no doubt because, as with Cincinnati, most central cities have limited "green space" to expand; thus land development and improvement must be part of their strategy. Overall, direct provision instruments are used by more cities and to a greater degree than each of the other types of economic development instruments.

Both exhortation and orders instruments follow the same usage pattern as direct provision instruments. Some variation exists from one instrument to the next across city types, but, for the most part, cities of all kinds pursue exhortation and orders. Nearly two-thirds of all cities make visits to businesses and develop promotional material for the city (see table 6.3). These instruments are largely in the control of the city, easy to produce, and vary considerably in cost and quality. Promotional materials can range from multicolored, multifunction packets covering every facet of the city to photocopied city fact sheets. The Beloit Economic Development Corporation offers a most attractive packet, containing a multicolored brochure, a thirty-page data book, a separate industrial park brochure, a brochure on its riverfront project, a tourism guide, a cultural events calendar, area maps, and other "filler."

Woodstock makes use of many exhortation and orders instruments. Examples of the former include weekly drop-in meetings by the mayor and manager to existing businesses, developing a short film on historic Woodstock and its current business climate, and creating an extensive portfolio of promotional brochures. The city uses orders instruments through an accelerated building inspection procedure, strict sign and facade standards, and the development of a zoning process that encourages industrial and commercial development in green areas designated in its master plan.

Table 6.3. Exhortation Development Instruments (percent)

Instrument	All	NM	SS	LS	CC
Visit existing business	65.0	64.8	59.4	64.0	86.4
Develop promotional material	62.9	63.4	55.1	61.3	90.9
Visit prospects	40.5	36.6	43.5	37.3	54.6
Attend conferences	34.6	32.4	20.3	41.3	63.6
Use community resource databases	32.1	29.6	23.2	33.3	63.6
Develop business roundtable	27.0	26.8	21.7	32.0	27.3
Use direct mail	27.0	33.8	17.4	24.0	45.5
Participate in trade shows	25.7	26.8	13.0	28.0	54.6
Advertise in media	24.9	25.4	15.9	28.0	40.9
Send videos to prospects	24.5	32.4	14.5	22.7	36.4
Host special events	15.2	16.9	8.7	16.0	27.3
Give achievement awards	14.4	15.5	8.7	17.3	18.2
Executive mentoring	7.2	8.5	4.3	4.0	22.7

Note: NM = nonmetropolitan cities; SS = small suburban cities; LS = large suburban cities; CC = central cities.

Approximately one-half of the cities regulate signs and facades, and streamline the building inspection and zoning processes (see table 6.4). Some of the variation in orders usage can be explained in terms of city age. A greater percentage of central cities adopt historic district regulations and condemn buildings because there is more of a land scarcity or more land that has prior use; also, more older buildings exist in larger central cities. Beyond these two orders instruments, apparently all city types (with some minor differences) work to develop better administrative processes in dealing with planning and zoning. Again, the use of these instruments involves government power and often few, if any, expenditures of tax dollars.

Tax reductions of some form are among the most popular subsidy instruments (see table 6.5). Cities will rarely provide tax credits or actually pay to relocate businesses, but offering bonds for development and loans to businesses is more common than most exhortation and orders instruments. The reason for this, perhaps, is that these funds are paid back to the city and they may be easier to "sell" to city councils and to taxpayers. Businesses, in turn, can pass these costs on as part of their costs of goods and services.

The two most popular subsidy instruments are tax abatement and tax increment financing, which are often visible in local newspaper stories about business locations. Although our case study

Table 6.4. Orders Development Instruments (percent)

Instrument	All	NM	SS	LS	CC
Adopt sign and facade control regulations	52.7	49.3	53.6	54.7	54.6
Improve building inspection process	52.7	42.3	60.9	52.0	63.6
Modify the zoning process	47.7	45.1	39.1	58.7	45.5
Consolidate permit issuance	35.0	39.4	30.4	34.7	36.4
Adopt historic district regulations	24.9	18.3	17.4	26.7	63.6
Use ombudsman to resolve problems	24.5	23.9	13.0	33.3	31.8
Adopt antilitter regulations and programs	17.3	14.1	17.4	17.3	27.3
Condemn land	14.4	14.1	8.7	10.7	45.5
Relax environmental regulations and procedures	4.2	4.2	4.3	2.7	9.1

Note: NM = nonmetropolitan cities; SS = small suburban cities; LS = large suburban cities; CC = central cities.

cities make considerable use of them, some place limits on these tax breaks. Woodstock reduces the abatement if the agreed-upon number of jobs are not created. Cincinnati's Tax Increment Financing Program is limited to the central business district. Salem, like many other cities, has used its state-authorized authority to engage in several subsidy activities: tax abatements for business locations in the city that provide at least twenty jobs, revenue bonds for the

Table 6.5. Subsidy Development Instruments (percent)

Instrument	All	NM	SS	LS	CC
Abate taxes	57.0	59.2	55.1	52.0	72.7
Provide tax increment financing	55.7	59.2	50.7	50.7	77.3
Sell land to developer	40.5	46.5	27.5	33.3	86.4
Issue bonds for private development	32.5	26.8	23.2	34.7	72.7
Offer direct loans to private businesses	27.4	43.7	13.0	16.0	59.1
Provide in-kind services	27.4	31.0	24.6	16.0	63.6
Provide grants	26.2	36.6	15.9	22.7	36.4
Contribute cash to projects	19.8	28.2	13.0	10.7	45.5
Offer historic preservation incentives	14.4	12.7	10.1	14.7	31.8
Subsidize loans	13.9	14.1	8.7	14.7	27.3
Donate land to developers	13.5	16.9	8.7	9.3	31.8
Guarantee loans	13.5	18.3	8.7	14.7	27.3
Donate unused real property	12.2	15.5	5.8	9.3	31.8
Relocate business from redevelopment areas	11.0	14.1	4.3	6.7	36.4
Credit taxes	10.1	12.7	2.9	8.0	31.8
Reduce utility rates	7.2	9.9	2.9	6.7	13.6
Relocate new businesses	4.6	8.5	1.5	2.7	9.1

Note: NM = nonmetropolitan cities; SS = small suburban cities; LS = large suburban cities; CC = central cities.

expansion of its industrial park, a revolving microbusiness loan fund, and such in-kind services as writing business plans and preparing subsidies or guarantees.

The frequency of subsidy instrument usage varies significantly across suburbs and central cities. Few subsidies are common in the sample cities—just two of the seventeen are used by a majority of cities—but subsidy use is clearly more common in central cities than in other cities. A central city is three times as likely to sell land to a developer or issue development bonds, more than four times as likely to offer direct loans to businesses, and fifteen times as likely to offer tax credits, in comparison with small suburban cities. Cincinnati, for example, engages in all of these practices to attract business. Central cities are in a similar position to Cincinnati in attracting businesses, as they compete with suburbs. Because they have little open, inexpensive land to offer and a poorer perceived business climate, they must sweeten attraction packages. Businesses often expect some form of subsidy today to remain or locate in a central city. The overall larger tax bases of central cities allow them to absorb the tax losses accrued by these subsidies. Thus, subsidies form part of the strategy.

Endogenous instruments are used by a lower percentage of cities than are other instruments (see table 6.6). The most frequently used endogenous instrument—building rehabilitation—is used by approximately one-fifth of all sample cities, and all but four of these instruments are used by fewer than 10 percent of the cities. As was noted above with regard to Cincinnati, these highly specialized business expansion instruments are much more popular in central cities than in other types of cities; whereas nearly three-fourths of all central cities report the rehabilitation of buildings, only a little more than 10 percent of suburban cities undertake such activity. Similarly, one-half of the central cities have created business incubators, but only four large suburbs and not a single small suburb have done so. Although a significantly greater percentage of nonmetropolitan cities compared with suburbs use the endogenous instruments of building rehabilitation, employee training, and management, the primary variation in endogenous usage is accounted for by their significantly greater usage in central cities.

Central cities may use these instruments more than others because their economic condition is so poor that they are more

Table 6.6. Endogenous Development Instruments (percent)

Instrument	All	NM	SS	LS	CC
Rehabilitate buildings	21.9	26.8	10.1	12.0	72.3
Employee training and retraining	19.0	28.2	13.0	8.0	45.5
Technical assistance to management	13.1	16.9	13.0	6.7	22.7
Share equity in projects	10.6	9.9	13.0	6.7	18.2
Business incubator	9.7	11.3	0.0	5.3	50.0
Manage industrial property	9.7	19.7	4.3	0.0	27.3
Sale–leaseback	7.6	8.5	4.3	6.7	18.2
Develop export markets	5.5	4.2	1.4	2.7	31.8
Trade missions abroad	5.5	4.2	1.4	5.3	22.7
Transfer development rights	5.5	4.2	4.3	5.3	13.6
Centralize management services	5.1	7.0	5.8	1.3	9.1
Manage office-retail property	5.1	5.6	5.8	0.0	18.2

Note: NM = nonmetropolitan cities; SS = small suburban cities; LS = large suburban cities; CC = central cities.

likely to try virtually everything. They also may have more professional staff, who see the efficacy of the emergent tools. More likely, however, greater endogenous use by central cities is due to the rapidly changing and, in many cases, deteriorating central city economy resulting from businesses locating in or relocating to suburban enclaves. Beloit presents a typical case in this regard. With a weak economy and threats from close-by towns and a different tax climate in another state, it engages in land development to encourage real estate development. It also engages in many job development linkages. At the time of the research, it was applying for a federal-state grant to develop flexible machinist training for Beloit Corporation, its largest employer, in cooperation with the local community college. Central cities thus employ the most sophisticated methods to grow internally and utilize the resources already in place.

The small city of Ithaca also employs endogenous instruments such as combined management of its economic development functions, assistance to providing small business management by its multicommunity local development corporation (LDC), technical assistance and training through three different industry consortia (food processing, plastics, metal working), and renovation of buildings in its central business district.

Aggregate development instrument usage is examined with two different measures: the *number* of policy instruments, which is an additive index of development policy instruments adopted by a city, and the *mix* of development policy instruments, which measures the qualitative dimension of a city's policy context by operationalizing usage of different instrument types as a proportion of the number of instruments adopted. The policy instrument mix is equivalent to a reliance measure and is calculated by dividing the number of instruments used from each of the five instrument classes by the total number of instruments employed by the city. For example, if a city adopted twenty total development instruments, and ten of these were endogenous instruments, the city's reliance measure for endogenous instruments would be 50 percent. Cities will have a reliance measure for each of the five development instrument types, the total of these five measures being 100 percent.

Economic development has become a nearly ubiquitous policy issue in cities, and the mean number of policy instruments used reflects this; on average, cities use approximately seventeen different instruments (see table 6.7). Total usage varies significantly across city types: small and large suburbs report using less than the overall city mean, whereas central cities use nearly twice as many as suburbs. The pattern of development effort as represented by total usage of the five instrument types is much the same; central cities report a significantly greater number of instruments used than do suburban and nonmetropolitan cities. Central cities use 50 percent more direct provision instruments, twice as many exhortation instruments, nearly three times as many subsidy instruments, and more than four times as many endogenous instruments as do small suburbs. Large central cities are working harder and employing more mechanisms to establish a more stable local economy.

The bottom part of table 6.7 addresses the actual instrument choices made by local officials, controlling for the number of instruments used. For the entire sample, approximately one-third of the total instruments used are direct provision instruments (31.6 percent), nearly one-fourth are exhortation instruments (23.4 percent), and more than one-fifth are subsidy instruments (21.4 percent). Given the relative ease with which cities may engage these approaches, this finding is not surprising. Conspicuous in its relatively low reliance is the endogenous instrument type, accounting for just above 5 percent of an average development effort. Clearly, endogenous instruments are the instruments least relied upon within the context of a city's overall development strategy.

Table 6.7. Total and Relative Usage of Economic Development Policy Instruments

Instrument	All	NM	SS	LS	CC
Total (mean number)	17.1	18.0	13.9	15.7	28.6
Direct provision	5.3	5.4	4.9	4.9	7.5
Endogenous	1.2	1.5	0.8	0.6	3.6
Exhortation	4.0	4.1	3.1	4.1	6.3
Orders	2.7	2.5	2.5	2.9	3.8
Subsidy	3.9	4.5	2.7	3.2	7.6
Mix (mean percent)					
Direct provision	31.6	29.4	36.7	30.9	25.1
Endogenous	5.2	6.6	4.0	3.0	11.7
Exhortation	23.4	24.4	20.0	25.2	24.2
Orders	16.3	13.3	17.3	19.4	12.4
Subsidy	21.4	24.8	17.6	20.0	26.6

Note: NM = nonmetropolitan cities; SS = small suburban cities; LS = large suburban cities; CC = central cities.

The mix of development instruments varies significantly across city types. Exhortation instruments are relied upon at roughly the same rate from one city type to another. Every city must let the business community know that it is out there. It thus must market itself and promote its virtues to some extent on a continual basis. Whether large or small, metropolitan or suburban, exhortation makes up approximately the same relative proportion of effort in all cities. This is not the case with the other instrument types. Suburbs, especially smaller ones, rely on directly provided instruments to a much greater degree than do central cities. Nearly 37 percent of an average small suburb's total development effort is made up of direct provision instruments, but the share of reliance on the same instruments in central cities is just 25 percent.

The primary focus of a central city's development strategy is subsidy instruments. The central city must offer more attractive features than just improving the physical location. As less attractive land parcels, congestion, high crime, long commutes, lack of parking, and other disincentives to attract business accrue to the central city, it must offer more by putting costly subsidies in the way of tax relief or low-cost loans to outbid the more attractive suburbs. For the growing suburb, offering incentives to prospective businesses is not as necessary as addressing the infrastructure, regulatory, and procedural issues that can attract financial and human resources, as evidenced in suburban cities' strong reliance on direct provision and orders instruments. Whereas 54 percent of all development instruments adopted by small suburbs are direct provision and orders instruments, just 37 percent of total instruments in central cities are direct provision and orders instruments. With the exception of exhortation instrument use, different circumstances lead suburbs and central cities to have substantially different packages of instruments.

Perhaps the most compelling variation in relative instrument usage is found in endogenous instrument use. Central cities use endogenous instruments at a rate more than twice the sample city average, nearly three times the rate of small suburbs, and nearly four times the rate of large suburbs. Endogenous instruments are relied upon in central cities to nearly the same extent that orders instruments are relied upon, making the former a legitimate, and not peripheral, part of the central city development strategy.

Nonmetropolitan cities also adopt endogenous instruments at a significantly greater rate than suburban cities. The evidence of endogenous instrument use does not signify the wholesale policy transformation toward endogenous development predicted by Eisinger (1988), but it does indicate that endogenous instruments are a significant strategic component of local economic development policy for those cities experiencing economic distress. The question of whether reliance on such instruments affects collaboration is addressed in the next section.

Development Strategy and Collaboration

Are particular patterns of policy adoption associated with collaborative policymaking and administration? Cities still rely most heavily on subsidy instruments like tax abatements and tax increment financing, and exhortation instruments such as promotions and business visits, but evidence also indicates that the use of endogenous instruments, and the strategic planning that such approaches entail, are on the rise (Blakely 1994; Levy 1990).

Because the literature on local economic development emphasizes policy *design* at the expense of policy *operation*, we do not know how the adoption of such policy approaches affects the policymaking and administrative processes in the city. If certain emergent policy approaches require more collaboration, are city officials prepared to operate in such settings as a consequence of being innovative? Given the nature of endogenous policy instruments—seeking and developing new products and markets—such usage may require contacting and collaborating with multiple actors.

We examined the relationship between the adoption of development policy approaches and the level of collaborative activity in cities in multiple ways. First, we generated bivariate correlation coefficients for variables measuring both policy and collaborative activity (from chapter 4). The hypothesis that "more means more"—the greater the level of policy activity, the greater the level of collaboration activity—is supported by substantial correlation coefficients that describe the relationship between the total number of all policy instrument types and the number of all collaboration types. Although there are certainly other determinants of collaborative activity, we discovered that the level of policy activity accounts for nearly 40 percent of the variation in collaborative activity. To examine the true effect of particular types of development activity on collaboration holding the level of policy activity constant, partial correlations of the policy and collaborative activity variables were calculated, controlling for total policy activity (reported in table 6.8).

Partial correlations were calculated both for the raw usage policy variables (the total number of policy instruments for each type) and for the instrument reliance variables (instrument usage as a ratio of total instrument usage). In addition, partial correlation coefficients were calculated both for variables measuring the five instrument types and the two collaborative environments, and for the collaboration dedicated to each of the five horizontal collaborative activity types. For this partial correlation analysis, statistically significant coefficients of correlation for total instrument use and collaboration represent a measure that is more specifically based on the type of policy and collaborative activity itself, rather than on overall activity. Significant coefficients between the policy variables measuring reliance and collaboration (the mix columns in table 6.8) suggest that reliance on a particular instrument type is significantly associated with collaboration.

Even controlling for total policy activity, as the number of endogenous instruments adopted by a city increases, the greater

Table 6.8. Statistically Significant Partial Correlations of Development Policy Use and Mix and Collaborative Activity (Controlling for Total Policy Activity)

Collaborative Activity	Endogenous		Direct Provision		Exhortation		Orders		Subsidy	
	Total	Mix	Total	Mix	Total	Mix	Total	Mix	Total	Mix
Vertical										
Information seeking					−.145					
Adjustment seeking	.128				−.131		−.141			
Total					−.148					
Horizontal										
Policymaking and strategy-making	.265	.144			−.211				.169	
Resource exchange	.211				−.141		−.140		.168	
Project-based work	.207				−.164				.134	
Total	.272	.142			−.212		−.131		.180	
Total for all	.144				−.148	−.129			.139	

Note: All correlations significant at $p < .05$.

the level of collaboration, measured in various ways. Although endogenous use does not appear to be significantly related to total vertical activity (it is only modestly correlated with adjustment-seeking activity, at $r = .128$, controlling for total activity), such use is positively and relatively strongly related to each horizontal activity. Regardless of whether a city is highly active in economic development or uses just a few policy instruments, the more endogenous instruments adopted by a city, the greater that city's extent of any type of horizontal collaboration.

Ithaca's economic development strategy, which relies on endogenous instruments, focuses on expanding its full industrial park to an equal-sized plot across the road from the original site. Targeted industries include agriculture research, value-added agricultural manufacturing, and other nonpolluting small manufacturing firms, although the city owns a "super site" held in reserve if the right large firm demonstrates interest. Emphasis is placed on business expansion, and thus the city wants to have proper siting available. Continued promotion of agriculture and agricultural services is also seen as important for Ithaca's economy. In this case, it involves city efforts to help retain existing agribusiness by infrastructure and site availability. Retail promotion is not an area of emphasis. Although the downtown is full, there is considerable shopping leakage to Alma, an industrial and college town of about 10,000 located 8 miles away, and Mount Pleasant, home of Central Michigan University and more than 30,000 persons, 25 miles to the north. Again, business retention is the aim. Collaboration to promote these interests through its LDC, Greater Gratiot Development Incorporated (GGDI), involves partnerships of many types, including industry cluster networks, with Michigan State University School of Engineering, and venture capitalists throughout the state.

The story is different for the other types of policy instruments. There is no significant relationship between the number of direct provision instruments adopted by a city and collaboration of any type. Such instruments do not appear to induce collaboration when controlling for total policy activity. Lack of association between development policy instruments such as infrastructure provision or construction and collaboration is no surprise, given the nature of direct provision. Contracting with private-sector firms is the extent of most extra-governmental interaction in this particular policy context. Subsidy instruments appear to be related to collaboration, although without the same scope (number of collaborative activity types), or to the strength (magnitude of the correlation coefficient) of the relationship between endogenous instruments and collaboration. Vertical collaboration is not significantly associated with subsidy use, suggesting that the ability to package and offer subsidies does not rest on the capacity to operate in the vertical environment. Even information-seeking collaboration, which includes seeking out program finances and interpretations from state and federal agencies, is not associated with subsidy usage or reliance.

If the case can be made that endogenous instrument use is associated with collaboration, an equally strong case can be made that exhortation (and, to a lesser extent, orders) instrument use is related to a low collaboration. For all vertical and horizontal activity types, the greater the number of exhortation instruments adopted by a city, the lower the level of collaboration. The ratio columns indicate that the more a city relies on exhortation instruments as part of an overall development strategy, the lower the level of total collaboration ($r = -.129$). The story is much the same for orders instruments use. Orders adoption apparently does not induce lower levels of overall collaboration, but adjustment-seeking and resource-exchange activity decreases as orders usage increases. Total horizontal activity is also negatively correlated with orders activity.

The relationship between exhortation or orders instrument usage and collaborative activity can also be viewed in the inverse: The lower the number of exhortation and orders instruments adopted by a city, the greater the level of collaboration in that city. Across all cases, and controlling for total policy activity, collaboration is apparently more prevalent in the absence of exhortation and orders activity. The partial correlation coefficients suggest that for both cities highly active or minimally engaged in economic development, collaboration is *greater* when cities adopt *endogenous* and/or *subsidy* instruments, *lower* when they adopt *exhortation* or *orders* instruments, and *unaffected* when they adopt *direct provision* instruments. Although causal linkages cannot be safely inferred from correlation analysis, we do have strong, albeit preliminary, evidence that the adoption of economic development policy instruments is a significant determinant of collaboration.

To further explore the hypothesis that development instrument adoption is associated with collaborative activity, the sample cities were divided into groups, according to each city's degree of reliance on each of the five types of development instruments. All cities at or above the 75th percentile (the top 25 percent) in reliance were identified and placed in one group for each instrument type, and the remaining 75 percent in another for each type. We thus placed 25 percent of the sample cities with the highest reliance on direct provision instruments in one group and the remaining 75 percent of the sample in another group, and repeated this grouping for the other four instrument types. Differences in the mean level of collaboration between the high and low groups in each development instrument type were examined. Difference-of-means hypothesis tests were conducted to compare the level of collaboration for the cities with the greatest reliance on each instrument type with the rest of the cities. Tests for all five instrument types were thus performed for each of the variables examined in the correlation analyses.

The results of the difference-of-means tests are consistent with, and perhaps even more revealing than, the findings presented in the two previous tables (see table 6.9). Cities with the highest reliance on endogenous instruments collaborate, on average, three times as much horizontally as do the rest of the sample cities (19.8 total activities, compared with 6.6), and nearly twice as much vertically (26.4, compared with 15.2) and overall (42.8, compared with 24.1). There is also a statistically significant difference in the mean level of vertical activities and horizontal linkages for every type of collaborative activity between cities with the highest reliance on endogenous instruments and the rest of the cities. Cities with the highest reliance on direct provision, exhortation, and orders instruments collaborate, on average, less frequently than do the rest of the cities. Although the cities with the highest reliance on endogenous instruments average nearly 43 total collaborative activities, cities with the highest reliance on direct provision, exhortation, or orders instruments averaged approximately 24, 22, and 21 activities, respectively—or roughly half as much activity. The mean level of collaboration for cities that rely the most on subsidy instruments is not significantly different from the mean level of collaboration for the rest of the cities, for most measures of collaboration.

Ithaca, through its multicity, county-level LDC, GGDI, illustrates the relationship between using endogenous instruments and high levels of collaborative activity. In its survey, it reported pursuing twenty-eight activities in the horizontal or interlocal system. It has pursued seven of the twelve endogenous activities: rehabilitation of buildings, employee training, technical assistance to management, shared project equity, business incubators, managing industrial property, and centralized management services. In the training and retraining area, for example, GGDI has collaborated in workforce development needs in the changing plastics industries, jointly sponsored a local upgrade and skill training program, and worked with school systems in an innovative school-to-work initiative.

Through GGDI, Ithaca is trying to compete in a changing global economy by promoting new jobs in the value-added agriculture and agriculture research arenas. It also regularly links local companies with Michigan's comprehensive industrial extension programs, which is organized on a regional basis. Both the City of Ithaca and GGDI also regularly collaborate on business expansion activities with the Ithaca Industrial Development and Economic Association, the county-level Chamber of Commerce, and the Gratiot County government.

Table 6.9. Difference-of-Means Tests, Cities with High Reliance on Development Instrument Types Compared with the Rest of Cities (mean number of activities)

Instrument Type	Information Seeking	Adjustment Seeking	Total Vertical	Policymaking and Strategy-Making	Resource Exchange	Project-Based Work	Total Horizontal	Total Collaboration
High endogenous use cities	13.9	12.5	26.4	12.7	2.2	4.8	19.8	42.8
Rest of cities	9.3	5.9	15.2	4.2	0.8	1.6	6.6	24.1
Difference	4.6*	6.6*	11.2*	8.5*	1.4*	3.2*	13.2*	18.7*
High direct provision use cities	10.0	5.7	15.8	4.3	0.4	1.7	6.4	24.2
Rest of cities	10.6	8.2	18.7	7.0	1.4	2.6	11.0	30.3
Difference	−0.6	−2.5**	−2.9	−2.7	−1.0*	−0.9	−7.6	−6.1**
High exhortation use cities	8.3	6.0	14.3	3.1	0.3	1.7	5.1	22.5
Rest of cities	11.2	8.0	19.2	7.4	1.4	2.6	11.4	30.8
Difference	−2.9*	−2.0	−4.9**	−4.3*	−1.1*	−0.9	−6.3*	−8.3*
High orders use cities	8.2	4.4	12.6	3.7	0.4	1.6	5.7	20.9
Rest of cities	11.2	8.6	19.8	7.2	1.4	2.6	11.2	31.3
Difference	−3.0*	−4.2*	−7.2*	−3.5	−1.0*	−1.0	−5.5*	−10.4*
High subsidy use cities	10.8	9.0	19.8	8.7	1.7	3.5	13.9	32.6
Rest of cities	10.3	7.1	17.4	5.5	1.0	2.0	8.5	27.5
Difference	0.5	1.9	2.4	3.2**	0.7	1.5**	5.4**	5.1

* = statistical significance at $p = .05$.
** = statistical significance at $p = .10$.

Policy Approaches and Collaboration

Cities clearly have many opportunities and means of reaching out. Industrial decline in central cities; the rise of second- and third-ring suburbs with their "edge cities" offering retail, finance, and service industry opportunities; and declining nonmetropolitan populations are evidence of the changes in urban economies. At virtually the same time, the federal government in Washington has begun to reduce its financial support for cities and substituted other means, such as loans and regulations, and states have become heavily involved with economic development (Eisinger 1988; Clarke and Gaile 1998). States have put many potential economic development instruments into the hands of their local governments, as well as small pots of money for venture capital, revolving loan funds, and capital fund grants. In combination with existing municipal powers to provide or produce urban services, big cities like Cincinnati can potentially use federal and state programs to their strategic advantage in attracting business or holding it within their borders.

We have shown that not all cities jump equally into these approaches. Not every city is a Beloit or Salem, nor do many cities use as many endogenous instruments as does Ithaca. Lower frequencies among responding cities in the survey show that some instruments are not as widely used as expected. But many—particularly some direct provision, exhortation, and subsidy instruments—are quite extensively used. They are available, and they are accessed. As expected, cities use these tools in relation to their economic condition; that is, less financially well-off central cities and nonmetropolitan cities are more likely to involve tools and approaches, including the least-used endogenous instruments.

Because our data do not include economic performance, we cannot test the effectiveness of one strategy versus another, although McGuire (1999) has attempted this in a separate study. Performance is beyond the scope of the book. However, we can and have examined the central relationship of policy to collaboration or to collaborative management. What a city engages in strategically is clearly connected to the pattern of collaboration, and it is thus no accident that Cincinnati and Ithaca are high networking cities. Promoting the city or improving public infrastructure mainly attracts business, but they are in-house strategies. By contrast, pursuing business retention and expansion strategies that involve endogenous approaches like workforce development, shared equity in development projects, business incubation, building rehabilitation, and promoting trade and export markets involves a high degree of external engagement with potential and actual partners.

Such tools for "growth from within" mean combining knowledge, capital, and human and other resources wherever they might be found locally, and working together—the city and other entities—to get businesses to adapt and grow in place. To take a hypothetical example, it means that city government and others are helping a local company adopt a new technology in chemical products manufacturing that will appeal to export markets. It also requires expanded space near the existing facility and new forms of workforce development. It may even tap some of the knowledge and technology from a city-sponsored business incubator project. In short, in this example the city is out there facilitating local capital's ability to capture new demands. These activities require the highest degree of collaboration.

The use of endogenous instruments can be viewed, particularly in cities like Cincinnati and Ithaca, as one indicator among many of jurisdiction-based management. If jurisdiction-based management is driven by a strategic rationale focused on the jurisdiction, then the use of endogenous instruments, like such other strategic approaches as planning and evaluation, is an important component of jurisdiction-based management.

Notes

1. In many cases, the choice of instruments determines the collaborative activity, whereas in some cases the collaborative linkages produce a choice of policy instrument(s). Time order was not explicitly addressed in the survey, but our observations suggest that mostly, but not always, the selection of an instrument leads to the collaborative structure. Either way, although the causal forces are incompletely determined, we can definitively speak to association.

2. Some endogenous instruments may, in general, also be classified in terms of the other four categories from Linder and Peters (1990). For example, managing industrial or office-retail property could also be considered as a directly provided instrument because the city government is

providing a service—management—directly. However, the strategic intent and operational process of the instrument are different than, say, infrastructure development. Because endogenous instruments have been viewed as a distinct category of development instruments and widely accepted by economic development scholars since Eisinger's description of demand-side instruments (1988), we separate these.

This conceptual grouping of the instruments into five categories is borne out with reliability analysis. Cronbach's alpha coefficients of .70 or above indicate a high degree of internal consistency and measurement reliability in the scales developed, and three of the instrument categories (direct provision, exhortation, and subsidy), as well as the additive scale of all sixty-three instruments, reach this level. Alpha coefficients for endogenous and orders instruments are .60, indicating an acceptable level of reliability in each instrument scale.

7

Jurisdiction-Based Management

The foregoing analysis documents thoroughly the extensiveness of the collaborative context for cities and economic development. A reconfiguration of intergovernmental relationships in the federal system as a result of the processes of devolution and dwindling resources, increased policy diversity and complexity, and institutional growth during the past few decades in areas affecting economic development has produced a system of interdependence that requires city governments to regularly operate across boundaries. Officials working within the development arena are collaborating formally and informally, vertically and horizontally. The significance of the contacts, one might say the collaborative loadings, shift from jurisdiction to jurisdiction, and from project to project. Collaborative management occupies about one-fifth of a city official's time and involves a complex grid of activities. The challenge for a city wanting to manage its local economy effectively encompasses both the networking and coalition-building activities at the horizontal level, as well as financing and regulatory activities with state and federal governments.

As a means to summarize our findings and shed light on their implications, in this chapter we discuss three components of the premise that has guided this book. First, we revisit the propositions stated in chapter 1 in light of our data. We do this by briefly synthesizing the vast amount of information contained in the tables. Second, we further explicate our theory of jurisdiction-based management and demonstrate its applicability by way of the case study cities. We do this by considering how probable future scenarios for these cities may either enhance the capacity of those cities already practicing jurisdiction-based management, or possibly stimulate jurisdiction-based activity in the cities not presently operating according to that model. Third, we suggest how the jurisdiction-based theory affects commonly held views of intergovernmental relations and federalism. The context for a new perspective of managing across governments and organizations is thus established.

A simple argument is made throughout the book: Collaboration is a routine, regular, and, in many cases, requisite activity in cities of all sizes, but we know too little about it. Past research on collaborative activity runs the gamut of scholarship, from how-to manuals for achieving successful collaborative processes to formal modeling of the impact of management on program outcomes. Each of these reports—and everything in between—provides a welcome stream of knowledge on collaborative activity, but they tell us nothing descriptively about the form and content of inter-governmental collaboration or how such activity is practiced. The intent of this book at the outset was to fill the gaps, at least partially, in our understanding of collaborative management. Some cities somehow manage to exploit their complex intergovernmental and interorganizational environment, but we simply do not know why and we do not know how. Here, then, we summarize some of the lessons learned from our research.

The Abundance of Collaborative Mechanisms

Collaborative management is more than an occasional task performed with a single partner. In economic development, on average, it involves 20 percent of the manager's time. The two dimensions we studied, horizontal and vertical, have many hidden aspects that we have been able to reveal. In the vertical realm, local managers do more than seek grants and comply with regulations. They manage programs through negotiations and pursue program adjustments with state and federal officials. Meanwhile, they manage horizontally by engaging other local governments and nongovernmental organizations in program developments and exchanges of specific development efforts. These joint engagement activities broaden the concept of interlocal cooperation and adjustment. Managing interdependencies has indeed become more pervasive, routine, and complex (Kettl 1996).

Managing grants, regulations, and cooperative arrangements continues to be part of the working core of city collaboration, but a great number of other activities can be added to this list. As city officials work within the vertical system, they pursue at least eleven discrete collaborative activities, encompassing nearly two-thirds of all the intergovernmental activity explored in this study. Working within the vertical system is important, as the literature suggests, but a more complex interactive process is occurring than what is typically portrayed in the literature.

Collaboration is more than seeking and managing grants or complying with regulations. Financial assistance in economic development also includes arranging loans, negotiating interest-rate adjustments, attempting to forge sale–leaseback arrangements, and a host of other financial transactions. It involves seeking relevant operating information, asking about interpretations related to running a program, seeking guidance regarding a proposed course of action on a program, as well as applying for technical assistance. Dealing with intergovernmental regulation does indeed include those activities related to compliance, but not every regulated government complies in every case. Some manage by seeking discretion. They do this by one of several means of "tweaking the system," learning how to ask for, negotiate, and perhaps bargain for greater measures of discretion. Though not every local government in our sample reported doing this, a notable percentage have done so. These managers have attempted some basic regulatory or statutory adjustment, sought a policy change, or tried another way to "loosen up" the compliance game. Many local managers are actually out there "working the system" to adapt federal and/or state programs to jurisdictional needs.

The horizontal plane of collaborative management also expands earlier notions of interlocal adjustments and cooperative agreements. By looking at the economic development arena, we are able to uncover additional aspects of interlocal activity. Governments at the local level not only work with one another in the form of city–county, city–township, or city–special district relations, but they also engage a variety of nongovernmental partners. Contacts and collaborations are between cities and chambers of commerce, public–private partnerships, local utilities, and, to a lesser extent, with job training programs, neighborhood associations, and a few other organizations. The work that is being done in economic development involves collaborative policymaking and strategy-making, exchange of resources, and project undertakings through a process of horizontal networking.

Managerial activity in a city entails nontraditional activities, such as seeking out policymaking information, negotiating partner arrangements, practicing interorganizational policymaking, leveraging and arranging multiple sources of financing, creating financial incentives, overseeing contracts management, finding and operating formal partnerships, and using and giving technical assistance of various kinds. Although these managerial actions are less often employed than those of a vertical nature, they are called upon nonetheless. These emergent mechanisms do not supplant the traditional list of interlocal managerial actions, structural adaptations, and joint purchasing or servicing, but they add to the expanding nature of what needs to be known about managers' collaborative activity within communities.

Interaction based on mutual need is more prevalent at the operating level, and it is an interaction that has become routinized on one hand but more political on the other. State government agencies are by far the most important components of the intergovernmental context, but the agencies include departments of transportation and environment, and political contacts like the state legislature and the governor, in addition to the more traditional contribution of commerce and development departments. County government is a strong intergovernmental player in local economic development, but cities also network with other cities, chambers of commerce, numerous public–private structures, and utilities. Such institutional fragmentation in the environment of a city can prove to be beneficial for a city, enabling any and all players to play an important collaborative role with the city, depending on the policy problem and context.

Variation in Collaborative Activity

There is certainly variation in the levels of collaboration across the sample cities; some cities are more active than others, and this has been a truism for intergovernmental relations and management research for decades. In this regard, collaborative activity is as variable as intergovernmental activity. The analysis presented here indicates that collaborative management varies according to the types of strategies, policies, and institutions adopted in the jurisdiction. Cities that attempt to gain strategic control over their local economies by planning and evaluating performance are also the most active cities. City governments that operate alongside a development corporation and that have a full-time director leading development activities have significantly higher levels of activity than cities that do not have such structures in place. In addition, multiple forms of analyses indicate that adopting specific policy approaches to economic development policymaking and administration is associated with significantly higher levels of collaboration. The findings offer an alternative view of economic development policy adoption and administration by examining the effect of certain adoptions on the role of the economic development professional.

The form and amount of collaborative activity vary substantially across cities. Cincinnati and Ithaca use 132 and 87 vertical and horizontal activities respectively, while operating within literally dozens of clusters. Another twelve cities reported absolutely no activity, while thirty cities collaborate either horizontally or vertically, but not both. Similarly, some cities, like Salem and Beloit, devote the majority of their vertical collaborative activity to seeking information, whereas others develop a strategy of seeking adjustments from state and federal government agencies through bargaining and other political means.

What leads to high levels of collaborative engagement in one city and none in others? The relationship between activity and the dimensions of strategy, structure, economic characteristics, and the set of players chosen by a city leadership is strong and undeniable. The strategic purpose of local economic development is critical for understanding the composition of a city's collaborative environment. Our data on clusters by categories of strategic activity show different densities for policymaking and strategy-making, resource exchange, and project-based purposes. Partnerships with county governments and local development corporations (LDCs) are most active for resource exchange, and with chambers of commerce for policy assistance and joint policymaking. Indeed, a collaborative network involved in producing local policies and strategies is most likely to include multiple entities: the chamber, LDC, and sometimes the utility or another city. Project networks are similar, involving the city government, an LDC, and often the local utility.

Resource-exchange networks are somewhat different, seldom involving chambers, but often including local foundations, private industry councils, special districts, and local utilities. In sum, it is probably inaccurate to speak of a single type of collaboration in cities. Rather, the series of connections in cities is determined by what the city is trying to accomplish strategically.

City involvement with each of the horizontal players flows from the varied roles they might play in economic development. The horizontal environment faced by the local development manager includes stakeholders and potential stakeholders located in a more lateral direction from the city. Within each community, economic development players depend a lot on the pattern of state-established local governments—cities, counties, townships, and special districts—and the pattern of activity of nongovernmental actors. The array of nongovernmental organizations involved in economic development in a given community likewise depends on the level of activity of other entities, such as the chamber of commerce, private developers, or neighborhood associations. These players are involved in numerous activities that include joint efforts in the formulation and implementation of development policy, seeking financial resources, contracting, developing joint financial incentives, and carrying through a jointly created development project.

Economic conditions certainly provide a partial explanation for the level of collaborative activity in a city; poor cities pursue more collaboration than rich cities. However, the correlation of activity and economic condition is weak. Although economic development policy effort is often viewed as being driven by need, related research demonstrates that the horizontal collaborative tasks of jointly designing policy, working on projects, and seeking resources may be associated with economic conditions, but they do not appear to be driven substantially by the number of development instruments used in the community (McGuire 1999). The positive but weak relationship between policy activity and collaborative activity is just about the same for the most active cities as for the average cities. In other words, all cities receive about the same effect from their respective levels of policy activity. A key predictor of the variation in city collaborative activity is thus not to be found in that city's economic development activity. Holding that variable constant reveals that strategic and structural forces are much more robust explanations for the variation in activity levels.

Distinct Models of Collaborative Management

Our data suggest that three different patterns or models of management exist in cities with moderate to high levels of collaborative activity. By implication, we argue that a dominant collaborative orientation in cities can be identified. One emergent model present in some cities is one that we have referred to as jurisdiction-based management. Such management is defined by the initiated actions of local officials and managers who seek out program adjustments and other actors and resources needed to serve the strategic aims of their governments. This model highlights the actions of multiple interdependent governmental and nongovernmental organizations pursuing joint action. Jurisdiction-based management involves problem resolution by facilitating and furthering interaction, as well as creating and changing collaborative arrangements for better coordination. An official in a jurisdiction-based city will spend a great deal of time and effort doing just that. Because the effectiveness of collaboration is as much a function of where and how the various parties are positioned, in the layers of other governments or in the community, as it is the actions of the actors themselves (Burt 1992; Provan and Milward 1995), the city official may seek new players and different resources when it proves impossible to solve problems within the existing structure (Kickert, Klijn, and Koppenjan 1997). The adept official in a jurisdiction-based city knows which configuration of players and what available resources are needed to achieve jurisdictional goals.

We also found evidence of two long-standing but still relevant models for active cities. The donor–recipient model emphasizes mutual dependence or shared program administration where two-party bargaining or reciprocal interactions among government officials is the norm. The top-down model emphasizes executive branch control and is embedded in enforcement and exchange related to the laws, regulations, funding rules, program standards, and guidelines associated with federal and state grant, procurement, and regulation programs. In addition to jurisdiction-based management, all three of the active city models appear to be alive and well on the intergovernmental scene, posing complex challenges for cities and their managers.

In many respects, the empirical confirmation of our hypothetical management models suggests a unification of theory with practice regarding the operation of state and local governments within the U.S. federal system. Elazar's matrix model of noncentralization appears to extend beyond policymakers to administrators (1984). On another level, however, the findings indicate that the extent of collaborative activity is much greater than even twenty years ago. Cooperation and collaboration in the intergovernmental system at one time consisted primarily of sharing resources vis-à-vis the grant-in-aid system. Identifying the sources of financial and technical support available for economic development was relatively simple: Contact those agencies, state but mainly federal, that had the words "development" or "commerce" in their title, follow instructions, and spend the money wisely. Today, resources are scarce, but potential partners in planning, policymaking, implementation, resource exchange, and delivering projects are numerous and active. Many other jurisdictions and organizations in the horizontal system are perceived as important for city development, resulting in a complex intergovernmental, intersectoral operating context that requires new political and managerial skills. In the vertical system, federal and state officials need winning programs and projects to show impact, and local officials need to attract resources and adjust regulatory frameworks to suit local requirements (Pressman 1975).

The most enduring models of public management in intergovernmental or interorganizational settings do not capture what our empirical research has found. The collaborative activities carried out in many cities—promoting adjustments to regulations and statutes, acquiring funds from sources other than the federal government, involving private-sector players in city policymaking—are not consistent with management models based in top-down compliance. Although some activity across governments is hierarchically ordered, jurisdiction-based, city-level activity is undeniably carried out to support the agenda of the city primarily, and only secondarily to comply with extra-jurisdictional conditions.

Furthermore, collaboration in some cities is associated with policy strategies that are locally determined, rather than externally imposed. Indeed, it appears that even when policymaking and administration are locally based, the city collaborates; that is, somewhat paradoxically, the more a city seeks solutions that benefit the city (as opposed to meeting state or federal requirements), the greater the level of collaborative management that extends beyond city hall. Our data certainly support the idea that vertical and horizontal collaboration by some cities in economic development involves multiple players, multiple activities, and multiple strategies, that is, first and foremost, jurisdiction-based.

Challenges for Jurisdiction-Based Cities

As more responsibilities are "left" to the local level to solve or are devolved by state and federal governments, and more policy decisions are decentralized, the incidence of jurisdiction-based management also should increase. If, over time, federal grant programs increasingly include elements that are broad or discretionary categorical and/or the block grant structure, and if, over time, local governments become more proactive and innovative at addressing environmental and other regulatory concerns, then jurisdiction-based management will become more relevant, displacing the remnants of existing management approaches. It should be noted that the jurisdiction-based model presupposes that a local jurisdiction wishes to assert its will in policy matters, that it is willing to bypass existing relationships and establish new relationships with bearers of resources for the purpose of achieving local goals. If such behavior is encouraged, either politically or administratively, jurisdiction-based managers will become more common.

Cincinnati, the prototypical jurisdiction-based city, exemplifies just how such management is relevant for its future success. The city government has developed "nonsource" intergovernmental programs that emanate directly from strategic and operational plans, involving extensive vertical and horizontal linkages with hundreds of collaborators. Bargaining and adjustment seeking with vertical players are regular activities in Cincinnati. Several local development corporations and a highly professionalized department of development promote economic development in the city. Moreover, the city is meeting the challenges of the global, informal economy by growing its economy with the liberal use of endogenous development instruments. Its long experience with intergovernmental programs and professional bureaucracy helps managers know when to comply, when to bargain and adjust, when to propose, and when to network. Cincinnati, with the highest level of activity in the sample, has its collaborative act together.

Cincinnati is not without problems, however, and its future economic success will depend greatly on its ability to maintain its jurisdiction-based approach to governing. Like other core metropolitan cities, Cincinnati faces tremendous challenges as it competes for business development with other cities in its region. It has lost core manufacturing jobs, levies relatively high local taxes, and has limited green space for industrial or commercial sites. Its immediate challenge is to capture its regional locational advantages, which will require new alliances to help its economy grow and prosper.

Another challenge for Cincinnati is to build on its earlier strength in automotive electronics manufacturing to branch out into new forms of electronics manufacturing. This strategy also will require innovative alliances with industry and educational institutions, as well as promotion of industrial cluster networks. Expanding its manufacturing will require working with area university research institutes, workforce development agencies, venture capitalists, and other economic interests to help replace older, less skilled labor factories with smart manufacturing technology.

The city also intends to maintain its status as a magnet for tourism, particularly for its major league franchises, and attract its share of retail commerce and business services. Far from relying on government promotion, however, the downtown LDC public–private partnership must assist the city in reaching out to the region and nation. Even greater intermetropolitan and interstate cooperation outside the city will be needed to take advantage of its regional airport, located in Kentucky, which is a major hub for one of the country's largest airlines.

Jurisdiction-based Cincinnati must not forgo the established relationships with state and federal agencies; indeed, it should expect these to accelerate. The city may find the U.S. Department of Commerce's Advanced Manufacturing Partnership Program useful. Also, venture capital and capital improvements programs from the state of Ohio are accessible to the city. Because cities like Cincinnati that seek to exploit their complex governing environment understand that vertical activity typically results in greater horizontal activity, links with county government, suburban governments in the county, the airport authority, and school districts all will be needed to support such an agenda. Given Cincinnati's location in a three-state region, links with other local governments will involve much formal and informal interstate cooperation.

Ithaca also can be classified as a jurisdiction-based city, but in a much smaller package than Cincinnati and with different economic challenges to overcome. Like Cincinnati, this small town experiences very high levels of horizontal and vertical activity, much like large central big cities. The city works closely with its lead development agency, Greater Gratiot Development Incorporated (GGDI), in planning. Its ability to mobilize local forces to pursue federal and state policymaking resources is a crucial component of its success. Through the professional staffing efforts of GGDI, its capacity to exploit the intergovernmental and interorganizational environment is considerable. Given its size and location, collaboration must be a continuing way of life.

Ithaca's future is tied directly to the continued success of its multicommunity strategic planning effort and the creative use of collaborative economic development tools. Officials in this forward-looking, jurisdiction-based city realize that regionwide advanced manufacturing programs need to be developed in conjunction with the Michigan Economic Development Corporation. Similarly, the city will seek to promote more small industry networks. Probable vertical targets include Economic Development Administration and Department of Agriculture Rural Development (USDA/RD) programs, Community Development Block Grants (CDBG) for small cities, and other assistance programs administered by the state Economic Development Commission. Existing interlocal connections will be enhanced and new ones established in an effort to keep other small cities in the county edging toward meeting the changes in manufacturing, communications, and the global basis of trade. Ithaca and GGDI serve as one important example of a kind of jurisdiction-based management that is needed for rural areas to stay alive and compete within a constantly transforming economy. Its jurisdiction-based approach for dealing with both local partners and with the state and federal governments will no doubt be an important determinant of a successful local economy.

Challenges for Donor-Recipient Cities

The donor–recipient model is another approach to managing that exists in moderately to highly active cities. The model remains relevant, as suggested by the numerous cities that regularly cooperate with state and federal governments but do not seek interlocal adjustments, and are not as active horizontally. Cities can certainly achieve economic development success by fulfilling federal and state aims, and develop further as a result, although a jurisdiction-based approach can help to focus federal and state resources. Exposure to federally stimulated local economic development processes leads to a corps of experienced locals who know how to deal with federal officials while seeking adjustments and pursuing local aims. Federal and state officials need local winners; their program successes ultimately depend on local government action in meeting program aims.

In turn, local governments want federal and state program authority and assistance and, as recipients, find a way to direct it to jurisdiction needs and priorities. Our field research substantiates that human engagement over federal or state programs in many cities moves beyond compliance to a form of negotiated adjustment or settlement that attempts to maximize solutions for the two parties. The donor–recipient model says that not everybody will comply and not everybody will defy. Some jurisdictions do find a way to manage a solution within the overall external policy framework.

Salem is an example of a donor–recipient city. Like Ithaca, the city is small yet involved in collaborative activity, particularly in seeking adjustments to federal and state programs. Unlike Ithaca, horizontal activity overall is not a major component of Salem's management approach. As a small city in a rural area, Salem is guided by a strategic plan and relies heavily on the Washington County Economic Growth Partnership (WCEGP) to maintain its mixed manufacturing, service, and retail economy. Along with WCEGP, the city takes advantage of external connections—state agencies, a regional planning body, and a grant-making consortium—to make this small city "big" in terms of planning, development, and intergovernmental assistance capabilities. Most important, it uses every opportunity to seek program adjustments that will move city projects along and/or secure funding.

Salem will need noncity resources to keep its rural-based manufacturing "up to speed" in industrial technology, communications infrastructure, workforce development, and physical infrastructure. Continuing its connections with state and federal transportation departments to "backfill" in transportation infrastructure is important because of Salem's location, some nineteen miles from an interstate highway. Salem must take advantage of federal and state funding opportunities to build a truck bypass and to make airport improvements. As a small city, Salem is eligible for USDA/RD low-cost long-term loans for public facilities, business development, and housing.

In addition, Salem receives state-administered discretionary CDBG small-cities money for the same purposes. Using these funding sources as leverage to expand community-level involvement will be imperative for a city whose tax base is growing only modestly. Finally, Salem should seek to take advantage of the experience it gained in its protracted negotiations and bargaining with the Indiana Department of Environmental Management over its municipal water system. It is now an adept donor–recipient small city with the potential to carry its intergovernmental adjustment-seeking abilities into many other areas. As Salem begins to realize that vertical activity can spawn beneficial horizontal activity, and vice versa, it will move toward a more opportunistic jurisdiction-based approach.

Woodstock administers economic development in a way that is similar to Salem. This donor–recipient city engages in various types of regulatory adjustments and bargains over major issues when costs or other burdens threaten them. However, horizontal activity is only moderate; it does not advance a current intergovernmental agenda designed to lead to new policy strategies. City government officials and leaders from the LDC do create alliances with local businesses for retention and expansion purposes, and an occasional small manufacturing firm locates there. The city works with the McHenry County government, the school district, and neighboring cities on issues of land use, infrastructure development, and coping with expanded service demands.

As an outer-ring suburb and small city at the fringe of the Chicago metropolitan area, Woodstock's critical issue is growth management rather than survival, as in the smaller towns of Ithaca and Salem. It does not depend on industrial promotion in the same way as do the other case study cities. Because McHenry County recently became an entitlement CDBG county, new funds will be available through this source for community development, and Woodstock plans to propose a somewhat flexible application. The city's more or less dormant connections with the state Department of Commerce and Community Affairs will have to be reestablished for access to funding, licensing, and other program supports. Existing collaboration with the Illinois Department of Transportation, one of its few regular state contacts, will also have to be exploited to deal with the problem of the main commercial thoroughfare at the edge of town that lies along a two-lane, multiple-access state highway. As commercial development follows residential expansion, the traffic problems will become acute. Because the city does not perceive a need to maintain a large manufacturing base, its major horizontal collaborative targets will continue to be primarily with businesses, other cities, and the county. The question remains, however: Can Woodstock really manage growth without a plan that includes a broad program of federal support? Woodstock is an active donor–recipient city that can gain better control of its economic destiny if it adopts a strategic, jurisdiction-based approach.

Challenges for Top-Down Cities

The top-down model of collaborative management retains a great deal of temporal relevance. Our findings indicate that a considerable amount of managerial time is spent in transactions relating to meeting program intent or expectations; nearly half of the cities do not seek regulatory or statutory adjustments, many cities do not regularly bargain, and a large proportion of cities choose not to operate—for one reason or another—in a complex web of players and resources. A large incentive exists for cities to comply when such activity is subject to reporting, review, evaluation, and audit. Though the momentum of federal program growth may have subsided since the 1980s, new programs for cities, particularly those of a regulatory nature, continue to emerge as a reflection of national intent, and managers remain in a position where they must deal with national and state aims. As was demonstrated in chapter 3, state government programming is very much alive, and it can be no less hierarchical in intent. For public managers, the top-down model is a clear manifestation of the bureaucratic tradition of the twentieth century. Whether or not the manager follows the federal or state legal template to the letter, programs are guided in a normative framework that implies substantial if not essential compliance. Local governments as creatures of their state governments are heavily supervised by their states, except in the case of substantial home rule situations, and operate largely within an extensive web of top-down expectations.

For example, the top-down city of Beloit collaborates primarily with the state, and only occasionally is this activity based in bargaining and adjustment. It is not active in creating the horizontal linkages common to jurisdiction-based cities. Beloit's collaboration challenges are not unlike those of Cincinnati, but it does not seek or initiate broad community effort. Its federal activity, mainly CDBG, is highly compliance oriented. The city economy is based largely in one large papermaking equipment factory. Fortunately for Beloit, the demand for paper has not decreased with increased electronic communication. The city government must nevertheless pay attention to creating the linkages needed to keep this firm and its plants at the most advanced level of technology and workforce skill.

If Beloit wishes to grow an economy from one of dependence to interdependence, it will have to plan and forge broad alliances in the community. Attracting new globally oriented businesses or getting existing businesses to expand into global markets will be an increasingly important part of Beloit's survival. Such activity will require communitywide strategic planning and a great deal more targeted and specialized intergovernmental assistance to new and expanding businesses. The city must continue to help smaller manufacturers access trained workers and attain advanced equipment, which of course means more contacts with community and vocational-technical colleges, as well as with the state of Wisconsin. These firms will need the city and its LDC to broker loans, tax adjustments, permits, licenses, and grants in a way that benefits the jurisdiction. Because the city is in such a competitive position with surrounding communities, it will have to continue to devote a fair proportion of its CDBG entitlement to infrastructure improvement, even if that proportion must be arrived at through negotiation with federal officials.

Another example of a top-down city is Garfield Heights. The city occasionally seeks adjustments from the state and federal governments, but it seldom bargains over statutory or regulatory issues. The city engages some but not a great number of horizontal linkages. In many ways, Garfield Heights faces the typical challenges of all inner-ring suburbs, with its older and declining industries, deteriorating housing stock, and retail exodus to the outer suburbs. It does this virtually alone, because it has no public–private development agency and its Chamber of Commerce was inactive in the years leading up to the field study. At the time of the research, it did not employ any endogenous policy instruments.

Garfield Heights must promote the type of horizontal linkages that will bring in new manufacturing operations to replace those that have exited over the past few decades. One important collaborative challenge for Garfield Heights is to forge connections (schools, businesses, universities, institutes, workforce training) designed to take advantage of the advanced manufacturing boom in the Cleveland area. The city's location near important interstate exits, its open space, and its three industrial sites offer some opportunities, although these cannot be exploited without targeted vertical and community-level collaboration. Garfield Heights is becoming one of several close-in suburbs with easy-off, easy-on access to the central city, and thus is viewed increasingly as an important site for business services complexes. Its older homes may have to be supplemented with high-rise apartment buildings, also to take advantage of its location. However, as was mentioned in chapter 1, a large portion of this land is contaminated as former landfill sites. Garfield Heights will have to forge extensive collaborative relationships with the Ohio Environmental Protection Agency and U.S. Environmental Protection Agency before this situation is remedied, but such linkages will not come about without strategic action by the city. To effectively address the problem of the landfills, local officials must mobilize county and private interests, develop a plan, offer it to the state and federal government, and then negotiate over it.

Finally, Garfield Heights's connections with Cuyahoga County government and the Cleveland office of the state Department of Development will have to be extended to support business attraction and expansion. It will have to accelerate regional linkages in the area of business attraction if it wishes to remain a viable actor in the metropolitan economy. The challenges for Garfield Heights are vast, but not insurmountable, especially if the city asserts itself in the increasingly complex intergovernmental environment.

Challenges for Low-Activity Cities

The temporal relevance of intergovernmental abstinence has no doubt increased as the potential for activity has increased. Federal grants to cities increased during the 1960s and early 1970s, then gave way to increased regulation and loans. At the same time, new funding programs have been created for nongovernmental organizations, which in many cases reduce or eliminate the direct interaction between the federal government and cities. States accelerated their own more diverse assistance programs from the 1980s, adding them to their long-standing programs of mandates and regulations. At the horizontal level, proliferation of federal and state programs contributes to a more dense set of actors that are involved in all program activity, including economic development. Thus, just as the potential for activity is there, so is the potential to back away. As potential opportunities increase, so also do the barriers, the potential real costs, and the opportunity costs. Some jurisdictions say it is rarely worth the cost. Others say it is never worth the cost.

The economic challenges faced by the low-activity cities are, for some, much different from those faced by the case study cities. Contented cities are typically suburban cities that are located in a strong economic corridor. They are not often involved in much collaborative activity because it is not viewed as being necessary. Any activity that does occur is almost always at the community or horizontal level with promoters and businesses. Contented cities employ few economic development tools, and when they do it tends to be low engagement exhortation.

Collaborative challenges may emerge if the local economy turns sour. Officials from contented cities may not have the capacity to regenerate under conditions of serious fiscal stress, unemployment, poverty, and regional competition. Like central cities and small towns before them, however, that capacity will have to be developed. Becoming adept at exploiting their collaborative environment is one way to expand its capacity.

Reactive cities are low activity by choice and often because of political barriers and constraints in the city. Such cities often are located in the heart of an industrial and transportation hub that makes job activity less pressing, but always results in caution and concern on the part of local officials. Reactive cities strike a balance between vertical and horizontal connections, but that balance is often determined by economic tides, which rise and fall with those of nearby large cities. As these cities realize their interdependence with other cities in the economic corridor, increased horizontal collaboration should occur. If the city seeks to pursue a local economic strategy that places the jurisdiction's needs on a par with those of the outlying cities, increasing collaboration will result. Because of their cautious and calculated pursuit of collaboration, reactive cities can more easily adopt a jurisdiction-based approach than can contented cities.

Abstainers come in all shapes and sizes, although the majority of such cities are small and rural. Abstaining cities will often have declining population due to a very poor economy. As a result of being in a nonurban corridor, they have very few jobs to replace their shrunken agricultural economies. The administrative capacity of abstainers is low, so there is rarely anyone in the city to promote economic development activity, write grants, apply for loans, or pursue nongovernmental organizations for policymaking or resource-exchange purposes. The challenge for abstainers is clearly survival, one that, unlike some of the more active small towns in the study, they do not meet with action. Without mobilizing the community and without seeking external investments and resources, abstaining cities will no doubt experience further population loss and, at best, perpetual sustenance without prosperity.

The Relevance of Jurisdiction-Based Management in American Federalism

Decades ago, writing in *The American System*, Morton Grodzins (1966) characterized the policentric nature of the political system and its party dynamics as one possessing the "multiple crack." He was referring not only to numerous openings or fissures through which individuals and groups make their views known, but also to the multiple opportunities for individuals and groups to strike at government in an attempt to influence policy. "The normal process of policy-making is one in which individuals and groups take their crack at influencing governmental policy at literally uncountable points in the legislative and administrative process" (pp. 14–15). Since Grodzins wrote these words, policymaking and administrative activity at all levels of government have accelerated, and the number of potential collaborators has clearly increased. He could not have anticipated how appropriate the metaphor of the multiple crack would be to jurisdiction-based governing in the twenty-first century.

This study demonstrates many manifestations of the multiple crack and suggests an extension of the "crack" to encompass policymaking and administrative activity in local jurisdictions. The findings presented in this book are unequivocal: Many city officials design and administer programs outside the "boundaries" of organizations and jurisdictions. But managers in jurisdiction-based cities go beyond simply spanning boundaries. These officials consciously and purposively exploit the multiple crack by allowing—indeed, inviting—groups such as other jurisdictions, government agencies, and nongovernmental organizations to take their "wallops or smacks at government" as part of the administrative process (Grodzins 1966, 14). For jurisdiction-based cities, the multiple crack is an opportunity for improving governance rather than simply a description of the complexity of the political process.

This research demonstrates that there is a substantial diffusion of federal power in multijurisdictional and multiorganizational programs. Some cities allow this diffusion to dictate local policymaking, others ignore it. Jurisdiction-based cities capitalize on it. Because each unit in the federal system is to some degree a legally independent jurisdiction (or a legally chartered organization), it logically follows that some power is retained within a unit that has a program role. Federal and state programs definitely influence subnational behavior and result in legal, fiscal, and policy compliance, but it is also a "variable, not a constant, and cannot be understood if the interactions between program managers and thousands of local or state implementing agencies are ignored" (Anton 1984, 45). If it were not so, we would not find such widespread evidence of bargaining, statutory or regulatory adjustment, or all of the actions that originate within jurisdictions.

Does the emergence of jurisdiction-based management signal a revival of cooperative federalism? The three active models of managing federalism portrayed in this book indicate that there is far more horizontal and vertical jurisdictional interaction than meets the eye. Our data suggest that managers regularly and often routinely work their way through the maze of federal and state programs, propose adjustments, live with impediments, and achieve some successes in advancing jurisdictional interests. Managers do comply with standards and regulations, but they also negotiate, propose adjustments, and network among one another. Though our quantitative research was unable to directly measure the degrees of success of local officials in working the system, the qualitative portion suggests that among active jurisdictions there are numerous instances of making accommodations along the implementation chain. So again, does this evidence, along with new federal and state program enactments, suggest a renewal of the old cooperative federalism?

During the early period in the formal study of intergovernmental relations, the dominant theme in grants and other means of interjurisdictional exchange was a more balanced "work your way through together" mode of operation. As was noted in chapter 2, Jane Perry Clark's research in the 1930s found that there was much mutual exploration and sharing of ideas between state and federal officials, offering a "solution of the difficulties caused by the governmental attempt to regulate the centripetal forces of modern industrial life and the centrifugal elements of state interest and tradition" (1938, 9). Two groups of scholars who studied the intergovernmental system in the 1950s advanced the model of cooperative federalism. The first group was headed by William Anderson at the University of Minnesota. They found that in areas of national government involvement, money was transmitted with some rules and standards but with a minimal amount of supervision and a maximum amount of interactive solution. "They usually worked together in trying to get changes in standards, rules, budgets and personnel requirements to advance the service" (Anderson 1960, 62). Also, there was an absence of "crackdown" orders from federal to state agencies. In fact state and local officials welcomed the presence, advice, and help of federal field officials.

The second group was Morton Grodzins's University of Chicago Federalism Workshop, where his *The American System* (1966) ushered in the "marble cake" analogy as a way of depicting multiple overlapping functions, where sharing of administration was the norm in grants and many other arenas. There was national supervision but with state and local discretion, through mutual accommodation, and with state and local officials participating in the setting of agendas. The most noted of this group was Daniel Elazar, who in several volumes introduced the idea of collaboration in federalism, a management approach he considered consistent with federal democracy. The key is the notion that in a noncentralized system, problems need to be worked out in ways that are not conducive to hierarchical supervision, but through adjustments that respected subnational, historical, and cultural traditions, invoking a political interaction: "*Most* important actors are involved in the *most* important details of *most* steps in problem definition, planning, programming, budgeting, implementation and evaluation of *most* post policies of mutual interest to them through the political process" (Elazar 1984, 9; italics in original).

Cooperative federalism is said to have been largely set aside by the growth of federal programs, the expansion of rules and regulations, and particularly the widespread use of intergovernmental regulation. Kincaid (1990, 148) concludes that federalism became less cooperative in the 1970s and 1980s due to numerous preemptions of state and local government authority, continued federal aid reductions, fewer constitutional barriers to federal actions, the weakening of the political party system, and media nationalization. Zimmerman (1992, 11) also accords the end of cooperative federalism to the growth of such national action, particularly to preemptions through minimum standards legislation. At the same time, states have also become more powerful vis-à-vis local governments. The increase of federal–state programming—particularly through the deemphasis of federal–local programs since the 1980s, the attempt to come to grips with more intractable problems of modern life, greater pressure on states to deal with metropolitan problems, and states' ability to raise greater amounts of tax money for revenue-sharing purposes—has put a strain on working partnerships on a state–local basis (Zimmerman 1995, 203–4).

The evidence presented here would suggest that beneath the surface appearance of an eroding cooperative federalism, daily and routine work also defines a system that is cooperative. It includes both enactments and actions. First, there is the new focus on the states. Three decades of institutional, procedural, and fiscal changes have moved states beyond the mere role of intermediary in the system to become policy actors and innovators in their own right (Walker 2000) in which interactive roles with local governments suggest "a continuance of pre-1964 cooperative federalism."

Second is the federally generated corresponding shift in collaborative venues to the state–local and interlocal levels identified throughout this study. The federal presence, while real, is limited in ability to control the chain of players like the state administering agency, a local government and nongovernmental organization contractee, the vendor and delivery agent, and the client and beneficiary. Reductions in the federal workforce, reduced travel and oversight resources, increased programming, and more detailed regulations might seem to work against the opportunity to cooperate but also against the ability to fully control.

Third, one must also factor in the growing sophistication of managers at the street level dealing with external programs. They are not only program technical experts, but have developed an "intergovernmental technology" that includes not only how to comply, but also how to interpret, propose, adjust, and maybe even sidestep. It is a cumulative working knowledge, passed on to subsequent generations, that is derived from working with grants, regulations, contracts, cooperative agreements, and the like (Agranoff 2001). So perhaps there is a persistence in intergovernmental cooperation, but with many essential interactions occurring steps away from the more visible and more dramatic federal–state contacts.

As Derthick recently observed, "In studying American Federalism, the analyst is forever asking whether the glass is half-empty or half-full" (2000, 27). Answers, she concludes, "are to be found more in the day-to-day operations of intergovernmental relations" than in highly visible national actions. Jurisdiction-based management extends our common ideas of cooperation in a federal system by showing how the day-to-day operations of city-level governing in the twenty-first century are the very essence of "federal" in practice. It is the very essence of autonomy under federalism. In this context, we find cities pursuing their strategic objectives while operating within a broader environment of multiple governments.

This exemplifies what the framers of the Constitution intended by the federal (i.e., nonnational) features of the new system. If local governments are totally bound to national obligations and completely subservient to "higher-level" objectives, federalism in the most basic sense does not exist.

8

The Future of Public Management and the Challenge of Collaboration

The contacts, activities, policy tools, and other connections discovered in this study lead us to conclude that the capacities required to operate successfully in collaborative settings are different from the capacities needed to succeed at managing a single organization. The classical, mostly intraorganizational-inspired management perspective that has guided public administration for more than a century is less directly relevant to multiorganizational, multigovernmental, and multisectoral forms of governing. If collaborative management is a function distinct from that of single-organization, hierarchical management, as our data clearly indicate and many eminent scholars have suggested (Kettl 1996; Milward 1994; O'Toole 1997c), then focused research on and improved conceptualization of this core public activity must be accelerated. However, it is not enough to demonstrate that collaboration exists. Public administration and management is an action field, what some have called a design science (Simon 1981), and research in this field should seek to provide workable knowledge and prescribe action, despite the limitations of doing so (Lindblom 1990).

This final chapter addresses such issues. The work being done in cities like Cincinnati and Ithaca suggests that collaborative management is in need of a knowledge base equivalent to the organizational paradigm of bureaucratic management that can both inform and improve practice. Using our empirical research as a guide, we here build on the theoretical approaches introduced in chapter 2 and present a future agenda for developing such a knowledge base for collaborative management. We ask a simple question: What does the field need to know to adequately prepare public managers to meet their need to engage in collaboration?

First, we consider the types of skills that might be important for collaborative management. Second, we investigate decision making in collaborative settings and speculate how it might differ from decision-making models derived from applied behavioral science models. Third, we consider factors that may help multiple players cohere into a workable structure to design and carry out programs, such as trust and the perception of a common purpose. Fourth, the issue of power, authority, and influence in collaborative settings is addressed. Fifth, the venerable accountability issue is discussed. Sixth, we explore the issue of whether collaboration produces results that would otherwise not have occurred; that is, whether collaboration adds value to the design and delivery of public programs. The light that is ultimately shed on these issues builds on our research. It should contribute to a greater understanding of collaborative management both for scholars considering the role of collaborative institutions in public administration and for public managers who must operate in such settings.

Future Research on Collaborative Management

Skills for Collaborative Public Management

When a public- or private-sector manager—perhaps a full-time director of a city department of economic development or an executive director of a chamber of commerce—is observed operating in his or her "home" organization, we can clearly describe, in the most general sense, what activities are being performed at any given time and, for the most part, why they are being performed. A vocabulary or nomenclature that has developed and has been refined over many decades can be used to describe the manager's daily activities within the single-organization, bureaucratic structure. Many textbooks devoted to single-organization behavior and public management describe tasks such as planning, organizing, and leading, and suggest time-tested remedies to fix intraorganizational problems. Managers know, for example, that if an organization appears to lack direction, better planning may be the answer; and if communication and coordination are poor across departments within an organization, a reorganization could be in order. To inform the practice of collaborative public management, future research must strive to develop a similar functional and conceptual parallel to traditional management processes.

How does a manager determine the right collaborative partners? Is there an identifiable calculus or set of decision rules that each manager has, or should have? Tapping the skills, knowledge, and resources of participants and stakeholders in the collaborative arrangement is a fundamental managerial act (Gray 1989; Innes and Booher 1999; Lipnack and Stamps 1994). Such players and resources are the integrating mechanisms of managing in collaborative settings. According to Scharpf, selective activation of potential participants in such collaborative arrangements as horizontal networks is "an essential prerequisite for successful interorganizational policy formation and policy implementation" and, if performed correctly, is based on "the correct identification of 'necessary participants'" as well as the willingness of these potential participants to devote resources and not be influenced by players who may have other interests at stake (1978, 364). We know from the urban regime literature (Stone 1989; Stoker and Mossberger 1994) that governing coalitions in cities must "bring together resources that are adequate to address the identifying agenda"; otherwise, the arrangements will not be effective (Stone et al. 1999, 3). Because the probability of involving the wrong player or the wrong mix of resources is greater than zero (see Landau 1991), this task is of crucial importance for managerial effectiveness.

How does the collaborative process begin, continue, and end? Can a city official establish and influence the operating rules and procedures of a collaborative arrangement without violating the prevailing values and norms of collaborative players (Kickert and Koppenjan 1997; Klijn 1996; Gray 1989; Mandell 1990; O'Toole 1997a)? If so, how is this done? Some suggest that a manager can frame the policymaking context by introducing ideas or offering an alternative perspective on the problem in hopes of creating a shared purpose or vision (Mandell 1988; Lipnack and Stamps 1994). Managers like the city manager of Woodstock must synthesize players—who may have conflicting goals, different perceptions, and dissimilar values—into a coherent whole charged with fulfilling a specific strategic purpose. They must achieve cooperation among actors while preventing, minimizing, or removing blockages to that cooperation, thereby lowering the costs of inter-action, which can be substantial in collaborative settings.

Previous theorizing about collaborative management suggests a number of synthesizing mechanisms that should be explored empirically: promoting information exchange (Innes and Booher 1999; O'Toole 1988; Mossberger and Hale 1999), changing incentives to cooperation (Kickert, Klijn, and Koppenjan 1997), changing the positions and roles of participants (Klijn 1996), and facilitating effective communication among participants (Mandell 1990). In addition, officials of the case study cities spoke of how it is often necessary to induce some players to make a commitment to the joint undertaking—and to maintain that commitment (Innes and Booher 1999; Mandell 1990). Officials sometimes must sell an idea to potential collaborative players to mobilize commitment and support for the collaboration and its purposes.

Although for analytical purposes researchers could distinguish among numerous behaviors or tasks, local officials indicate that the act of managing collaboratively should not be viewed as a series of distinct encounters. Just as a manager in a single organization may lead, plan, and organize simultaneously within the context of a particular goal, so too are multiple behaviors utilized in collaborative settings. For example, the removal of a player can have myriad effects on the network. Alternatively, if the attitudes and behaviors of some players are stifling productive interaction, the manager must somehow create an environment within which greater interaction can take place. Similarly, synthesizing the players into a collaborative whole is often accompanied by a conscious attempt to frame the players' perceptions of the interaction.

Beyond identifying these tasks, research must discover the set of managerial decision rules that collaborative managers currently follow in their quest for performance. What does a public manager do when trust is lacking among the many players? What should she do? What does a public manager do when the goals of the collaborative players are conflicting? What should he do? What are the best mechanisms to improve decision making, to increase productivity, or to address a slacker in vertical or horizontal collaboration? Broadly, what are the critical occurrences or situations affecting collaborative operations, and what are the preferred responses to these situations? Extensive observation and in-depth interviewing are required to answer these critical questions.

Group Development in Collaboration

Hierarchies have long been viewed as an effective means to coordinate and control actions across people, knowledge, time, and space. Even before bureaucratization emerged as the organization form of choice during the Industrial Revolution, hierarchical, top-down structuring of production processes was in widespread use as a coordinating mechanism. The coordinating properties of markets and hierarchies are well-documented (Powell 1990), but we know little about the scale of group development that is required to make decisions and reach solutions jointly. Weiner (1990, 456) suggests that in transorganizational (collaborative) management, techniques similar to organization management are normally employed: group problem solving, force-field analysis, action planning, team building, process consultation, and others. However, the two domains are distinctive in at least two ways.

First, in collaborative management, empowerment is based on information rather than authority. As has been shown, there are no formal subordinate relationships in collaboration. Second, collaboration involves representatives from several organizations working together to fashion new systems, using the flow of information to link the overall system. Multiple cultures, procedures, and divisions of labor, even in small towns such as Salem or Ithaca, are incorporated into the collaboration (Clegg and Hardy 1996). Organization representatives must shed some of their ideology and forge a multiorganizational implementation technology to reach a mutual understanding that transcends the coordination and communication resulting from hierarchy. Operating collaboratively clearly requires the application of standard applied behavioral science techniques—but is more required? We speculate that a kind of "groupware" must be developed in successful collaborative settings. Groupware refers to intergovernmental, interorganizational, and interagency task group development for jointly reaching solutions, but which incorporates principles that are qualitatively different from interorganizational coordination or mutual adjustment.

One possible ingredient in the information flows that are necessary for developing groupware is social capital (for related definitions, see Coleman 1990; Fountain 1998; and Putnam 1993). Social capital is essential to enable groups of disparate representatives to work toward sharing resources held by individual organizations. Fountain (1998) argues that the important elements of social capital are trust, norms, and operations of the network. She suggests that tools to enhance the creation of social capital need to be a part of policies promoting innovation and productivity growth. Because social capital has been associated with increased innovation in many industries, it seems likely that in policy contexts where service production is required, a critical determinant of collaboration may be the quantity and quality of social capital developed through interaction.

Shared learning is another potentially fundamental component of groupware, and thus of effective collaboration. Collaborative processes among organizational representatives can be viewed as joint learning systems. That proved to be an important product of the Beloit 2000 riverfront development process. The idea is similar to Senge's (1990, 3) learning organization, "where people continually expand their capacity to create the results they truly desire, where new and expansive patterns of thinking are nurtured, where collective aspiration is set free, and where people are continually learning how to learn together." To Innes and Booher (1999), the most important consequences occur not at the end, but during the discussion process itself. An environment conducive to learning is created when collaborative players follow principles of civil discourse, where all are listened to, and where conditions of sincerity, comprehensibility, accuracy, and legitimacy are met. The jurisdiction-based manager facilitates collaborative discussions that create shared meaning, result in mechanisms other than arguing and debating, bring out added knowledge, and enable participants to formulate ideas and processes for joint action. Senge (1990) suggests that learning organizations require five core disciplines: personal mastery, mental models, shared vision, team learning, and systems thinking. Like learning organizations, perhaps, collaboration may require similar collective cognitive capabilities.

Groupware may also be developed through negotiation. Bardach (1998, 232) refers to a "culture of joint problem solving" that includes an "ethos that values equality, adaptability, discretion and results." Part of this ethos is to overcome bureaucratic tendencies (hierarchy, stability, obedience, procedures). Bardach even suggests that negotiation is the core of collaboration when he argues that "collaboration is a matter of exhortation, explication, persuasion, give and take. To collaborate is to negotiate" (p. 238). Negotiations have to take into account all interests—personal, organizational, and the collective (Galaskiewicz and Zaheer 1999). Collaborative managers, as is the case with the mayor of Garfield Heights, help players reach a mutual understanding of a latent opportunity to create public value and recognize that collective efforts and risks are manageable so that the process of collaboration can proceed (Bardach 1998). The success of a collaborative effort may depend on players negotiating and exploring the critical issues, and in general making a significant effort to find creative responses to differences (Innes and Booher 1999). Such processes are supported by the dualism of the agency delegate to the network and the network delegate to the agency being the same person—the collaborative manager. Researchers could draw from Weiner (1990), who suggests that such dual loyalty necessitates a totally new mind-set and value stance for managers working collaboratively.

A number of behavioral process questions remain that must be addressed if scholarship hopes to inform practice. Previous observation and our empirical evidence suggest that information is an important ingredient in interorganizational transactions. Is the information that participants bring to the network an empowering or overpowering force in collaborative discussion? Social capital's contribution to groupware also raises questions. Is social capital necessary to reach collaborative results, or can other features (resources, legal requirements, and a perception of mutual gain) make up for capital deficiencies? Is social capital sufficient to reach mutual outcomes? Can collaboration occur when social capital is low or absent from an interagency situation? Does joint learning have new and different dimensions? If joint learning through process is the key, what is the process? If negotiations are part of the collaborative process, to what extent are collaborative negotiations different from those between organizations? In the process, when does mutual decision making based on joint learning end and negotiation begin? Does a negotiation imbalance (too much negotiation) reduce the chances of creative synergy? Most important, how does negotiation within the network contribute to the development of group abilities to recognize and solve problems?

Cohesion in Collaboration

Since Max Weber, scholars and public managers have explicitly or implicitly accepted that legal authority vested in a hierarchy keeps people operating in a bureaucratic structure and is the reason why they allow themselves to be led, as long as expectations are within a zone of acceptance. Collaboration is not based on the legal authority paradigm, however. When people from different organizations are not in legally bounded authority relationships, why would they decide to come to the table, work together on problem clarification and solutions, reach agreement, and follow through on implementation? The evidence on linkages presented in chapter 5 demonstrates that cities establish collaboration for many purposes, but often involving certain players for most purposes. This multiple contact with particular players suggests that trust, common purpose, mutual dependency, and other factors of collaborative management may be analogous to the cohesive force of legal-rational authority in bureaucracies.

The most tangible and thus most plausible explanation for cohesion is found in the resource-dependent relationship of the manager and the collaborative players. Cities function in an interactive, dependent environment based in resource exchanges (Pennings 1981). Most collaborative players are thus strategically interdependent; but, as shown throughout the book, some are more resource dependent than others (Yuchtman and Seashore 1967). This orientation is the defining activity and becomes a force of cohesion within the collaboration. Although the extent of commitment and resources shared may vary greatly, all players possess some measure of resources (funding, expertise, support, and human resources), to move the collaborative process forward.

It is commonly accepted that, in the absence of the legal charter, people join, work, and remain together because some element of trust exists. Trust in collective behavior is linked to the obligation not to do unnecessary harm to another party's interests. Such fiduciary obligations are said to be essential in holding collaborative linkages together because it involves the obligation to attend broadly to the concerns of specific others beyond the boundaries of specific, measurable transactions (Barber 1983). Trust does not require common belief, but rather obligation and expectation. In addition to being competent and aware of how and where to attain needed resources, collaborative managers must certainly take great care not to exploit or betray purposes and to show respect and fairness to collaborative players (Ferguson and Stoutland 1999). When there is more trust, there is less need to constantly monitor compliance (Alter and Hage 1993). Indeed, Fountain (1994) suggests that trust as a social relation may be on a par with exchange as a lubricant of collaborative behavior.

Managers may also find that the public or collective good, as manifested in a shared belief or common purpose, contributes to holding the collaboration together (Alter and Hage 1993). Mandell (1999, 46) refers to the sum of these qualities as a *program rationale*, which describes the "mind-set" or commitment to the whole that holds a linkages network together when traditional methods of coordination and control are not operative. From this perspective, program structures are not merely aggregates of individual organizations; the collaborative management itself is more critical than the players, and focus on the individual players is relevant only for gaining understanding of how and why each player contributes to the overall effort (Provan and Milward 1991).

Leadership and/or guidance ability is another potential contributor to collaboration that is suggested by our research but has not been explored empirically. Collaborative leadership and management require the "principles of 'soft' guidance" as a replacement for command and control (Windhoff-Héntier 1992), but the degree to which they are critical in holding the linkages together is unknown. All the managerial tasks discussed above take advantage of network self-management propensities, using minimal coercion and resources, "balancing social forces and interests and enabling social actors and systems to organize themselves" (Kooiman 1993, 256). Bardach's (1998) thorough examination of success and failure in collaborative settings relies heavily on various aspects of capacity building, but points most heavily to leadership as the central factor holding interagency collaboration together. It is important to note that these are not personal attributes, talents, or conditions of individuals, but roles in a system of strategic interactions. Cohesion in the network from this perspective is thus dependent on the integrative, creative, and purposive opportunities seized by those applying the craft of collaborative public management.

Clearly, any prescriptions regarding collaborative cohesion must offer an equivalent to hierarchical authority. But the answer may not lie along a single channel. Is it possible that more than one of these cohesive forces can be at work within the same network configuration? Mutual dependence clearly holds collaborative linkages together; we have indicated throughout this book the types of resources that are exchanged in local economic development. A program rationale is easily established when a collaborative venture benefits all players. The obligations and expectations regarding trust within the collaboration developed over time, even among competing players. Our site visits revealed the occasional catalytic leader or project manager who builds collaborative capacity and holds together the various linkages on behalf of the city. If numerous factors help to cohere disparate linkages, then questions other than "What is it?" may be relevant. For example, what measures of shared purpose, trust, resource dependence, and steering or collaborative capacity are needed to hold networks together? How do jurisdiction-based managers use each cohesive force to help attain collaborative goals? Is an operating deficit in one cohesive area complemented by a surplus in another? At what point do deficits in one or more of these cohesive factors contribute to a functional collapse of cohesion, and thus to a collapse of the network?

Power and Influence

Our data do not shed light on a neglected and often misunderstood aspect of collaborative processes: power. One of the weaknesses of our empirical approach and the approaches of many researchers before us is to treat linkages as if power and influence are a constant. A continuation of this empirical oversight could prove to be a major obstacle to explaining collaborative public management. Power is typically viewed as the ability to compel action by players under circumstances where all persons have dual responsibilities to both home organizations and the joint effort. A focus on joint decision forces implies coequal, interdependent, patterned, and ostensibly equally weighted relationships.

Indeed, our tendency in this research has been to weight each linkage the same; collaborating with the chamber of commerce is viewed as one linkage, county government another linkage, and so on. Different players bring different resources, but our quantitative measures—and the measures of other research—do not capture the level of power and influence that various players may possess, thus masking the possible existence of coercive behavior in collaborative management. It is possible that in some cities a chamber of commerce or a local development corporation will occupy different role positions and wield a mightier sword than the city government or other collaborative players. Some sit in positions with extensive opportunity contexts, filling "structural holes" (Burt 1992, 67), creating unequal opportunity, while others may be less willing or able players. Ithaca's local development corporation, Greater Gratiot Development Incorporated, appears to occupy such a niche. Organizational representatives also differ with regard to the resource dependencies they may bring to the network (Rhodes 1981), leading to power differences. Clegg and Hardy suggest that "we cannot ignore the facade of 'trust' and the rhetoric of 'collaboration' used to promote vested interest through the manipulation and capitulation by weaker partners" (1996, 679). Power concerns should be at the core of any general theory of public management in collaborative settings, because we must know whether power moves hinder the kind of synergistic creativity that reciprocal relationships are purported to produce.

Power in collaboration can be portrayed neutrally, or at least dualistically, as a property that either prevents or facilitates action. Schapp and van Twist refer to individual veto power in collaborative networks because "actors in the network are able to cut themselves off from the steering interventions of other actors" (1997, 66–67). Such veto power could be used in different ways: to exclude certain actors, to ban certain points of view, or to put potential actors outside of the network. Conversely, there is an enabling component to network power. The use of power does not always include getting players to act. In the "social production" model identified by Stone and his associates (1999, 354), it is assumed that social forces (and society's most vexing problems) are characterized by a lack of coherence and that many activities are autonomous and require numerous middle-range accommodations instead of a cohesive system of control.

In any collaborative setting where one player does not and cannot develop control over another, the main concern is how to bring about enough cooperation among disparate community elements to get things done. This is a "power to" that, under most conditions of interdependence and complexity, characterizes situations better than "power over." The social production model juxtaposed against veto power illustrates just two dimensions of power in networks. As any political scientist can relate, power has many faces. At a minimum, it can inhibit or facilitate collective action, including action within networks.

We must learn how power is acquired and challenged in the formation of collaborative efforts. Some observers characterize collaboration explicitly as power sharing. Different types of power are critical to collaboration: (1) the power to mobilize; (2) the power to organize; (3) the power to strategize; (4) the power to control information; and (5) the power to exercise influence or authorize action, which is paramount to implementation (Alinsky 1971; Gamson 1975; Gray 1999; Bachrach and Baratz 1963). The same player will rarely exercise all types of power in truly coequal settings. Instead, temporary redistributions of power will occur throughout the process, enabling stakeholders with differential power levels to engage in domain transformation. In less than coequal settings, alternative strategies of engagement can also characterize involvement—for example: compliance, when one organization bows to the wishes of the other (or others) because of resource leverage or undermining of legitimacy; contention, the act of challenging practices held or decisions made by more powerful players; and contesting, or engaging other stakeholders, particularly more powerful ones. Also, equality of power can be eroded when a player invokes formal or legal authority, controls the flow and distribution of resources, or co-opts the lower power players. Power is clearly a property that can facilitate or inhibit collaborative action.

Power is obviously a more complicated concern in collaboration than can possibly be depicted with our data. We raise it as an important attribute of management because so much of the rhetoric of collaboration emphasizes processes that imply mutuality or where interests are checked (or expected to be) at the door. One popular book on network management, for example, extols five key features of mutuality: unifying purpose, independent members, voluntary links, multiple leaders, and work at integrated levels (Lipnack and Stamps 1994). It says much less about the ability of key stakeholders to dominate or how such domination may erode unifying purpose, the independence of members, and so on.

Some empirical research has revealed the reality of power. The work of Milward and Provan (1998) found that network effectiveness was associated with a single player—community mental health centers—acting as a monopoly provider that dominated both service delivery and funding provisions for others in the network. Harrison and Weiss (1998) also demonstrated the utility of using a central, powerful player at the head of a network (hub and spoke configuration) to connect the residents of low-income neighborhoods to employers with training positions.

The power issue is an important aspect of collaboration that managers must understand, much like they must know leadership skills in single organization settings. However, there is much that we do not know. What techniques can be used to channel negative engagement from players into positive engagement? Do collaborative administrators manage power discrepancies differently than they would in hierarchies? Is it possible to recognize when collaboration is breaking down because the power balance is breaking down? What can public managers do to channel power from players protecting their interests into social production? What are the negative effects on creative problem solving of the unequal application of power? Power concerns must be part of future research if scholars hope to provide realistic guidance to public managers.

Accountability of Collaborative Management

The issue of accountability involves the question of control and the difficulty of establishing accountability in collaborative management. Indeed, this is one of the most frequently raised questions in the public administration field in general (Kettl 1996; Milward 1996; Frederickson 1997; Radin 2002). In single-organization settings, do bureaucrats operate in accordance with executive direction and the policy preferences of those in authority to whom they report, melding personal responsibility with constitutional duty (Rohr 1989)? Or do they contradict the norms of representative democracy by assuming "too much" discretion and disregarding the important direction of legislators and elected officials of the executive branch (Burke 1986)? Such venerable issues are magnified for more complex collaborative settings, where multiple parties operate with limited authority and even less direct contact with executives and legislators. Is this strong concern with accountability issues in collaborative management warranted? Is there a demonstrable "leakage of authority" in collaborative settings (Bardach and Lesser 1996, 198)? If there is, can its impact be determined through empirical study?

The concern for loss of accountability in multiorganizational settings first emerged as contracting relationships were becoming plentiful. In such arrangements, there is some fear that the employees of contracting organizations will pursue purposes inconsistent with those of elected officials (Milward 1994). Because contractors assume a critical intermediary position in service delivery systems, they have autonomy from each of the other governmental players (Kettl 1993). Kettl describes the discrepancy between intent and reality in the contracting relationship:

> The philosophy of contracting out presumes that the basic relationship between government and contractor will be that of principal and agent. The contractor's job is to act as agent of the government's policy. The relationship is fractured, however, if contractors create independent political ties with policymakers and thus outflank their administrative overseers. In such cases contractors are less agents than partners, helping to shape the very design of the program, free of any significant oversight, and beneficiary of state and local governments' dependence on their performance. (1993, 176)

Two important factors render discussions of accountability in collaborative management unique. First, accountability relationships in multiactor collaboration are quite different from those found in the dyadic linkages of contracting or the bi-level interaction of layers of government. Myriad applications of principal–agent theory to contractual and extrajurisdictional activity exist in the literature (Waterman and Meier 1998). However, for settings where multiple interests—jurisdictional, organizational, sectoral— are involved in policy design and/or implementation, establishing just who is the principal and who are the agents is a near impossible, maybe even meaningless, exercise. As O'Toole points out in his description of interorganizational networks, "they do not have the formal wherewithal to compel compliance with such cooperative undertaking" (1997b, 445).

Second, because there is no obvious principal or agent in collaboration, and no exigent authority to steer the activities in harmony with elected officials, the issue of accountability is miscast. With no single authority, everyone is somewhat in charge, and thus everyone is somewhat responsible; all collaborative players appear to be accountable, but none is absolutely accountable. In addition, the expectations of being accountable to a legally constituted democratic entity are not consistent with collaborative linkages that may possess insufficient democratic legitimacy; interaction like the kind we have documented among civil servants and representatives of private interests, other governmental layers, and partnership organizations makes it very hard for representative bodies to influence policy. In general, perhaps the public sector's responsibility for affecting the public interest is compromised and limited by the use of collaborative policymaking and management.

However, it may be that collaboration forces us to shift our concern away from hierarchical accountability to notions of responsibility, responsiveness, and the fostering of democratic ideals. From this perspective, O'Toole asks, "Does networked public administration pose a threat to democratic governance or offer the prospect of its more complete attainment?" (1997b, 458). He suggests that consideration of the aforementioned dimensions offers a more complete assessment of the effect of networks and collaboration on democratic governance, and concludes that network management "provides both complications and opportunities to facilitate parts of the democratic ideal" (p. 458). In a similar call to redirect traditional public administration concerns with accountability, some argue that accountability means organizational systems based in oversight and reporting arrangements. This "accountability to" concern obfuscates issues of effectiveness and performance (Bardach and Lesser 1996). Accountability *for* means accountability for results, for setting wise priorities, for targeting, and for system modification and design. Accountability for these outcomes is the objective of the collaborative, and accountability *to* is the means to that objective. From this perspective, bureaucratic notions of accountability simply do not apply to collaborative processes, if they ever did in bureaucracies.

Because a control orientation is problematic for collaborative structures, how do managers maintain the advantages of collaboration while ensuring accountability? We cannot determine from our data whether the linkages instigated by city administrative officials are representative of the wishes of local elected officials. Recent research on natural resource management by Wondolleck and Yaffee (2000) suggests that collaborative processes should be developed as supplemental to, not exclusive of, normal decision-making processes. Regardless of which players are involved, decisions made collaboratively "still need to pass muster under legally derived administrative procedures" (p. 237). They also recommend that decisions could be reviewed by independent, ostensibly objective, sources and, where possible, that collaborative managers establish performance measures that capture the intent of policy objectives. Standard setting can create incentives for collaborative players to seek solutions that achieve the standard. Finally, elected officials and other stakeholders are too often uninformed about the results of collaborative decision making. Wondolleck and Yaffee suggest that home agencies of collaborative managers should monitor and evaluate the effectiveness of solutions created collaboratively.

Many descriptive and normative issues still must be sorted out. To whom or what *do* (should) collaborative players feel responsible? To whom or what *do* (should) collaborative players feel responsive? If we analyze a set of collaborative linkages as a single entity rather than as many pieces, how does personal responsibility get translated into accountability? Are there certain collaborative structures, such as hub–spoke structures (Harrison and Weiss 1998) and collaborative clusters built by jurisdiction-based managers, that are (or are perceived to be) more accountable because there is a single organization through which most information passes and from which the collaborative manager emerges? If so, does collaboration still require some single player who can be held accountable?

We must be able to measure the outcomes and performance of networks to assess how accountable a particular network is to its stakeholders and for achieving its stated goals (Wondolleck and Yaffee 2000). The groundbreaking work of Provan and Milward (1995; Milward and Provan 1998) and Meier and O'Toole (2001) in this regard is very important. How do we know if a collaboration is shirking its responsibility if we do not know what the players are doing or how well they are doing it? If there is variation within and across collaborative linkages in the level of personal responsibility assumed by the players, is performance affected? The most basic issues of network management are bound up in our ability to assess effectiveness and then compare that effectiveness against some baseline to which the network can be held accountable. The research presented in this book cannot assess the effectiveness or productivity of the many linkages we have discussed. As we show in the next section, the issue of collaborative effectiveness is fundamental yet has been incompletely addressed.

Effectiveness of Collaboration

Several questions concerned with effectiveness lead to consideration of the origin of collaborative public management. The critical issue is whether collaboration produces solutions and results that otherwise would not have occurred through single, hierarchical organizations. Is collaboration *required* to achieve solutions to particular problems? When the public demands action on certain issues, are multiple players drawn together to fulfill that demand because, if it is to be fulfilled, it can only be done through collaboration? Or when the public demands action on certain issues, do multiple players work jointly to fulfill that demand because governments will not do it?

Some dominant perspectives argue that the pace and quality of social change at this point in history are the primary determinants of the emergence of collaboration or that the types of problems societies face require collaborative responses. Over and above societal changes and the shift in the types of acceptable policy instruments used in governing, perhaps decisions made in collaborative arrangement are simply better decisions. Not better in the sense of more efficient—there is nothing particularly efficient about making decisions jointly—but better in the sense of being more effective, because those involved in any collaboration ideally are not merely steerers but also stakeholders, suppliers, clients, and even customers. If the basic problem and challenge of policymaking and strategy making in many policy settings is for multiple governmental and nongovernmental organizations to jointly steer courses of action and to deliver policy outputs that are consistent with the multiplicity of societal interests, then a policy decision that laboriously, even painfully, meets that test is bound to be viewed as the best decision. When all relevant interests are considered in decision making, then, at a minimum the decision will gain wider acceptance, which still may be the test of the best policy (Lindblom 1959).

To some degree, collaborative decision making can be viewed as more rational than individual decision making. Multiple parties means multiple alternatives to suggest and consider, more information available for all to use, and a decision system that is less bounded by the frailties of individual thinking. And decisions in such settings may not only be the product of a more rational process but may also occur as a result of a synergy that can develop when multiple players pursue a common solution. Synergy means that the commitment and interaction of the participants stimulate new alternatives that otherwise would not have been considered.

It is necessary to discover the key determinants of collaborative effectiveness. One critical independent variable in modeling the effectiveness of collaborative policymaking and administration is the actions of the manager (McGuire 2002). What is the explanatory value of the public manager in collaborative settings in comparison with the explanatory variables such as strategy and structure discussed throughout this book? How much of the variation in the effectiveness of collaborative arrangements is explained by these variables? This key variable—the manager—has been neglected in most empirical studies of collaborative public management. Current research focuses on strategy, structure, linkages, and players as potential correlates of collaborative effectiveness without measuring the value—positive or negative—of the actions taken by the public manager. If scholarship is intended ultimately to inform action, to provide guidance to managers operating in an increasingly complex and rapidly changing environment, more must be learned about the effectiveness of collaborative arrangement.

More empirical research is necessary to sort out the distinctive contribution of collaborative decision making. Is the emergence of collaboration in public policy and administration due to a shift in the types of policy instruments used by governments, as is suggested in chapter 6? Do we see a greater incidence of collaboration because of a shift in the level of political acceptability of some forms of governance? Conversely, do collaborative processes select policy instruments that are fundamentally different than those selected by bureaucracies? Does the choice to utilize collaboration emerge from the political calculus of government institutions, or is that choice predetermined by the natural forces of change? Research that examines how and why collaborative processes are effective within the context of particular policy and program areas is necessary to better understand what can be expected from such managerial forms in the future.

The Challenge to Collaborate

The core nature of collaboration as a task for public managers is clearly established. It is a natural consequence of the shift in work from labor intensity to knowledge-based production, with its emphasis on human capital. As was mentioned in chapter 2, Reich (1991) refers to this type of work as symbolic-analytic, with an emphasis on problem-identifying, problem-solving, and strategic brokering activities. Clarke and Gaile (1998) document the importance of this type of work in today's cities. In this study, we have established the importance of symbolic-analytic work in cross-organization venues. Collaboration is not something that is an "add on" to the job, but has become the job itself. The complexity of the task is also clear, when one considers the technicalities of public work (law, finance, engineering, planning, and politics, to name a few) along with the numerous government organizations, nongovernmental organizations, programs and instruments, and cross-cutting concerns (e.g., economic development now has a heavy environmental component) faced by the local manager. Shifts in policy and economic directions are expected to lead to even greater expectations to collaborate.

The challenge is partially fed by the many changes in the U.S. federal system indicated throughout. Moreover, as more federal programs change, potential opportunities to collaborate will further increase. Recent program changes such as the Temporary Assistance for Needy Families block grant, Children's Health Insurance Program, the amended Intermodal Surface Transportation Efficiency Act, and the Environmental Protection Agency's partnership agreements are expected to engender more linkages with the nonprofit and for-profit sectors, and to place more program responsibility in the hands of state and local officials (Schram and Weissert 1999). President George W. Bush's faith-based initiatives also fall into this category.

The picture cannot be completed without accounting for the actions of state governments, where new programs for social services, health, transportation, the environment, and economic development will also accelerate collaboration. In economic development, Eisinger (1995) reports a continuing increase in new state programs as well as a shift in program emphasis over time toward a more balanced approach among the new endogenous policies and the older industrial recruitment strategies. The increase in the number of new programs overall suggests that the pressure for collaboration will not abate. A national opinion survey of officials in cities with a population over 100,000 found that though local officials do not feel that greater flexibility or a large reduction of mandates, rules, and regulations exists, they are more positive in experiencing the involvement of private-sector and nonprofit organizations, and greater regional and interjurisdictional cooperation (Cole, Hissong, and Avidson 1999).

Collaboration expectations also increase because the substantive policy areas within which managers work become more complex and interdependent. The research discussed in this book shows the direct effect of the four-decade shift among states from exclusively locational strategies to encouraging and stimulating mixed approaches that include various entrepreneurial policy tools. Economic transformations faced by states and localities include globalization, a shift to knowledge and ideas as the source of competitive advantage, and the increasing importance of regional agglomerations and clusters (Toft and Audretsch 2000). These forces are putting greater pressure on governments to work with many entities: (1) businesses, as a way to enhance information technology infrastructure; (2) university clusters, to develop products and markets for science, engineering, and technology; (3) investors, to create research parks and to promote other place-friendly venues as potential industry clusters; and (4) whole industries, by using these other linkages to keep them prosperous. More and more devolution from state to local governments will compel cities to forge alliances with education and workforce development agencies, linkages between business and industry clusters, agreements with university research facilities, partnerships with schools, and general collaboration with regional bodies.

The need to survive within an ever-changing economy and evolving federal system works hand in hand with new approaches to public management—it has changed the nature of the enterprise. Cities like Cincinnati have to find new ways to manage with old partners and forge new alliances. Other central cities not only fight to remain afloat within their metropolitan areas and become globally competitive but also must deal with the loss of core manufacturing jobs, relatively high taxes, and limited green space for development. As a result, vertical links with state and federal governments accelerate, and more lateral contacts must be made with university research institutes, workforce development agencies, venture capitalists, and local entrepreneurs. The same holds true for smaller, nonmetropolitan cities like Salem. Partnerships with local development corporations and regional planning agencies, and extensive state and federal contacts, make small cities "big" in their strategic intergovernmental programs. But they will only be successful in terms of maintaining their rural economies if they can orchestrate collaboration with local manufacturers, educational institutions, and training providers, and can gain access to information infrastructure and emergent technology. Only these collaborative strategies will enable a small city to maintain its economy with new generations of manufacturing and commerce.

The expectation that there will be more of this type of activity in future public management leads us to a concern for future research and practical attention to theory and process. This study has empirically documented the frequency and regularity of collaborative management. Although not every public entity is so involved, not only are more and more entities collaboratively linked, but these boundary-spanning activities outside the formal organization involve increasing amounts of managerial time and effort.

The study has also advanced a new conceptual approach to understanding management across the boundaries of public organizations, that of jurisdiction-based management, which we consider to be a meaningful addition to intergovernmental and public management research. Intergovernmentally, it says that when managers act they do not just react or act within a constrained framework—top-down compliance or donor–recipient bargaining—but act strategically on their own behalf, or on behalf of their communities. In terms of management, the jurisdiction-based model suggests the importance of purposive, strategic activation that steers a course of action among partners, a form of managing for results through one's partners and contacts. In addition, many important findings about the activities and players in collaborative management have been advanced.

Together, the findings suggest that collaboration is a mighty complicated enterprise, for which we know there is more and more to be discovered, but its commonplace occurrence makes it a main arena of study in public management. Jurisdiction-based management is new and at the state of the art in this arena. There is no other conclusion but that the study of collaborative management is just beginning.

APPENDIX A
SURVEY DESIGN AND
ADMINISTRATION

This research is from a study of collaborative contacts and activities in 237 cities from the five states located in the East North Central (ENC) Census Bureau geographic division: Illinois, Indiana, Michigan, Ohio, and Wisconsin. The cases are drawn from a sample of localities in these states that responded to a nationwide mail survey sent out to 7,135 cities and 3,108 counties by the International City/County Management Association (ICMA) in May 1994. Questions on this survey addressed general economic development policies and practices. The questionnaire was sent to the chief administrative officer of all cities and counties with populations of 2,500 or more and to those cities and counties with populations under 2,500 that are recognized by ICMA as providing for an appointed position of professional management. This study restricts the analysis to the responding cities in the ENC census division.

Of the 1,349 cities in the ENC census division surveyed by ICMA, 313 responded. A second questionnaire addressing collaboration and economic development was designed and mailed in November 1994 by the authors to the chief administrative officers of the cities that responded to the ICMA economic development survey. All respondents from the 313 cities in the survey universe were aware that they were being surveyed again because of their response to the ICMA survey and that the results from both questionnaires would be linked and used to study collaboration and local economic development. The intent of this purposive sampling and multisurvey design was to capture the collaborative management actions of cities for which we had extensive local development data. Only five months separated the initial ICMA mailing and the mailing of the collaboration surveys, which contributed to the very high response rate of the second survey: 237 cities or 76 percent of those cities responding to the economic development survey. The final data set of 237 cities represents 17.6 percent of all ENC cities surveyed by ICMA.

The survey is buttressed by six in-depth case studies. A systematic, comparative case study methodology was employed (Agranoff and Radin 1991). After the mail survey was completed and tabulated, site visits were made to six responding cities that were high in collaborative activity. They were drawn from the five states and represent a mixture of small, medium-sized, and large cities. Also, the case study selections include both council–manager and mayor–council forms of government, as well as differences in metropolitan status. The cities selected, in descending order of size, are Cincinnati; Beloit, Wisconsin; Garfield Heights, Ohio; Woodstock, Illinois; Salem, Indiana; and Ithaca, Michigan.

It is important to underscore that both surveys emphasize managerial actions rather than attitudes. The ICMA survey is primarily designed to discern what development strategies cities actually adopt, whereas the second survey looks at collaborative actions involved in the pursuit of such strategies. Although such managerial functions are intuitively important to development officials, they are not well understood in any systematic way. Through the lens of city development policymaking, we hope to reveal vertical and horizontal intergovernmental dimensions to public management. Thus, the major concern is not with what officials think, but with how they carry out these dual actions.

The ENC geographic division of states being studied is an appropriate population for many reasons. First, these five states contain more cities than each of the other eight divisions, so the municipal composition of the division is broad and expansive. Second, the ENC division comprises states with a relatively large number of "small towns" with populations under 10,000. Small cities are often excluded from policy research, because, in most cases, data are unavailable, but this data set is able to include them. Third, the sample distribution of the cities utilized in the research "looks like America" in terms of the various sizes of the cities (see table A.1). In addition, the sample population proportions of each state vis-à-vis the entire sample are nearly in balance with the ENC population as a whole (see table A.2). Finally, the distribution of sample cities among the three location classifications used by the U.S. Census Bureau is similar to the national distribution, and the sample is divided evenly between cities that have a council–manager form of government and cities that have a mayor–council or some other form. The sample of 237 cities from five states compares surprisingly well with the ENC division as a whole and with the rest of the nation. The analyses conducted with these data can be expected to illustrate issues common to many cities across the country.

Table A.1. Comparative Sample Distribution by City

Classification	No. of Cities	Percentage of Cities	No. of Cities Reporting	Percentage of Cities Reporting
Total, all cities	6,571		237	
Population group				
More than 200,000	76	1.2	3	1.3
100,000–199,999	119	1.8	5	2.1
50,000–99,999	310	4.7	12	5.1
25,000–49,999	566	8.6	27	11.4
10,000–24,999	1,290	19.6	68	28.7
5,000–9,999	1,566	23.8	51	21.5
2,500–4,999	2,036	31.0	59	24.9
Less than 2,500	608	9.2	12	5.1

Note: The table includes all cities with populations of more than 2,500 and of less than 2,500 that are recognized by the International City/County Management Association as providing for an appointed position of professional management.

Table A.2. Comparative Population Distribution

State	Regional Population	Percentage of Regional Population	Sample Population	Percentage of Sample Population
Illinois	11,697,000	27.2	1,437,000	26.0
Indiana	5,713,000	13.3	1,085,000	19.6
Michigan	9,478,000	22.0	899,000	16.2
Ohio	11,091,000	25.8	1,557,000	28.1
Wisconsin	5,038,000	11.7	560,000	10.1
Total	43,017,000		5,539,000	

Note: "Regional" refers to the Census Bureau geographic division; see text.

APPENDIX B
ECONOMIC CHARACTERISTICS
OF THE SAMPLE CITIES

The sample cities that are located in the five states of the East North Central (ENC) Census subregion have experienced geographical and structural shifts in their economic base during the past several decades that figure prominently in the strategic direction of their development activity. What Eisinger calls the "decentralization of people and industry" describes the drastic shift since 1950 in population and jobs from the states located in the Northeast and Midwest Census Regions of the country to states in the South and West (1988, 55). Three of the sample states—Illinois, Michigan, and Ohio—experienced a net loss of persons from 1950 to 1995. The distribution of jobs throughout the country from 1970 to 1994 also shifted decidedly away from the East and Midwest sections of the country—including the sample region—toward the South and West (see table B.1). In 1970, the five sample states possessed nearly 21 percent of all nonfarm jobs in the United States, the most of any subregion, but by 1994 just 17.4 percent of all U.S. jobs were located in these states. During this period, the sample states experienced the second lowest job growth of the nine subregions (36.3 percent), a rate lower then the national mean growth rate and much lower than that in most South and West subregions.

Economic restructuring—the systematic shift in the distribution of jobs across industrial sectors—has also occurred over time in the sample cities. The vast bulk of the net job growth in the sample cities from 1970 to 1990 can be attributed to the service and finance sectors of the economy (see table B.2). Controlling for the rate of change in total employment during the same period, these were the only two sectors that saw jobs being created at a rate substantially greater than the overall rate of growth. Sample cities experienced a 50 percent loss in the number of manufacturing jobs

Table B.1. Historical Employment Distribution in Nine Census Subregions

Subregion	Percentage of U. S. Nonfarm Employment			Percentage of Job Growth	
	1970	1980	1994	1970–94	Relative Index
Northeast	6.4	6.0	5.4	37.0	60.2
Mid-Atlantic	20.0	16.5	14.5	17.0	27.7
East North Central	**20.6**	**18.5**	**17.4**	**36.3**	**59.1**
West North Central	7.6	7.6	7.6	62.8	102.1
South Atlantic	14.8	16.1	18.3	99.4	161.7
East South Central	5.4	5.7	6.0	78.5	127.7
West South Central	8.5	10.3	10.3	96.7	157.4
Mountain	3.8	4.9	5.9	153.3	249.4
Pacific	13.0	14.4	14.6	80.9	131.7
United States	100.0	100.0	100.0	61.5	100.0

over and above the total job loss in these cities, and suburban cities lost manufacturing jobs at a rate much greater than central cities (65 percent loss in small suburbs, 75 percent loss in large suburbs, and approximately 27 percent loss in central cities). However, compared with central cities, suburbs experienced nearly three times as much employment gain in the finance sector and more than twelve times as much growth in the services sector. Because the industrial sectors of manufacturing, finance, and services account for approximately two-thirds of all sample city employment, the significant differences between suburbs and the other cities are notable.

The cyclical shifts and fundamental changes in both the condition and overall structure of the Midwestern economy are extremely important for understanding the policy context of these sample cities. As a result of these changes, the states and their cities have become extremely active in pursuing economic growth through the development of innovative products and state-of-the-art manufacturing technologies. The 1994 State Policy Index compiled by the Corporation for Enterprise Development ranked all five sample states in the top eleven in terms of the quality and quantity of the state's overall development policy strategy. All of the states ranked in the top five in at least one subindex, with the subregion showing particular strength in the *Technology and Innovation* and *Local Economic Development Assistance* subindexes. Whereas

Table B.2. Mean Net Sectoral Employment Change by City Type, 1970–90

Industrial Sector	All	NM	SS	LS	CC
Manufacturing	−50.3	−19.0	−65.0	−75.9	−27.0
Wholesale and retail	4.7	−1.8	1.6	11.7	6.5
Construction	−10.8	−14.2	−10.6	−6.2	−16.1
Transportation, communications, and utilities	2.8	−3.0	−11.7	17.7	−3.0
Finance	87.7	58.0	102.6	120.0	36.9
Services	57.6	38.4	73.9	80.2	6.7
Government	−22.7	−9.3	−29.9	−33.3	−12.0

Note: NM = nonmetropolitan cities; SS = small suburban cities; LS = large suburban cities; CC = central cities. Figures are displayed as the mean percentage of gain or loss in each employment sector.

in 1985 the states ranked just fifth as a subregion in terms of new facilities and expansions, more new facilities and expansions as a proportion of employment were located in the sample states in 1994 than in any other subregion except for the East South Central one. In 1994, Ohio opened or expanded the most facilities of any state, whereas Wisconsin was ranked fifth. Although the sample cities experienced varying levels of economic distress and thus put forth varying levels of policy effort, the policy context of the five states as a whole was one of activity, innovation, and a strong focus on local government capacity.

REFERENCES

ACIR (U.S. Advisory Commission on Intergovernmental Relations). 1977. *Improving Federal Grants Management*. Washington, D.C.: U.S. Government Printing Office.

Agranoff, Robert. 1986. *Intergovernmental Management: Human Services Problem Solving in Six Metropolitan Areas*. Albany: State University of New York Press.

———. 1990. Managing Federalism Through Metropolitan Human Services Intergovernmental Bodies. *Publius: The Journal of Federalism* 20(1): 1–22.

———. 1998. Partnerships in Public Management: Rural Enterprise Alliances. *International Journal of Public Administration* 21(11): 1533–75.

———. 2001. Managing Within the Matrix: Do Collaborative Intergovernmental Relations Exist? *Publius: The Journal of Federalism* 31(2): 31–56.

Agranoff, Robert, and Valerie A. Lindsay. 1983. Intergovernmental Management: Perspectives from Human Services Problem Solving at the Local Level. *Public Administration Review* 43(3): 227–37.

Agranoff, Robert, and Michael McGuire. 1999. Expanding Intergovernmental Management's Hidden Dimensions. *American Review of Public Administration* 29(4): 352–69.

———. 2000. The Administration of State Government Rural Development Policy. In *Handbook of State Government Administration*, ed. John J. Gargan. New York: Marcel Dekker.

———. 2001. American Federalism and the Search for Models of Management. *Public Administration Review* 61(6): 671–81.

Agranoff, Robert, and Alex N. Pattakos. 1979. *Dimensions of Services Integration*. Rockville, Md.: Project SHARE.

———. 1985. Local Government Human Services. *Baseline Data Report* 17(1):1–20.

Agranoff, Robert, and Beryl A. Radin. 1991. The Comparative Case Study Approach in Public Administration. In *Research in Public Administration*, vol. 1., ed. James L. Perry. Greenwich, Conn.: JAI Press.

Alinsky, Saul D. 1971. *Rules for Radicals*. New York: Vintage Books.

Alter, Catherine, and Jerald Hage. 1993. *Organizations Working Together*. Newbury Park, Calif.: Sage.

Anderson, William. 1960. *Intergovernmental Relations in Review*. Minneapolis: University of Minnesota Press.

Anton, Thomas. 1984. Intergovernmental Change in the United States: An Assessment of the Literature. In *Public Sector Performance*, ed. Trudi Miller. Baltimore: Johns Hopkins University Press.

Austin, James E. 2000. *The Collaboration Challenge*. San Francisco: Jossey-Bass.

Bachrach, Peter, and Morton S. Baratz. 1963. Decisions and Non Decisions: An Analytical Framework. *American Political Science Review* 57: 641–51.

Barber, Benjamin. 1983. *The Logic and Limits of Trust*. New Brunswick, N.J.: Rutgers University Press.

Bardach, Eugene. 1998. *Getting Agencies to Work Together*. Washington, D.C.: Brookings Institution Press.

Bardach, Eugene, and Cara Lesser. 1996. Accountability in Human Services Collaboratives: For What? and For Whom? *Journal of Public Administration Research and Theory* 6(2): 197–224.

Bartik, Timothy J. 1989. Small Business Start-Ups in the United States: Estimates of the Effects of the Characteristics of States. *Southern Economic Journal* 55(4): 1004–18.

———. 1991. *Who Benefits from State and Local Economic Development Policies?* Kalamazoo, Mich.: W. E. Upjohn Institute of Employment Research.

Blakely, Edward J. 1994. *Planning Local Economic Development*, 2d edition. Thousand Oaks, Calif.: Sage.

Borins, Sandford. 1998. *Innovating with Integrity*. Washington, D.C.: Georgetown University Press.

Bowman, A. O'M. 1988. Competition for Economic Development Among Southeastern Cities. *Urban Affairs Quarterly* 23(4): 511–27.

Bozeman, Barry, ed. 1993. *Public Management: The State of the Art*. San Francisco: Jossey-Bass.

Bryson, John M. 1988. *Strategic Planning for Public and Nonprofit Organizations*. San Francisco: Jossey-Bass.

Bryson John M., and Barbara C. Crosby. 1992. *Leadership for the Common Good: Tackling Public Problems in a Shared-Power World*. San Francisco: Jossey-Bass.

Bryson, John M., and William D. Roering. 1996. Strategic Planning Options for the Public Sector. In *Handbook of Public Administration*, 2d edition., ed. James L. Perry. San Francisco: Jossey-Bass.

Burke, John P. 1986. *Bureaucratic Responsibility*. Baltimore: Johns Hopkins University Press.

Burt, Ronald. 1992. *Structural Holes: The Social Structure of Competition*. Cambridge, Mass.: Harvard University Press.

Cable, Gregory, Richard C. Feiock, and Jaehoon Kim. 1993. The Consequences of Institutionalized Access for Economic Development Policy Making in U. S. Cities. *Economic Development Quarterly* 7(1): 91–97.

Campbell, Andrew, and Michael Gould. 1999. *The Collaborative Enterprise*. Reading, Mass.: Perseus Books.

Campbell, Colin, and B. Guy Peters, eds. 1988. *Organizing Governance, Governing Organizations*. Pittsburgh: University of Pittsburgh Press.

Chrislip, David D., and Carl E. Larson. 1994. *Collaborative Leadership*. San Francisco: Jossey-Bass.

Clark, Jane Perry. 1938. *The Rise of New Federalism*. New York: Columbia University Press.

Clarke, Susan E., and Gary L. Gaile. 1989. Moving Toward Entrepreneurial Economic Development Policies: Opportunities and Barriers. *Policy Studies Journal* 17(3): 575–98.

———. 1992. The Next Wave: Postfederal Local Economic Development Strategies. *Economic Development Quarterly* 6(2): 187–98.

———. 1998. *The Work of Cities*. Minneapolis: University of Minnesota Press.

Clegg, Stewart R. 1990. *Modern Organizations: Organization Studies in the Postmodern World*. London: Sage.

Clegg, Stewart R., and Cynthia Hardy. 1996. Conclusion: Representations. In *Handbook of Organization Studies*, ed. Stewart R. Clegg, Cynthia Hardy, and Walter R. Nord. London: Sage.

Clingermayer, James C., and Richard C. Feiock. 1990. The Adoption of Economic Development Policies by Large Cities: A Test of Economic, Interest Group, and Institutional Explanations. *Policy Studies Journal* 18(3): 539–52.

Cole, Richard L., Rodney V, Hissong, and Enid Avidson. 1999. Devolution? Where's the Revolution? *Publius: The Journal of Federalism* 29(1): 99–112.

Coleman, James S. 1990. *Foundations of Social Theory*. Cambridge, Mass.: Harvard University Press.

Conlan, Timothy J. 1998. *From New Federalism to Devolution: Twenty-Five Years of Intergovernmental Reform*. Washington, D.C.: Brookings Institution Press.

Dahl, Robert A., and Charles E. Lindblom. 1953. *Politics, Economics, and Welfare*. Chicago: University of Chicago Press.

Derthick, Martha. 1970. *The Influence of Federal Grants: Public Assistance in Massachusetts*. Cambridge, Mass.: Harvard University Press.

———. 2000. American Federalism: Half-Full or Half-Empty? *Brookings Review* 18: 24–27.

Drucker, Peter. 1995. *Managing in a Time of Great Change*. New York: Truman Talley Books.

Dunsire, Andrew. 1993. Modes of Governance. In *Modern Governance: New Government-Society Interactions*, ed. Jan Kooiman. London: Sage.

Eisinger, Peter K. 1988. *The Rise of the Entrepreneurial State*. Madison: University of Wisconsin Press.

————. 1995. State Economic Development in the 1990s: Politics and Policy Learning. *Economic Development Quarterly* 9(2): 146–58.

Elazar, Daniel J. 1962. *The American Partnership: Intergovernmental Cooperation in the Nineteenth Century United States.* Chicago: University of Chicago Press.

————. 1964. Federal–State Collaboration in the Nineteenth-Century United States. *Political Science Quarterly* 79 (June): 248–81.

————. 1984. *American Federalism: A View from the States,* 3d edition. New York: Harper & Row.

Elmore, Richard F. 1985. Forward and Backward Mapping: Reversible Logic in the Analysis of Public Policy. In *Policy Implementation in Federal and Unitary Systems,* ed. Kenneth Hanf and Theo A.J. Toonen. Dordrecht: Martinus Nijhoff.

————. 1987. Instruments and Strategy in Public Policy. *Policy Studies Review* 7(1): 174–86.

Farr, Cheryl. 1989. Encouraging Local Economic Development: The State of the Practice. *Municipal Yearbook.* Washington, D.C.: International City/County Management Association.

Feiock, Richard C., and James C. Clingermayer. 1992. Development Policy Choice: Four Explanations for City Implementation of Economic Development Policies. *American Review of Public Administration* 22(1): 49–63.

Ferguson, Ronald F., and Sara E. Stoutland. 1999. Reconceiving the Community Development Field. In *Urban Problems and Community Development,* ed. Ronald F. Ferguson and William T. Dickens. Washington, D.C.: Brookings Institution Press.

Fleischmann, Arnold, and Gary P. Green. 1991. Organizing Local Agencies to Promote Economic Development. *American Review of Public Administration* 21(1): 1–15.

Fleischmann, Arnold, Gary P. Green, and Tsz Man Kwong. 1992. What's a City to Do? Explaining Differences in Local Economic Development Policies. *Western Political Quarterly* 45(3): 677–99.

Fosler, R. Scott. 1992. State Economic Policy: The Emerging Paradigm. *Economic Development Quarterly* 6(1): 3–13.

Fountain, Jane E. 1994. Trust as a Basis for Organizational Forms. Paper presented at a conference on Network Analysis and Innovations in Public Programs, University of Wisconsin, Madison, Sept. 30–Oct. 1.

————. 1998. Social Capital: Its Relationship to Innovation in Science and Technology. *Science and Public Policy* 25(2): 103–15.

Frederickson, H. George. 1997. *The Spirit of Public Administration.* San Francisco: Jossey-Bass.

————. 1999. The Repositioning of American Public Administration. *PS: Political Science and Politics* 32(4): 701–11.

Fry, Earl H. 1995. North American Municipalities and Their Involvement in the Global Economy. In *North American Cities and the Global Economy*, ed. Peter Karl Kresl and Gary Gappert. Thousand Oaks, Calif.: Sage.

Furdell, P. 1994. *Poverty and Economic Development: Views of City Hall.* Washington, D.C.: National League of Cities.

Galaskiewicz, Joseph, and Akbar Zaheer. 1999. Networks of Competitive Advantage. *Research in the Sociology of Organizations* 16(1): 237–61.

Gamson, William O. A. 1975. *The Strategy of Social Protest.* Homewood, Ill.: Dorsey Press.

Goggin, Malcolm L., Ann O'M. Bowman, James P. Lester, and Laurence J. O'Toole, Jr. 1990. *Implementation Theory and Practice: Toward a Third Generation.* Glenview, Ill.: Scott, Foresman/Little Brown.

Gray, Barbara. 1989. *Collaborating: Finding Common Ground for Multiparty Problems.* San Francisco: Jossey-Bass.

———. 1999. Theoretical Perspectives on Collaboration. Paper prepared for Collaboration Research Group, Technology University of Sydney, Sydney.

Green, Gary P., and Arnold Fleischmann. 1991. Promoting Economic Development: A Comparison of Central Cities, Suburbs, and Nonmetropolitan Communities. *Urban Affairs Quarterly* 27(1): 145–54.

Grodzins, Morton. 1966. *The American System*, ed. Daniel J. Elazar. Chicago: Rand McNally.

Gross, E. P., and J. M. Phillips. 1997. The Effect of Economic Development Agency Spending on State Income and Employment Growth. *Economic Development Quarterly* 11(1): 88–96.

Gulick, Luther. 1937. Notes on a Theory of Organization. In *Papers on the Science of Administration*, ed. Luther Gulick and Lyndall Urwick. New York: Institute of Public Administration.

Hale, George E., and Marian L. Palley. 1981. *The Politics of Federal Grants.* Washington, D.C.: Congressional Quarterly Press.

Hanf, Kenneth. 1978. Introduction. In *Interorganizational Policy Making: Limits to Coordination and Central Control*, ed. Kenneth Hanf and Fritz W. Scharpf. London: Sage.

Hanf, Kenneth, Benny Hjern, and David O. Porter. 1978. Local Networks of Manpower Training in the Federal Republic of Germany and Sweden. In *Interorganizational Policy Making: Limits to Coordination and Central Control*, ed. Kenneth Hanf and Fritz W. Scharpf. London: Sage.

Hanson, Russell L., and Michael B. Berkman. 1991. Gauging the Rainmakers: Toward a Meteorology of State Legislative Climates. *Economic Development Quarterly* 5(3): 213–28.

Harmon, Michael M., and Richard T. Mayer. 1986. *Organization Theory for Public Administration.* Glenview, Ill.: Scott Foresman.

Harrison, Bennett, and Marcus Weiss. 1998. *Workforce Development Networks.* Thousand Oaks, Calif.: Sage.

Henderson, Lori M. 1984. *Intergovernmental Service Arrangements and the Transfer of Functions*. Baseline Data Report 16. Washington D.C.: International City/County Management Association.

Hjern, Benny, and Christopher J. Hull. 1985. Small Firm Employment Creation: An Assistance Structure Explanation. In *Policy Implementation in Federal and Unitary Systems*, ed. Kenneth Hanf and Theo A. J. Toonen. Dordrecht: Martinus Nijhoff.

Hjern, Benny, and David Porter. 1981. Implementation Structures: A New Unit of Administrative Analysis. *Organization Studies* 2(3): 220–33.

Howitt, Arnold. 1984. *Managing Federalism: Studies in Intergovernmental Relations*. Washington, D.C.: Congressional Quarterly Press.

Howlett, Michael. 1991. Policy Instruments, Policy Styles, and Policy Implementation: National Approaches to Theories of Instrument Choice. *Policy Studies Journal* 19(1): 1–21.

Hull, Christopher J., with Benny Hjern. 1987. *Helping Small Firms Grow: An Implementation Approach*. London: Croom Helm.

Ingram, Helen. 1977. Policy Implementation Through Bargaining: The Case of Federal Grants-in-Aid. *Public Policy* 25(4): 499–526.

Innes, Judith E., and David E. Booher. 1999. Consensus Building and Complex Adaptive Systems: A Framework for Evaluating Collaborative Planning. *Journal of the American Planning Association* 65, autumn: 412–23.

Jennings, Edward T., and JoAnn G. Ewalt. 1998. Interorganizational Coordination, Administrative Consolidation, and Policy Performance. *Public Administration Review* 58(5): 417–28.

Jennings, Edward T., and Dale Krane. 1994. Coordination and Welfare Reform: The Quest for the Philosopher's Stone. *Public Administration Review* 54(4): 341–48.

Kanter, Rosabeth Moss. 1995. *World Class: Thriving Locally in the Global Economy*. New York: Simon & Schuster.

Kaplan, Abraham. 1964. *The Conduct of Inquiry*. San Francisco: Chandler.

Kaufmann, Franz-Xaver. 1991. Introduction: Issues and Context. In *The Public Sector Challenge for Coordination and Learning*, ed. Franz-Xaver Kaufmann. Berlin: Walter de Gruyter.

Kettl, Donald F. 1993. *Sharing Power: Public Governance and Private Markets*. Washington, D.C.: Brookings Institution Press.

———. 1996. Governing at the Millennium. In *Handbook of Public Administration*, 2d edition, ed. James L. Perry. San Francisco: Jossey-Bass.

Kickert, Walter J. M., Erik-Hans Klijn, and Joop F. M. Koppenjan. 1997. Introduction: A Management Perspective on Policy Networks. In *Managing Complex Networks*, ed. Walter J. M. Kickert, Erik-Hans Klijn, and Joop F. M. Koppenjan. London: Sage.

Kickert, Walter J. M., and Joop F. M. Koppenjan. 1997. Public Management and Network Management: An Overview. In *Managing Complex Net-*

works, ed. Walter J. M. Kickert, Erik-Hans Klijn, and Joop F. M. Koppenjan. London: Sage.

Kincaid, John. 1990. From Cooperative to Coercive Federalism. *Annals of the American Academy of Political and Social Science* 509(May): 139–52.

Klijn, Erik-Hans. 1996. Analyzing and Managing Policy Processes in Complex Networks. *Administration and Society* 28(1): 90–119.

Kooiman, Jan. 1993. *Modern Governance: New Government-Society Interactions*. London: Sage.

Krumholz, Norman. 1995. Equity and Local Economic Development. In *Exploring Urban America*, ed. Roger W. Caves. Thousand Oaks, Calif.: Sage.

Landau, Martin. 1991. Multiorganizational Systems in Public Administration. *Journal of Public Administration Research and Theory* 1(1): 5–18.

Leicht, K. T., and J. C. Jenkins. 1994. Three Strategies of State Economic Development: Entrepreneurial, Industrial Recruitment, and Deregulation Policies in the American States. *Economic Development Quarterly* 8(3): 256–69.

Levine, Charles H., ed. 1980. *Managing Fiscal Stress: The Crisis in the Public Sector*. Chatham, N.J.: Chatham House.

Levy, John. 1990. What Economic Developers Actually do: Location Quotients Versus Press Releases. *Journal of the American Planning Association* 56(2): 153–60.

Liebschutz, Sarah F. 1991. *Bargaining Under Federalism: Contemporary New York*. Albany: State University of New York Press.

Lindblom, Charles E. 1959. The Science of Muddling Through. *Public Administration Review* 19: 79–88.

———. 1990. *Inquiry and Change*. New Haven, Conn.: Yale University Press.

Linder, Stephen H., and B. Guy Peters. 1990. The Design of Instruments for Public Policy. In *Policy Theory and Policy Evaluation*, ed. Stuart Nagel. Westport, Conn.: Greenwood Press.

Lipnack, Jessica, and Jeffrey Stamps. 1994. *The Age of the Network*. New York: Wiley.

Mandell, Myrna P. 1988. Intergovernmental Management in Interorganizational Networks: A Revised Perspective. *International Journal of Public Administration* 11(4): 393–416.

———. 1990. Network Management: Strategic Behavior in the Public Sector. In *Strategies for Managing Intergovernmental Policies and Networks*, ed. Robert W. Gage and Myrna P. Mandell. New York: Praeger.

———. 1999. Community Collaborations: Working Through Network Structures. *Policy Studies Review* 16(1): 42–64.

Marlin, Matthew R. 1990. The Effectiveness of Economic Development Subsidies. *Economic Development Quarterly* 4(1): 15–22.

McGuire, Michael. 1999. The "More Means More" Assumption: Congruence vs. Contingency in Local Economic Development Research. *Economic Development Quarterly* 13(2): 157–71.

———. 2002. Managing Networks: Propositions on What Managers Do and Why They Do It. *Public Administration Review* 62(5): 571–81.

McGuire, Michael, Barry Rubin, Robert Agranoff, and Craig Richards. 1994. Building Development Capacity in Nonmetropolitan Communities. *Public Administration Review* 54(5): 426–33.

Meier, Kenneth J., and Laurence J. O'Toole. 2001. Managerial Strategies and Behavior in Networks: A Model with Evidence from U.S. Public Education. *Journal of Public Administration Research and Theory* 11(3): 271–93.

Milward, H. Brinton. 1994. Mapping the Linkage Structure of Networks. Paper presented at a conference on Network Analysis on Innovations in Public Programs, LaFollette Institute of Public Affairs, University of Wisconsin, Madison, September 30–October 1.

———. 1996. Symposium on the Hollow State: Capacity, Control, and Performance in Interorganizational Settings. *Journal of Public Administration Research and Theory* 6(2): 193–95.

Milward, H. Brinton, and Keith G. Provan. 1998. Principles for Controlling Agents: The Political Economy of Network Structure. *Journal of Public Administration Research and Theory* 8(2): 203–21.

Mossberger, Karen, and Kathleen Hale. 1999. Information Diffusion in an Intergovernmental Network: The Implementation of School-to-Work Programs. Paper delivered at the Annual Meeting of the American Political Science Association, Atlanta, Sept. 2–5.

Nathan, Richard P., and Fred C. Doolittle. 1987. *Reagan and the States.* Princeton, N.J.: Princeton University Press.

Osborne, David, 1988. *Laboratories of Democracy.* Cambridge, Mass.: Harvard University Press.

O'Toole, Laurence J. 1988. Strategies for Intergovernmental Management: Implementing Programs in Intergovernmental Management. *International Journal of Public Administration* 11(4): 417–41.

———. 1996. Hollowing the Infrastructure: Revolving Loan Programs and Network Dynamics in the American States. *Journal of Public Administration Research and Theory* 6(2): 225–42.

———. 1997a. Implementing Public Innovations in Network Settings. *Administration and Society* 29(2): 115–34.

———. 1997b. The Implications for Democracy in a Networked Bureaucratic World. *Journal of Public Administration Research and Theory* 7(3): 443–59.

———. 1997c. Treating Networks Seriously: Practical and Research-Based Agendas in Public Administration. *Public Administration Review* 57(1): 45–52.

O'Toole, Laurence J., and Kenneth J. Meier. 1999. Modeling the Impact of Public Management: Implications of Structural Context. *Journal of Public Administration Research and Theory* 9(4): 505–26.

O'Toole, Laurence J., and Robert S. Montjoy. 1984. Interorganizational Policy Implementation: A Theoretical Perspective. *Public Administration Review* 44(6): 491–503.

Pagano, Michael A., and Ann O'M. Bowman. 1992. Attributes of Development Tools: Success and Failure in Local Economic Development. *Economic Development Quarterly* 6(2): 173–86.

Parks, Roger G., and Ronald J. Oakerson. 1989. Metropolitan Organization and Governance: A Local Public Economy Approach. *Urban Affairs Quarterly* 25(1): 18–29.

Pasternack, Bruce A., and Albert Viscio. 1998. *The Centerless Corporation.* New York: Simon & Schuster.

Pelissero, John P., and David Fasenfest. 1989. A Typology of Suburban Economic Development Policy Orientation. *Economic Development Quarterly* 3(4): 301–11.

Pennings, Johannes M. 1981. Strategically Interdependent Organizations. In *Handbook of Organization Design*, ed. Paul Nystrom and William O. Starbuck. New York: Oxford University Press.

Peters, Tom. 1992. *Liberation Management.* New York: Knopf.

Pierce, Neal R. 1993. *Citystates: How Urban America Can Prosper in a Competitive World.* Washington, D.C.: Seven Locks Press.

Powell, Walter W. 1990. Neither Market Nor Hierarchy: Network Forms of Organization. In *Research in Organizational Behavior*, ed. Barry Staw and Larry L. Cummings. Greenwich, Conn.: JAI Press.

Pressman, Jeffrey L. 1975. *Federal Programs and City Politics: The Dynamics of the Aid Process in Oakland.* Berkeley: University of California Press.

Pressman, Jeffrey L., and Aaron Wildavsky. 1973. *Implementation.* Berkeley: University of California Press.

Provan, Keith, and H. Brinton Milward. 1991. Institutional-Level Norms and Organizational Involvement in a Service-Implementation Network. *Journal of Public Administration Research and Theory* 1(4): 391–417.

———. 1995. A Preliminary Theory of Interorganizational Effectiveness: A Comparative Study of Four Community Mental Health Systems. *Administrative Science Quarterly* 40(1): 1–33.

Putnam, Robert. 1993. *Making Democracy Work: Civic Traditions in Modern Italy.* Princeton, N.J.: Princeton University Press.

Radin, Beryl A. 2002. *The Accountable Juggler: The Art of Leadership in a Federal Agency.* Washington, D.C.: Congressional Quarterly Press.

Radin, Beryl A., Robert Agranoff, Ann O'M. Bowman, Gregory C. Buntz, Steven J. Ott, Barbara S. Romzek, and Robert H. Wilson. 1996. *New Governance for Rural America: Creating Intergovernmental Partnerships.* Lawrence: University Press of Kansas.

Reese, Laura A. 1993. Categories of Local Economic Development Techniques: An Empirical Analysis. *Policy Studies Journal* 21(4): 492–506.

———. 1997. *Local Economic Development Policy*. New York: Garland.

Reich, Robert B. 1991. *The Work of Nations*. New York: Alfred A. Knopf.

Richter, Arthur J. 1976. Federal Grants Management: The City and County View. *Urban Data Service* 8(10): 1–13.

Rhodes, Roderick A. W. 1981. *Control and Power in Central–Local Relations*. Adershot, England: Gower.

Rohr, John A. 1989. *Ethics for Bureaucrats: An Essay on Law and Virtue*, 2d edition. New York: Marcel Dekker.

Rose, Richard R. 1985. From Government at the Center to Nationwide Government. In *Center–Periphery Relations in Western Europe*, ed. Yves Meny and Vincent Wright. London: George Allen and Unwin.

Ross, Doug, and Robert E. Friedman. 1991. The Emerging Third Wave: New Economic Development Strategies. In *Local Economic Development: Strategies for a Changing Economy*, ed. R. Scott Fosler. Washington, D.C.: International City/County Management Association.

Rubin, Herbert J. 1986. Local Economic Development Organizations and the Activities of Small Cities in Encouraging Economic Growth. *Policy Studies Journal* 14(3): 363–88.

Sabel, Charles F. 1992. Study Trust: Building New Forms of Cooperation in a Volatile Economy. In *Industrial Districts and Local Economic Regeneration*, ed. Werner Sengenberger and Frank Pyke. Geneva: International Institute for Labor Studies.

Schapp, I., and M. J. W. van Twist. 1997. The Dynamics of Closedness in Networks. In *Managing Complex Networks*, ed. Walter J. M. Kickert, Erik-Hans Klijn, and Joop F. M. Koppenjan. London: Sage.

Scharpf, Fritz. 1978. Interorganizational Policy Studies: Issues, Concepts, and Perspectives. In *Interorganizational Policy Making*, ed. Kenneth Hanf and Fritz W. Scharpf. London: Sage.

Scheberle, Denise. 1997. *Federalism and Environmental Policy: Trust and the Politics of Implementation*. Washington, D.C.: Georgetown University Press.

Schrage, Michael. 1995. *No More Teams: Mastering the Dynamics of Creative Collaboration*. New York: Doubleday.

Schram, Sanford F., and Carol S. Weissert. 1999. The State of U.S. Federalism: 1998–1999. *Publius: The Journal of Federalism* 29(1): 1–34.

Senge, Peter M. 1990. *The Fifth Discipline: The Art and Practice of the Learning Organization*. New York: Doubleday.

Shanahan, E. 1991. Going It Jointly: Regional Solutions for Local Problems. *Governing* 5(1): 70–76.

Sharp, Elaine B. 1991. Institutional Manifestations of Accessibility and Urban Economic Development Policy. *Western Political Quarterly* 44(1): 129–47.

Simon, Herbert A. 1981. *The Sciences of the Artificial*, 2d edition. Cambridge, Mass.: MIT Press.

Smith, Hendrick. 1995. *Rethinking America: Innovative Strategies and Partnerships in Business and Education*. New York: Avon.

Sternberg, Ernest. 1987. A Practitioner's Classification of Economic Development Policy Instruments, with Some Inspiration from Political Economy. *Economic Development Quarterly* 1(2): 149–61.

Stever, J. A. 1993. The Growth and Decline of Executive-Centered Intergovernmental Management. *Publius: The Journal of Federalism* 23(1): 71–84.

Stoker, Gerry, and Karen Mossberger. 1994. Urban Regime Theory in Comparative Perspective. *Environment and Planning C: Government and Policy* 12(2): 195–212.

Stone, Clarence. 1989. *Regime Politics*. Lawrence: University Press of Kansas.

———. 1993. Urban Regimes and the Capacity to Govern: A Political Economy Approach. *Journal of Urban Affairs* 15(1): 1–28.

Stone, Clarence, Kathryn Doherty, Cheryl Jones, and Timothy Ross. 1999. Schools and Disadvantaged Neighborhoods: The Community Development Challenge. In *Urban Problems and Community Development*, ed. Ronald F. Ferguson and William T. Dickens. Washington, D.C.: Brookings Institution Press.

Study Committee on Policy Management Assistance. 1975. Executive Summary. *Public Administration Review* 35(6): 700–705.

Sundquist, James L., and David W. Davis. 1969. *Making Federalism Work: A Study of Program Coordination at the Community Level*. Washington, D.C.: Brookings Institution Press.

Taylor, Frederick W. 1947. *Scientific Management, Comprising Shop Management, the Principles of Scientific Management [and] Testimony Before the Special House Committee*. New York: Harper & Brothers.

Teitz, Michael. 1994. Changes in Economic Development Theory and Practice. *International Regional Science Review* 16($^{1}/_{2}$): 101–6.

Thompson, James D. 1967. *Organizations in Action*. New York: McGraw-Hill.

Toffler, Alvin. 1980. *The Third Wave*. New York: Morrow.

Toft, Graham, and David B. Audretsch, 2000. Creating a New Indiana Economy. Unpublished paper, Institute for Development Strategies, Indiana University, Bloomington.

Walker, David B. 2000. Rebirth of Federalism: Slouching Toward Washington. New York: Chatham House.

Waterman, Richard W., and Kenneth J. Meier. 1998. Principal–Agent Models: An Expansion? *Journal of Public Administration Research and Theory* 8(2): 173–202.

Weiner, Myron E. 1990. *Human Services Management*, 2d edition. Belmont, Calif.: Wadsworth.

Weiss, Janet A. 1990. Ideas and Inducements in Mental Health Policy. *Journal of Policy Analysis and Management* 9(2): 178–200.

White, Leonard D. 1939. *Introduction to the Study of Public Administration*, revised edition. New York: Macmillan.

Windhoff-Héntier, Andriene. 1992. The Internationalization of Domestic Policy: A Motor of Decentralization. Paper prepared for European Consortium of Political Research Joint Sessions, Limerick, Ireland, March 12–16.

Wondolleck, Julia M., and Steven L. Yaffee. 2000. *Making Collaboration Work: Lessons from Innovation in Natural Resource Management*. Washington, D.C.: Island Press.

Wright, Deil S. 1978. Understanding Intergovernmental Relations. Belmont, Calif.: Duxbury Press.

———. 1983. Managing the Intergovernmental Scene. In *Handbook of Organizational Management*, ed. William B. Eddy. New York: Marcel Dekker.

———. 1988. *Understanding Intergovernmental Relations*, 3d edition. Belmont, Calif.: Wadsworth.

Wright, Deil S., and Dale Krane. 1998. Intergovernmental Management (IGM). In *International Encyclopedia of Public Policy and Administration*, ed. Jay M. Shafritz. Boulder, Colo.: Westview.

Yuchtman, E., and Stanley E. Seashore. 1967. A System Resource Approach to Organizational Effectiveness. *American Sociological Review* 32: 891–903.

Zimmerman, Joseph F. 1973. Intergovernmental Service Agreements for Smaller Municipalities. *Urban Data Service* 5(1): 1–12.

———. 1992. *Contemporary American Federalism: The Growth of National Power*. New York: Praeger.

———. 1995. *State–Local Relations: A Partnership Approach*, 2d edition. Westport, Conn.: Praeger.

INDEX